MOMENT OF SURRENDER

My journey through prescription drug addiction to hope and renewal

Pj Laube

Copyright © 2016 Pj Laube
Published by Ant Press, 2016

The author asserts the moral right under the Copyright, Designs and Patents Act 1988 to be identified as the author of this work.

All rights reserved. No part of this publication may be reproduced, stored in a retrieval system, or transmitted, in any form or by any means without the prior written consent of the author, nor be otherwise circulated in any form of binding or cover other than that in which it is published and without a similar condition being imposed on the subsequent purchaser.

Doctors' names have been changed. The intent of this book is not to put focus on the individual physicians themselves, but to raise awareness to addictive prescription drugs, withdrawal and recovery. The road is a long and bitter one.

Dedication

This book is dedicated to my mother, Pearl Marie. Born into a family of twenty children, she later had a dozen of her own. Four of them died from cystic fibrosis. My mother devoted herself to hard work, raising children and caretaking. She never complained about her life. "It's just how it is," she would say. I often wondered what her life would have been like if she had become the nurse she had dreamed of becoming. Mom did not plan on so many children, or of being a caretaker until the age of 72. In some respects, caring for her children paralleled the nursing career she always wanted, although Mom's patients seldom went home to live full lives.

I often observed her and questioned if she thought much about the possibilities; she never put much conversation into it. What was the point? Even without her acknowledgement, I, at times, felt like she longed for more and never really felt she was truly happy. I am not sure she ever discovered her authentic self. I graduated from college and pursued a career, which seemed to strengthen our bond. To some degree, she lived part of that through me.

Since her death, my outlook and focus in life have taken a drastic change. A new person emerged, a person who wanted to make the most out of life and not get short-changed by staying inside the box. I did not want to end up like my mom. I needed to find my true, authentic self—not just for me, but for her, too.

Lifesavers

At times our own light goes out and is rekindled by a spark from another person. Each of us has cause to think with deep gratitude of those who have lighted the flame within us.
~Albert Schweitzer

Two primary people stood by my side, enabling me to not only survive the trauma, but to prosper from it. A great injustice would be served not to give each of them their due. I am forever grateful.

The first to be named is my partner of 23 years and primary constant. Bonnie has been at my side through thick and thin, smooth or troubled waters. An unwavering means of love and support throughout this entire ordeal, Bonnie gave up her wants and needs to tend me until I was able to stand on my own again. Life and substance have well been embodied into the phrase "in sickness and in health." New meaning comes into play in a relationship when a health crisis is encountered, especially one involving a lack of understanding and support from family, friends and society. Bonnie stayed and braved the storm when many would have bailed. Who could ask for a greater love from her?

Lisa, the licensed psychologist, has been one of the most influential people in my life for two decades running. She first came into my life in 1992 after the breakup of my first long-term relationship, followed by my sister's death a year later. We remained in contact off and on as I dealt with losses in my life. Because of her genuine concern for my well-being, knowledge and support during many difficult phases of my life, a greater sense of individual strength and growth has been achieved.

My parents ingrained in me from childhood into early adulthood that life was primarily black and white. In early meetings with Lisa, I understood that to be false. Life, instead, is shades of gray with continual daily choices, followed by the natural consequences of each choice made. Working to continually self-improve, I came to trust myself no matter the circumstances life dealt. That is the single most invaluable lesson learned from my years with Lisa.

Over the years, I have not thought of Lisa as a psychologist, but a special friend. Her confident words in withdrawal and recovery bolstered hope in consummating a new, quality-filled life. With medical avenues closed, no other viable alternatives were visible. Lisa soothed my fears and gave me a ledge to stand on when the earth had fallen out from underneath me.

Gratitude need also be noted toward the specialists in holistic healing who assisted me. Several physicians abandoned me on this journey, but natural healers stepped to the forefront without any preconceived notions or conditions. Aside from their individual areas of expertise, each served as an appreciated listening board giving valuable guidance from their own experiences and from others they treated.

Words are not enough to express how invaluable each of these people is—each one an integral component of my lifeline. I will never forget and will be eternally grateful. God bless each.

Contents

Prologue	1
1 The Barbarian	3
2 Mr. Know-It-All	9
3 Dark Night of the Soul	11
4 Depersonalization and Derealization	15
5 First Responders	17
6 Oh, to Remember	21
7 Poker Face	25
8 No Turning Back Now	29
9 Date With Destiny	35
10 The Abyss	41
11 Opening the Floodgates	45
12 The Hardest Breath	49
13 The Most Shameful	53
14 Violent Ideations	57
15 A Term Overused	59
16 Box of Crayons	61
17 White Knuckles	63
18 Did You Ever Really Know Me?	69
19 Holy Grail	73

20 Protracted Withdrawal	79
21 Rape	83
22 Take My Breath Away	87
23 My Toolbox	89
24 My Physical Tools	91
25 My Mental Tools	99
26 Moment of Surrender	105
27 The Dark Horse	107
28 Reaching Out	113
29 Phoenix Rising	119
30 Belief System	123
31 Boogeyman Cometh	127
32 Baby Steps	129
33 Tug of War	135
34 Christmas: Waiting on a Gift	137
35 A New Year	143
36 Someday	147
37 First Anniversary	151
38 Return to Teaching	155
39 Original Injury	157
40 Next Prescription	165
41 Rear-View Mirror	173
42 On the Shelf	177
43 The Perfect Storm	181

44 Grace	187
45 Role Reversal	191
46 No Words	197
47 Watershed	203
48 Authenticity	209
49 Last Drug	215
50 Desperation Looms	219
51 Post-Benzo Chaos	223
52 Lost Time	229
53 Fourth Anniversary	235
54 Single	239
55 The Miracle	247
56 Perseverance	249
57 Meaning of Full Recovery	253
58 Aftermath	259
Contact the Author	261
Acknowledgements	263
Appendix A—Food for Thought	265
Appendix B—Timeline of Events	267
Ant Press Books	269

Prologue

My human frailty comes to light. I cannot control movements with any part of my body and lose the ability to feed myself. This disability causes a major emotional reaction in having to rely so fully on another human being. Trust issues instigate rebellion like ill-treated prisoners. I quickly identify how I bank solely on myself in dire straits. No longer capable, the brick wall begins to crumble one block at a time, spoonful by spoonful.

Moments of anger and stubbornness have me crawling short destinations without asking for or taking assistance. My hand is forced—literally—if I want to eat. Tears emanate from my eyes as one small spoonful after another feeds me. I feel powerless; my heart breaks.

The strong-willed fighter in me accepts "feeding" only whenever absolutely necessary, even though my eyes have been opened to trust issues I am free to relinquish. I hold tightly to whatever level of functioning I possess whenever possible. In my fearful eyes, letting go means admitting defeat. I am worse than I could ever imagine and refuse to question how much lower I can go.

1 The Barbarian

Even though I walk through a valley of deep darkness, I will not be afraid because you are with me. Your rod and your staff—they comfort me!
~Psalm 23:4

Monday, April 27, 2009: I knew this day would be anything but typical. Finally, a medical observation day—one I had wanted for more than two years. Forty-eight hours of suffering during a three-day taper off 1.5 milligrams of Lorazepam brings me to the moment of truth. The original prescription began with a daily dose of 3.0 milligrams in the fall of 2005. I had been prescribed a roller coaster series of prescription drugs following a back injury in 2004. Pain from the injury influenced my primary doctor to prescribe Neurontin for nerve pain. Difficulties with Neurontin and repeated misdiagnosis caused years of prescriptions, side effects and withdrawals. Lorazepam represents the last drug to be removed from my system.

The doctor who prescribed it instructed me in 2007 to take the drug "as needed" as I sensed I no longer wanted or required it. Six months later, I realized the travesty of his suggestion in relevance to an addictive drug and moved my level back to a daily dosage of 1.5 milligrams. Too late! Now, more than three and a half years since the initial dose and surviving a multitude of symptoms, I achieve the final taper off the drug.

I have spent the entire weekend in bed, caged in the confines of the upstairs bedroom. Bonnie acts as my motivational support, waitress and crutches. With each daily 0.5 milligram taper off the drug, a higher level of chaos ensues. By Sunday, I question a 911 call and a ride with flashing lights. Should I stay or should I go? My body convulses violently with feelings of nausea. Blurred vision hinders my sight and pain saturates my body. I gaze into the digital numbers of the nearby clock, but staring into the numerals fails to speed up the process. Time becomes my nemesis.

As Monday morning arrives, Bonnie checks on me repeatedly as she readies our transport to the hospital for my scheduled arrival. How will I make the 7 a.m. hospital appointment for admittance? Prayers answered, my body calms just enough to get there. Body vibrating, my full concentration focuses on checking in, filling out necessary paperwork and maintaining control until I obtain a room and hit the hospital bed. Life moves in slow motion.

A staff member rolls me by wheelchair to a lower level for electroencephalogram (EEG) hook-up. My body sits eerily still. Applying the electrodes constitutes a slow process and I fear the re-emergence of body shaking. I hold faith that I am in the right place should anything occur. An EEG is a procedure designed to measure and record electrical brain activity using electrodes attached to the scalp. It is a primary diagnostic test for epilepsy and other brain disorders.

The technician measures my head and marks designated spots to attach electrodes in accordance to my head size. She cleans each of these scalp areas with a solution that feels like abrasive sandpaper, then places electrodes on my head one by one, gluing them on with a sticky gel. Each of the wires connects to a central box, which is placed on my lap. After attaching all of the electrodes, the technician instructs me to push the button each time my body shaking occurs. The attached recorder will measure the electrical activity in my brain on a tickertape printout, and pushing the button will mark the spots where the shaking occurs.

She returns me to my room. I take one quick glance into the mirror as I pass, which invokes a lasting, undesirable image. The applied electrodes have displaced my hair and created large strands that stick straight up all over my head. I wear a metal wig with free-flowing wires pulled back into a ponytail as a dark mane. I look like one hot mess and the day is just beginning.

Soon after, my newfound doctor arrives. Dr. Tyson is a younger, dark-haired man possessing an air of confidence that borders on arrogance. Shedding the white medical jacket, he is dressed in a well-fitting, expensive-looking suit. His brown hair is parted to one side—not a strand out of place. Clean-shaven, his exterior appears flawless. I characterize our first meeting three days prior as confrontational due to his five-minute rush to a diagnosis and his attempt to wean me off the remaining 1.5 milligrams of daily Lorazepam in cold-turkey fashion. I questioned the notion of quitting an addictive drug with a haphazard taper—especially after my previous attempt. My primary physician referred to him as a "quick mover."

Dr. Tyson's plan tapered the Lorazepam down 0.5 milligrams per day, and began after my first appointment with him late Friday afternoon, with the last intake Sunday morning—some 24 hours ago. He intends to observe my body's response to the stoppage of the drug. Gauging my reaction over the weekend and past several months, I know I am in for a bumpy ride. I embrace the thought of switching to a longer-lasting drug to taper off once the flurry begins. I see a switchover as my only option to minimizing drug-induced side effects. My thinking is not his thinking. I ask what alternative drug might be used to help me adjust if I experience difficulty.

"None," he says, raising my alarm.

"None?" I stare in shock, unsure of what to say or do. This is not what I want; I don't know what to do. I naively convince myself that, once he observes how bad I react, he will change his mind. There is only one problem with my plan. In order to witness the aftermath, he must be present.

I will forever remember the words Dr. Tyson spoke with a big smile on his face prior to exiting my room. "This is going to be nasty, but don't worry, we'll take good care of you." Speechless, I watch him vanish into the hallway.

Three hours have passed by calmly, but I can tell if my body is about to act up. I lie down and the technician plugs in the EEG box over the bed behind me. The cord length affords just enough slack in the wires to reach the restroom toilet directly in front of the bed. Nothing like dragging a cord of wires around attached to the back of your head to make life difficult. Shackled to the tangle, I must pre-plan each restroom trip. Luckily, I am afforded the luxury of wearing panties under my gown for such ventures so passersby won't be exposed to my rear.

I have a single room with typical hospital walls—bleak white. I notice an audio visual camera in the upper-left corner of the room. An electrocardiogram (ECG) monitor sits off to my left; it will measure the electrical activity in my heart. An elevated tray sits directly to my right with a glass of water. Looks like the party is all set up and ready to begin. *Why didn't I decline this invitation? Why? Why? Why?*

Arriving right on time for the festivities, tremors, shaking and jerking commence. Having undergone a prior EEG, I know the test does not show all tremor or shaking activity. My body fires up and I push the button on the monitor to mark the spots on the film as the technician instructed. I question how often I should push the handheld button, doing so only when an aura is present. An aura denotes a perceptual sensation signaling the beginning of an attack. Sensations in my brain alert me. For me, an aura moves way beyond tremors and signifies "coherent" seizures combined with severe dystonia. "Coherent seizure" became my label for severe body shaking.

Surely if medical personnel are watching, they are aware that I could push the button a majority of the day based on tremors alone. Since earlier physicians questioned my anxiety levels, I press the button only when severe body shaking presents itself. I wonder if anyone is watching. Or is it just me and the machine? Is all of my shaking recorded, or only when I push to mark it? I begin to worry.

My body periodically stiffens like a board and teeter-totters back and forth, rapidly out of control. The arms I try to keep still at my side swing to and fro in an upward and downward motion like chicken wings.

Attempts to lock them together cause them to fly in unison. Sporadically, I feel as if I wet my bottom and the pad placed under me. The sensation causes me to sheepishly head to the restroom when my body allows to check. *Just a sensation; thank goodness.* I would suffer embarrassment no matter the circumstances should I wet myself. Within an hour and a half, a nurse comes in to put in an IV (intravenous) line. I ask her the purpose. "It's in case they want to run tests," she says.

Close-mouthed, I question that rationale. *Really? Come on! You can do better than that. I'm not here for any tests. This is an observation. The IV line is precautionary? What's going on?* I know she will not have answers to these questions, so I keep them bottled up inside as I await the doctor's arrival.

The tremors and shaking become unmanageable. Seconds of repeated bursts feel like continual five-minute intervals, separated by two- to three-minute breaks. With continued contractions, pain rifles through me. It is non-stop! The feeling of nausea ensues, but the sensation of puking never turns to action. My mind is uneasy. I feel my body faltering and sense no one cares. Every system in my body surges to full throttle. I inform Bonnie on two separate occasions that I feel I have reached my threshold. I am not sure what the threshold is other than my perception of the inability to undergo more before something outrageous happens—such as a heart attack or seizure. My body screams from the inside out, and I am fearful of not making it through the day.

Bonnie and I dialogue with repeated questions throughout the day. *Is anyone keeping close monitor? Are they going to wait until something happens before they stop this? What are the proactive measures? Are there any? Will someone tell me why I feel like this? What's happening to me?*

Dr. Tyson guaranteed my care. How does he figure that? His definition of care is far different than mine. I keep my eyes on the door. I anxiously await his return all day and evening, upset about the turn of events. He never comes. I don't hear a word from him, not even through the nurses who attend to me at their regular scheduled times, unless I call for one. I see no value in asking questions. It will only be lip service from a silent movie. No information will be given. I need the doctor.

I consider the level of care a disgrace and method of drug removal barbaric. Bonnie is the one and only person at my side all day. The observation and care Dr. Tyson said I would receive is all through monitors. I can't tell you how special that makes me feel.

Shortly after visiting hours end, my symptoms decrease, so I tell Bonnie to go home and get some rest. Fatigued, but not wanting to leave me alone, she begrudgingly says goodbye. The nurses turn the lights out shortly after 9 p.m. and close the door. Strangely, the closed-off room bothers me; I don't know why. Feeling alone all day, maybe closing the door exacerbates the isolation. At 10 p.m., another episode strikes. Instinctively, I hit the EEG button as I had several times during the day. Two nurses burst through the door, one to each side of my bed. They seem to be treating this like an emergency—unlike the casual attention I received all day. Startled by their entrance, all I hear is, "Yes, she is!"

Speechless, I watch them hover over my bedside. "Wait a minute," I finally say. "Yes, I am what? I have been doing this all day, people." My eyes scan back and forth to each of them, awaiting a reply. One nurse checks vitals while the other begins asking the same series of questions I was asked earlier today. "What's your name? Where are you? What day is it? Who is the president?"

I'm freaked out. They are treating me as if I have had a full-blown seizure. Needless to say, I never touch that button again the rest of the evening and as little as possible the next day. During the night, weird sensations come over me. Hard to explain; something is happening inside me. Something is not right. I find sleep troublesome and not just because of the intermittent blood-pressure checks. I awake gasping for air as if I had stopped breathing. Stunned, I remain awake until fatigue overtakes me. My body periodically jerks, not allowing me to fall asleep. I am eager for daylight and Bonnie's arrival. After my experience yesterday, I do not trust the medical staff. The doctor tops the list. Surely he tried to kill me and I somehow survived.

I feel disappointed by the medical report for that 24-hour period, which inaccurately reflects the hell I suffered. My medical chart states I had 33 stereotypical spells during the first 24 hours. They occurred primarily during the first ten hours. Most were marked as a maximum of twenty seconds in length. The evaluated recorded movements were those marked by none other than the push of the button. Medical records displayed these so-called "spells" to be consistent with non-epileptic convulsive activity.

I was awake, alert and conversing during these episodes. This is exactly what I have described to every doctor previously, including Dr. Tyson. Every single one looked at me with a shit-ass grin, obviously thinking I am crazy. "It isn't possible to be awake during a seizure," they said. I have had more than four years living that kind of crazy. Surely any doctor would recognize my term for "coherent seizure" as a convulsion. It is possible to be awake and coherent during a convulsion.

The chart also noted occasional premature ventricular contractions, which is probably why I was more aware of my heartbeat and feeling like it was going to jump out of my chest.

Anxiously, I await the doctor's arrival to analyze plan B because plan A was a hellacious failure. Upon Dr. Tyson's arrival, I am stupefied to find that no alternative plan exists. He does not want to switch me over to another drug to help me through my withdrawal. This has been my wish from the outset. In his mind, I made it through the worst and, while not yet well, day two will be a better day. I am deflated. I drop any hope of a switchover. I resign to getting through these next few days and out of this place.

I try to explain the jerking that awoke me at every onset of sleep, but the doctor shrugs this off as a normal phenomenon everyone experiences. It is not the same. I decide to keep my mouth shut and never mention awaking from sleep and choking. Like everything else I frustratingly tried to describe, it would be blown off. No need to waste more energy on him or anyone else here.

Day two is better, considering I thought I was going to die the day before. Not much of a leap. Tremors, dystonia and convulsive episodes occur on a smaller scale with issues stemming around nausea, dizziness and physical and emotional fatigue. I am haunted by a feeling in the pit of my stomach that something is wrong, but I can't put my finger on it. It is another long day staring at monitors, the non-conversational blank walls and retrieving medicine to calm my queasy stomach. I have no interest in watching television. I welcome simply lying motionless.

Bonnie, sitting at my side, keeps a part of her body in contact with me all day. I am unsure whether or not I want visitors, though friends have stopped by. The expression on each face says it all. Some can hardly look at me, appearing dismayed. *Do I look that bad?* Their demeanor makes me uneasy. Hearing voices in the hallway is sufficient for me. Inquiring calls from family and friends to check on us gives me a sense of life. Somehow I made it. I am so abundantly thankful.

2 Mr. Know-It-All

The whole problem with the world is that fools and fanatics are always so certain of themselves, and wiser people so full of doubts.
~Bertrand Russell

Originally, Dr. Tyson told me the hospital observation would last a week. Imagine my surprise when he enters my room on day three and asks me if I want to go home. I stare, unsure of the legitimacy of the question. *Is he joking? Is he serious?* Realizing he is waiting for my answer, I am relieved, yet shocked. "Of course I want to go home."

Again, that aura. I knew what was happening to me was beyond his full understanding even though he would not admit to it. All he had were those damn monitors. I knew I wasn't going to get better quickly even though he tells me it will only take three to four more days. I think him clueless and want out of this place. I will not let another doctor lay hands on me. Dr. Tyson is at the helm of a runaway train. I want off before it completely derails. He has done enough to me, and yet sits in the chair with a smug grin on his face like he wished he could have watched. Is he ignorant in his arrogance? How I wish we could have reversed roles. The smile would be wiped from his face.

The only emotional relief I feel comes when he calls my reaction a "drug-withdrawal phenomenon."

Now he has my attention. Sitting higher in the bed, I acknowledge his statement. "Thank you!"

Puzzled, he asks, "For what?"

With redemption in my eyes, I say, "For actually saying it."

The smug smile leaves, yet he delivers no response. Dr. Baker, my primary, makes her entrance to check on me. They move off to the side for discussion. Before leaving the room, Dr. Tyson tells Dr. Baker I should never receive a benzodiazepine prescription again. I do not fully understand what that means other than the obvious. He instructs me to schedule a follow-up appointment with Dr. Baker. I am so relieved to be going home that I do not question why the appointment is with Dr. Baker and not with him.

Since my back injury in 2004, Dr. Tyson is the fourth neurologist and eleventh doctor. After he is gone, Dr. Baker briefly discusses my situation. Shaking her head, she tells me how my body reacted to the withdrawal in numerous ways, beginning on day one of my hospital stay. In a hurry to get discharged, I never ask exactly what she means.

Never once during the three-day stay did Dr. Tyson, or anyone else, explain to me what was happening to my body. Not once did anyone make any attempt to reassure me all would be okay. Not once did anyone take time to visibly observe the event. In their minds, all seemed to be taken care of.

Now, the reverse of day one is about to occur. The scene resembles a beauty shop as I am moved to a single chair located in front of the mirror. The same technician who attached the electrodes removes them one by one. My hair feels gross. Strands twist wildly in every direction not only from the electrodes, but from lying in bed for two and a half days, and pressure from convulsive activity. The technician works to remove the electrodes from the paste, and the paste from the scalp, before cleansing the area of scalp itself. It itches and feels tender. Glue residue clings to my scalp, sticky in my hair. Raking the brush through my hair to remove the paste serves as a reminder of younger days when Mom would brush my hair back into a ponytail. The strong tug on the hair settles a tear or two in the corner of my eyes. The tears may be from the emotional undercurrent of the nightmare I survived. I acknowledge the battered person staring back at me in the mirror.

During this process, the technician asks the purpose of my hospital stay. When I inform her it was to observe me after a quick removal from Lorazepam, she inquires, "I thought you were supposed to slowly taper off those things?"

In agreement, I exclaim, "Yeah, me too."

The technician removes the last electrode, but residue remains in my hair. Continually brushing only serves to hurt my sore head and scalp. I do my best to calm down my unruly hair. Once the technician leaves, I move to get dressed, notify family members and anxiously await my departure. The wheelchair to take me to the car cannot get here soon enough. Finally, after all of the searching for answers and abandonment, I am drug-free. In my mind, it will be a long, long time before I see a doctor again.

3 Dark Night of the Soul

Being able to survive it doesn't mean it was ever okay.
~Unknown

The moment I arrive home, I promptly throw out every card and plant from the hospital stay. I want no reminders. Out of sight, out of mind—or so I think. I open the last remaining bottle of Lorazepam and dump the pills in the kitchen trash can. I manage a shower, scrubbing profusely to cleanse myself of the event. Afterward, I spend a great deal of time staring into the mirror and brushing through my hair, sure it will take days to rid myself of the residue. When finished, I toss the brush and wide-tooth comb into the trash. I don't want to bother cleaning either one. I don't want to look at them.

Earlier, while lifting my right arm overhead to brush and blow dry my hair, I realized I had pulled a muscle in my right shoulder. I know how I injured it—the ever-flapping chicken wings in the hospital.

That evening, Bonnie and I decide to carry on with our weekly family rendezvous to watch an episode of *Lost*. It is my blind illusion that all is well. I am trying to move past the events as though they never occurred and quickly return to my normal life.

All imaginings of how life will transpire shift when I retire for bed. The aura I felt in the hospital comes to light. I fall asleep easily exhausted from earlier events. After a few hours of sleep, I awaken in a frantic state, not knowing where I am or what is happening. Sitting up, I flash side to side to recognize my surroundings. Now cognizant, cravings for the drug just removed from my body become horrendous. I want the drug! I want it now! Temptation calls me to sift through the downstairs kitchen trash to retrieve the previously discarded Lorazepam pills and devour them as if they are decadent bonbons. I don't care about the length of time the pills have lingered in the trash or what disgusting remnants may be on them. My mind is frantic. *What the hell is happening? How can the night get any harder?* I have never experienced anything like this in my life.

Never ask questions. I soon discover things can always get worse. I contemplate suicide. Overwhelming graphic thoughts and images of slitting my wrists with a kitchen knife prevail. My "computer chip" brain continues to send visualizations. I see long slits, horizontal across my wrists. With arms raised, red blood flows freely off the sides and down my forearms. No harmful consequence is present; no pain, no distress, no death. After these self-harm images emerge, I decide it will be best to stay in bed. In disbelief and fear, I wrap my arms around Bonnie's closest left leg, grasping for some piece of life to sustain me. Teary-eyed, I fight to keep my focus, praying for the morning twilight to erase the black hole of the night.

Bonnie, with the ability to sleep through a tornado, never stirs. I make no attempt to wake her. Is it shame, shock, fear, or confusion? I don't know the answer.

Immediately upon rising, I tie the kitchen trash bag and move it to the garage, distancing the pills farther. I consider it my only pre-planned task today, other than keeping myself alive. I conceive the latter to take every ounce of energy and focus within me. With wrist-slicing thoughts present, my anxiety flies off the charts. Bonnie and I momentarily discuss hiding any harmful kitchen utensils. We both realize that, if I am going to injure myself, I will find something to use. I lack control of my topsy-turvy mind.

Bonnie calls Dr. Tyson's office the moment it opens and hands me the phone. I talk with his secretary, informing her of my ever-increasing anxiety, drug cravings and inappropriate thoughts.

How can I say suicidal? What will they think? I fear action by Dr. Tyson. *Will he attempt to medicate me again?*

I feel ashamed. The drug caused this—not me. But it doesn't matter. After the treatment I received in the hospital and from previous doctors, I need help, though I remain skeptical. The secretary tells me someone from the office will call back after she speaks with the doctor. I envision a call back within a half hour to an hour considering my dilemma.

Bonnie's work schedule takes the forefront. Her worrisome decision of going to work or staying home takes precedence. One phone call to her boss relieves her dilemma with the gift of a flex-schedule. She heads off for a few hours of work with my promise to call her if I cannot maintain stability. I cling to the couch for protection from the relentless darkness as I impatiently wait for the phone to ring. The internal fight rules constant, each moment an eternity.

I do not want to kill myself! I do not want to die!

I fear my harmful thoughts; I cannot stop them. Bonnie calls frequently and comes home by noon. No call back yet. I remain on edge waiting for the ring. I finally receive the long-awaited call midafternoon. First, the secretary asks if I have pitched the pills.

"I did that immediately upon arriving home from the hospital yesterday," I tell her.

"Good," she says, then relays once again the message to hang in there, this is not unusual and I will be better in a few days.

My thoughts race. *Hang in there? That's it? That's the best you have? Do they know what I mean by inappropriate thoughts?*

Dr. Tyson's office shows no other concern, asks no more questions. *Did they send me home as a high risk? No one made sure someone would be with me. No one prepared Bonnie for this. What the hell? No one prepared me. How do they know I won't kill myself? Surely they don't understand. It's all I can do to get through to this point. A few more days? How will I get through the rest of today? How will I get through the next few moments—never mind tomorrow and the day after?* A life seemingly so simple and controlled turns into an everlasting fight for existence.

I decide Dr. Tyson is no different than any other doctor appointed to me. Panic-ridden thoughts coat my brain. He abandoned me, too. I do not trust myself. I do not know how I will get through this. God help me!

Bonnie and I closet ourselves into the privacy of our home. She leaves when work demands, stays in constant contact, returning home to be of any support possible. I cannot imagine how emotionally draining and scary the plight for her to know my condition, yet leave. Then again, coming home to me is no picnic. It is really just the beginning for both of us.

Drug-withdrawal symptoms seize every part of my being. I look anorexic. Muscle waste gives the appearance of meat eaten off my bones seemingly overnight. I already dropped weight and strength markedly over the past several months. This, however, hits an all-time low. I appear extremely unhealthy, skin hanging from my bones. Dark raccoon-like circles shadow my eyes. I look like death warmed over.

I shut down neurologically. Movement consists of limited walking. Otherwise, my arms and legs remain motionless. Walking is shuffling in distances of feet, not miles. I can move downstairs to the couch or restroom and back. That's it. My energy stands depleted. I exhibit no gestures. I stare out with little recognition of my surroundings, yet totally aware of my condition.

Withdrawal affects my entire body, but primarily my left side. My left arm hangs, lacking proper strength or coordination of movement as if my nervous system does not exist. I place my arm slightly in front and against my body for carriage. I lightly clasp the bottom of my shirt to keep it secure. I frequently wear my favorite dark blue Nike hoodie with a through pocket in the front. I stick my hand in it as support and to mask the malfunction. Awkward and weak, I find it impossible to carry the slightest object, dropping any item attempted. Almost all function: vanished.

The tremors, dystonia and convulsions appear periodically, but seem more merciful. My limbs fall asleep excessively, equating to a deadened touch. I acknowledge a pins-and-needles sensation that dwells throughout, again more noticeable on the left side. The left side of my tongue has dropped significantly lower. I stick my tongue out to have it drift off to one side. It protrudes unevenly from my throat. Numbness serves as an additional feature.

I am a zombie. A living blob—a shell of a being. All my life, I've possessed picture-perfect recall. Now, my memory plays hooky. I understand what I am told, but forget seconds later. I have no thoughts. No feelings. I am just here—all meaning lost in the depths of my mind.

I display zero word recall and the inability to make a sentence. I model a lot of "yes," "no" and head-nodding. When speaking, words scuffle out of my mouth, as if in partials. They get entangled in my throat. Spoken words chunk together in unusual syllables. My speech patterns and rhythm have changed altogether. I begin to say a word, but it gets chopped and I abruptly spit out the end of it with an increased intensity and a higher volume as if yelling. I communicate one word at a time, if the word pulls up in my file at all.

Brain activity appears non-existent. Bonnie asks me a question and I stare back comatose. My eyes appear vacant of life. *My brain is surely damaged. Is it permanent?* Even with the question, no emotions stir.

In this zombie state, I suffer overwhelming anxiety. Immobile, I find it difficult to sit or lie still. My brain is stressed. So is my body. Thoughts do not cause the uneasiness. I feel like I have been in an accident. Fully aware of my dysfunction, I do not react to my circumstances. I am incapable. I am unable to feel any emotion, with the exception of fear. When suicidal thoughts pass through, I highlight fear of acting on them. Other than that, I feel nothing.

Bonnie, my primary caretaker, lacks outside emotional support. Without complaint, she juggles work and manages my shortcomings. The heavy load carries a great deal of emotional stress. We do not update many family or friends, informed by Dr. Tyson that this process would be over before we knew it. In over our heads, will this be the case?

4 Depersonalization and Derealization

Even the darkest night will end and the sun will rise!
~Victor Hugo, *Les Misérables*

Who is staring back at me? Adding insult to injury, I do not recognize the person in the mirror. I look deeply into my eyes, trying to find some warmth, some sense of being. I find nothing. I trace my brown hair, brown eyes, olive-tone skin, face and nose, what I always referred to as chicken lips, and every part of my being that is visually present. Diddly squat. I exhibit no attachment to this person. None. I feel cold. This is depersonalization.

I feel no attachment to the people around me, family or friends, including Bonnie. I recognize faces, but I can't remember names. One moment I can pull someone's name out of a hat, but the next it is a crapshoot. I cannot give a descriptor of someone and often confuse who people are and the relationship I have with them. Bonnie coaches me in all aspects.

The order of events in my life confuses me. I cannot distinguish the difference between what happened yesterday from a decade ago. So baffling. I cannot determine whether I am with my ex of nearly a decade, who I haven't seen in years, or Bonnie. Even though my ex isn't present, I don't know which person will come back into a room after Bonnie has exited. I cautiously wait to catch view of which one so they will not notice my dilemma. I communicate this to Bonnie, but have no feelings connected to it other than frustration from the confusion itself.

I think of my sister, Norma Jean, who died of cystic fibrosis in 1993 and my father, who succumbed to cancer and heart complications in 1998. Confused, I ask Bonnie if both died. When she informs me of Norma Jean's death, I do not question it. Somewhere in my mind I register it. However, I contemplate the news of dad's passing. I anticipate my next visit with him under the assumption he is really still alive, though told otherwise.

When I need an escape from the house, Bonnie takes me for a drive. I live in a bubble, occasionally seeking fresh surroundings only to retreat back home. Each time I go out, I feel as if it is my first visit to Columbia. While vaguely familiar, everything appears new. Columbia doesn't feel any more like my home than Dallas, Miami or Seattle—though I've never visited or lived in any of them. Any jaunts outside the city give me a heaven-like feel of floating. The roads, countryside and earth itself open up for me and I can travel across them for days.

I come to learn that my altered state of perception has a clinical term: derealization. It is an alteration in perception leading to the feeling that the reality of the world has been changed or lost. I feel totally detached and alienated from all around me. I live in a dream as an observer—never an interactive participant. I stand in the backdrop of a picture, watching the unknown world go by. The concept never bothers me. Too much is going on within me and keeps me busy.

Less than a visitor, I am a stranger in my own home. I find no warmth, no coziness and no comfort. I am just here. Rooms, furniture, pictures and wall hangings mean nothing to me. Bonnie took some of these pictures on our vacations. They do not trigger recall. She shows me pictures of our large, home renovation. Still nothing. I have just enough recollection to know everything she says is true, but nothing more.

I move through space and time with the inability to touch things, nor them to touch me. I am flying solo on autopilot over uncharted waters. I do not know my coordinates, how I arrived here, or my future destination. I pray for enough fuel in my tank to make the journey.

5 First Responders

I am very picky with whom I give my energy to. I prefer to reserve my time, intensity, and spirit exclusively to those who reflect sincerity.
Dau Voire

To top off anxiety and suicidal thoughts, panic attacks rush in and take me for an overpowering ride. I have suffered them twice prior to this. Both were within a couple of months of each other after Norma Jean's death at the age of 26. More frequent and severe, I can't find a resourceful means of stopping them. I do not form thoughts to materialize them. They blitz out of nowhere without warning, making minutes seem like hours. My heart races; breathing is difficult. Dizziness and faintness set in, accompanied by an inability to visually make sense of my surroundings. Oh, to run and escape. From what and to what I have no clue. Worst of all, I feel no control over it, never knowing when it will hit. Already in isolation, I feel even more leery around people now these attacks are further complicating my life.

A new sleep pattern emerges. I refer to it as "sleepless in Columbia." I nap one to two hours nightly for three to four days then, in pure exhaustion, sleep one whole night. The pattern then repeats itself. Who knew one's body could be so sleep deprived, yet stay charged like an Energizer bunny for days on end? An electrical presence keeps my brain and body on high alert. With the feel of being plugged into a wall socket, I experience the juice flow non-stop. I don't know how to break the circuit.

I perceive begging as a feasible option. Nine days after release from the hospital, the doctor's flawed prognosis leaves me in a predicament. I am not better. In fact, I am far worse. I cannot go on like this. I need answers and assistance. Not trusting doctors, I turn to Lisa, a licensed psychologist. Bonnie dials the number, then brings me the phone as I lie in bed.

Lisa responds to my call with two simple questions. "Who did this to you?" and "Can you get in here today?"

Within hours, I begin the 45-minute drive to see Lisa. The decision to go alone may not represent the smartest thing under the circumstances. Bonnie has already missed several hours each day of work to be at my side. We knew she would miss more. I told her I would be okay as long as

I was sitting, exerting no physical energy. The independent drive serves as a strong-willed attempt to stand back up and handle the cards dealt. I promise Bonnie that, if I encounter difficulty, no matter where I am, I will immediately pull off the road and call her.

The majority of the trip consists of interstate and highway. I remember the general neighborhood Lisa's office is located in, not specifics. I find myself driving up one street and back down a parallel one until I recognize the house where her office is located. Lisa meets me at the door. I sit in her office loveseat waiting for her to take her spot in her chair directly across from me. With communication difficult for me, Lisa carries much of the conversation. She asks questions and I do my best to give a nutshell version of events.

On first observation, Lisa presumes I have experienced a stroke. The pain is visible in her eyes as she observes my state. She looks shocked. Sitting motionless, I show signs of neurological impairment. I sit to the back of the seat with my arms to my side and legs bent directly in front of me. I never cross my legs as I once deemed natural or move them in any way. My arms remain at my side the entire visit, never raising either in a display of emotion or gesture. I never change my posture. No signs of emotion leak to the surface; my face remains expressionless. My eyes appear spiritless.

I stumble with speaking, words not able to be pulled up, the organization of thought impossible. The intake and release of my breath, the blink of my eyes, the movement of my mouth upon speaking and heartbeat are my bare illustrations of life. I realize how bad a spot I am in by the expressions on Lisa's face and the tone of her voice. I register emotional pain, but I am unable to display it. I sit like a bump on a log, shedding no tears.

A much bigger story starts to unfold. Traumatized, I ask how to reinstate Lorazepam. I stick to the illusion that eventually switching to Diazepam from Lorazepam will aid my taper and rid me of symptoms. Surely this nightmare will then disappear. To my disbelief, Lisa informs me I have surpassed the point of no return. Bottom line, too much time has passed since my last drug intake and reinstating gives no guarantee of ridding symptoms, possibly increasing them instead. Now nine days since leaving the hospital, and twelve since my last drug intake, my one hope vanishes into thin air. Already hollow, I feel nothing else can be taken from me.

Lisa has working experience with drug withdrawal and recovery. I decide to use her as my point person to guide me through this hell. For whatever reason, I have no trouble remembering her or the trust I have always had in her. This makes the decision easy. She puts a plan into place, suggesting I see her one to two times per week. Bonnie will be my set of wheels if I cannot drive on my own. I hope to gain insight into what happened and learn about the obstacles to my recovery. More important, I need a great deal of emotional assistance to deal with this trauma. Lisa's knowledge prods me to endure and heal from the symptoms themselves and the emotional pain inflicted upon me by them.

She instructs me to find a person I feel comfortable with for acupuncture, and also wants me to have deep tissue massages followed immediately by Epsom salt baths. Bonnie and I put the plan into play immediately. I resolve to use natural healing methods throughout the recovery process.

I call Steve, my chiropractor, for an acupuncture appointment. He worked with my hip subluxation a few years earlier. Familiarity with him and his work make the decision easy. In my condition, I do not want anyone new. Trust is huge. I begin appointments within a week and continue bi-weekly. Thankfully, the acupuncture takes the edge off insomnia, pain and withdrawal-induced anxiety. Liver detox acts as a complementing benefit. Initially, the relief feels short-lived. However, I accept any benefit. *Maybe it will take several months for a longer-lasting payoff to occur?*

As Steve put it, "Acupuncture either works for you or it doesn't. There is no in between." I see benefits and will stay with the process.

I consider Pam, once connected with Steve's office, the quick pick of the litter for my masseuse. Again, familiarity. The deep tissue massage to be performed focuses on muscles located below the surface of the topmost muscles. It helps alleviate pain and increases circulation, which diminishes inflammation, helps release chronic muscle tension and promotes relaxation. The concept for drug withdrawal is to have the toxins—the leftover drug particles—moved from the lower tissue levels closer to the surface.

I realize my newfound hypersensitivity to touch once the deep tissue massage begins and fight the angry urge to tell Pam to keep her hands off me. After all, I am here for a massage. The 60-minute appointments cause internal havoc. Pain overwhelms me physically and emotionally. Nothing calms my mind. Finally, after a month, touch loses its hold. Physical pain, however, remains for several months to come.

When I return home from a massage, I immediately take an Epsom salt bath to remove those toxins from my body. The skin, using sweat, is the largest detoxification organ from which toxins can be drawn out. I take an Epsom salt bath every other day as recommended by Lisa, daily if possible, watching closely to take good care of my skin. During the daily regimen, Bonnie frequently needs to help me into and out of the tub. She stays in close proximity as a safety precaution. The pull of the salts tempts my symptoms. Not only weak, my body can shift into body shaking at the drop of a hat. I have no intentions of drowning in the tub.

The appointments with Pam serve a vital purpose in helping me realize misperceptions in my relationship with Bonnie. For a year prior to Lorazepam removal, difficulty with touch served as an emotional divide with her. I could not stand to have her sit up against me, lie next to me in bed or touch me in any way. Putting her hand on my leg while seated on the couch caused immediate anger. I now know why. Bonnie asks me if it is okay to initiate contact, no matter how trivial it may seem, or I inform her of my difficulty with it once it is applied. The communication from both sides settles any misperceptions before they crop up.

With excessively long days on the couch, I use background noise to drown out the increasing chatter in my brain. My brain zips around on overdrive. I cannot communicate, yet my mind runs rampant.

During my first appointment with Lisa, she instructed me to keep everything positive. She said to watch feel-good movies and hang around only positive friends and family. She rightly predicted I would have difficulty coping with the negativity as it would cause too much stress on my brain.

I fill my time with ESPN and HGTV. While a couple of perceived favorites, these choices are not based on my interests. I need a soft tone with no drama. Programming that contains conflict, violence, horror, fear or darkness sends me over the top. Drama-filled reality shows cause uneasiness. Crime or investigative shows immerse my mind with negative scenarios. My brain shifts the storyline into my own. My overly vivid mind overstates the drama and magnifies the graphic nature as if it is happening in front of me. No stop button exists.

6 Oh, to Remember

Memory is a way of holding on to the things you love, the things you are, the things you never want to lose.
~Kevin Arnold

Bonnie and I keep everything under tight wraps. I stay isolated. It keeps me from putting added stress on myself for expectations I am nowhere near capable of attaining. I don't know myself. I don't know people or understand relationships. Incapable of feelings, I desire to see no one. I constantly try to understand what happened to me and deal emotionally.

I continue my weekly appointments with Lisa. Work begins on redeveloping my memory. I am clueless to the world around me, past and present. Step one consists of exercising my brain like any other muscle in my body. I realize this process will be slow and ongoing. My project takes illumination in May. Lisa advises me to view photo albums, looking at family and friends. Bonnie and I have a large, burgundy antique chest full of albums. It sits in our living room for ease of access. I will not run out of photos any time soon. I focus on one or two albums daily.

I glance through pictures without pressure to remember, simply seeking familiarity with faces. People are highlighted, not the location or event behind each picture. Anesthetized, I flip through page after page. I feel no degree of connection toward one face over another. Some appear recognizable, others distant. They are nothing more than pictures. I hold no appreciation of the albums storing my closest memories. The pictures serve as no more than a key to healing.

Game-playing is another pivotal ingredient in the recipe. With the exception of cards, I normally do not enjoy playing many games. My typical response when asked to play a game is "no" or "one and done." Many board games last two or three hours. I'm ready to change activities long before that point. My even more limited attention span from the drug withdrawal deters me farther. When Lisa listed game-playing as a recovery tool, I had no reaction to it. Numb, I gear my focus to exercising my brain in hopes of getting full function back.

I play word- and number-memory games daily, typically one player. A classic game consists of modified Concentration. Seated on the floor, I lay out four pairs face down in random order from the 52-card deck. I flip over one card, then another, trying to match pairs. The goal is to match pairs with few errors. Once I master four-pair, I gradually increase the number of pairings. The ultimate goal is to play multi-player competitively.

Bonnie enjoys finding suitable word games for me. I adapt multi-player word-building games for my individual needs. With Bananagrams, I remove a series of tiles and make simple two-, three- and four-letter words. If I cannot construct a word, I add another tile. Once all of my tiles are used, I consider the game over, though I do not consider myself a winner. Winning holds new meaning for me now. To be the ultimate winner, I must reacquire my brain. I envision undertaking whatever it demands. My primary focus in all game-playing is nothing other than to train my brain.

In all discussed recovery plans up to this point, Bonnie has internally battled to find a means to be more fully involved. She fails to realize she has been a means of constant support since this trauma began and need look no farther. She experiences guilt in what she feels as a failure to establish a stronger voice as my advocate. She questions whether she should have made a stand. I see her at my side 24/7 – how could I possibly hold any animosity toward her? I hold the doctors 110 percent liable.

My game-loving Bonnie finds the addition of game-playing right up her alley and it induces her involvement. An avid Scrabble player, she was nearly unbeatable before any of this happened. She plays her own modified version, trying to keep a level playing field. My shortcomings apparent, the scenario epitomizes a special-needs teacher encouraging her student to succeed. Bonnie sits back and patiently instructs me to take my time as she sips on her glass of dry red wine. My brain crippled, I save attempts at anything other than individual games for a later date. I do not want to play her.

I stay clear of strategy-based games. It isn't an option. I cannot remember; therefore, I cannot plan ahead. My only strategy is to improve my brain by continual repetition. Beyond that, I fathom nothing. I think one step at a time if I can think at all. I cannot devise a pyramid of moves or understand consequences thereof. I activate math skills by counting. I count to ten forward, then backward. Any pause causes a memory fart. If I can, I start over. If my brain shuts down, I stop. Once I succeed with ten, I try twenty and continue increasing the goal until I reach 100.

Math flashcards initiate the next stage. Bonnie, a former elementary teacher, stashed her cards here at home. They appear just like any other deck, but have single-digit addition, multiplication, subtraction and division on them. Addition sets the tone. Simple two-plus-two does not register four. I count one, two, then add one, then another to equal four. Larger single digits cause me to use my fingers or tallies. Repetition.

Repetition. Repetition. Fatigue sets in as my brain exhausts easily. Once overwhelmed, my brain is finished for the day. I decide it will serve a dual purpose to write the numbers instead of using flashcards.

Next task: subtraction. It is a slower process. I use fingers and paper to calculate. A calculator sits beside me for answer checks. When multiplication begins, I stick with a multiplier of five and under. Once recall occurs, I move up to ten. I persist with single-digit math problems in all areas and decide I will not bother with division right now. I want to move on to other things.

Reading is sour grapes and a major frustration. I continually re-read words, not remembering what word I just read or the meaning thereof. I read a few words, lifting my head to repeat them aloud. Sounds so simple, yet so difficult for me. Three weeks of practicing every day and I think I have it down. I transition from words to sentences, moving gradually to a paragraph. I read each and attempt to paraphrase. Word, sentence and paragraph comprehension remain a big issue. With that being said, then comes retention. I feel like a kindergartner. I am starting all over again and going through each grade level little by little with fallbacks along the way. No matter what, every day, without question, I practice. What are my choices?

With all of these activities, I gauge myself. I notice improvements and fallbacks. Slow as they are, I try to applaud even the smallest improvements. I remember where I started and try not to be harsh toward myself with all of the difficulties. However, the possibility of longtime or lifetime damage constantly hangs over me.

Once functionally possible on a minor level, I begin writing, primarily in a journal. I place no focus on grammar, punctuation, spelling or sentence structure. Writing begins as nothing more than getting words down on paper. No sentences. Difficulty with word recall in writing parallels word recall in speaking. Journaling becomes a twofold treatment. First, I want to pull files from my brain and hopefully get my circuitry working properly again. Second, and just as important, I want to release emotions. I misspell the simplest of words. I stare at a word I am unsure of and then decide to continue on without concern over it. I also appear dyslexic, rearranging letters. I do not realize my letter changes during actual writing, but have the ability to self-correct upon re-reading.

Many of the words have the same formatting. Much of the writing is angry and hateful. Some pages have nothing more than "fuck" and the like written all over them. When I finish, I rip the pages out of the journal. I tear them into shreds and toss them into the trash. Something about that feels good. I may not be able to showcase my emotions, but anger and pain are definitely present. To add salt to an open sore, my eyes bounce words and whole sentences, making it necessary to refocus frequently.

Isolation can only last so long. I am alive, for God's sake. At some point, friends and family begin questioning their inability to talk with and see me. My communication skills barely existent, I have Bonnie handle most of the talking over the phone. For now, I remain hidden, working on skills to re-enter the world.

Moving through my sessions with Lisa, my concern turns to the length of recovery. School lets out for the summer in a month, with start-up again two months later. Wow! Seems unattainable, but I never question not making it to teach next school year. With the inability to think, worry never takes center stage. In my mind, diligence with my exercises will enable me to recover quickly. I question Lisa as to not only my return, but full recovery. With each and every question, she keeps the focus on the present day, the present moment. Her words—always encouraging and optimistic—have yet to match the tone of her facial expressions.

7 Poker Face

I like to pretend that everything's alright, because when everybody else thinks you're fine, sometimes you forget for a while that you're not...
~Unknown

May is coming to a close. In the four weeks since my release from the hospital, I have hidden within the confines of the house. Bonnie and I direct all of our energy into getting me through the day. Except for phone conversations or email, little communication has been held with the outside world. I pick time periods when I can handle a phone call; otherwise, Bonnie manages the health updates. I am not ready to have everyone observe the whole damaged package.

Only a handful of people have been allowed to catch a glimpse of me. When they visit, Bonnie gives few details and, asking no further questions, conversation remains surface level. Their facial expressions and demeanor illustrate their uneasiness. They direct a majority of the conversation to Bonnie. My facial recognition shows improvement, but is not guaranteed. With that said, I may not match the name with the face. If I can, nine out of ten times I will draw a blank on our relationship or anything about them.

At some point, I know the outside world will force itself upon me. But if people see my ailments, their questions will follow. *How can Bonnie or I possibly explain what has happened? Neither of us fully comprehends. How would anyone else?* I do not have the capacity to explain. I cannot relate to people or my environment and have lost my memory, yet I am fully aware of my predicament. I compare my dilemma to someone in a coma who is coherent of all that is going on in the nearby vicinity. I'm not lying in a bed with my eyes closed. Eyes open, however, I stumble through similar darkness. Without close observation, I look normal in appearance except for significant weight loss and overcast eyes. Dysfunction glows in the dark when I attempt to talk, walk or think.

My speaking and thinking abilities have improved over the course of the month. Whether it is natural healing or that the daily brain exercises have paid off, I don't know. Either way, I'll take it. My strengthened thinking abilities, however, have their downside. For the first time since entering the hospital, my thoughts create stress. I trouble myself with other people's perceptions. I carefully place myself in situations that demand very little of me. I don't want anyone noticing anything different. Dysfunction outweighs performance. Family members, Bonnie, my ex, Lisa and a handful of friends remain in my memory bank. All else is at a loss. I instill the objective to get out amongst people with little to no interaction. I want to feel like I am living, even though I don't know what that entails anymore. Parks, grocery stores and the health club emerge as viable solutions.

I give standard responses when meeting someone. "Hello! How are you doing?" No one really expects a response other than the same back in return, along with the standard, "good," even when they are not. When I struggle speaking, I simply smile and nod. I can avoid people, but be near them. I retreat to my home once I accomplish my mission of visiting one place per day. With anxiety over the top, I struggle to get out of the house, let alone be around other people. I push myself to do so, keeping my long-term goal of healing in mind.

I took medical leave in early May after my release from the hospital. Nearing the end of the month, staff friends contemplate my status and inquire about a visit prior to school letting out in June. Oh, my! There are moments during a day when I feel human. During these instances, I want to push the boundary. These are rare. *How can I pull this off? How can I pick a day ahead of time when I never know moment-to-moment how I will be? Will I be able to connect names to faces immediately upon greeting someone? If I can't, how will I cover it? How will I make conversation with my limited abilities?* I don't remember anything about most of them. While I may recognize their faces and know their names, their personalities and lives will remain a mystery to me.

I choose to utilize this opportunity, hoping a visit to the middle school will trigger my memory. This alone renders the social call worth it, as does the feeling of isolation that I, myself, have caused. For this task to be of value, I need to find the school environment familiar. Some friends must be distinguishable. I bank on both occurring and hope my world comes flooding back to me. *On the other hand, what if everyone witnesses my obvious mental shortcomings? How will I respond to that? What if I no sooner arrive and have to leave?* Though scared, I feel it is the next step.

Allowing flexibility for myself, I schedule several dates to attempt a visit. The first crashes and burns. Not functional enough to pull it off, I cancel. Day by day I await the second date, unsure of my probability. When the day arrives, I precariously decide to give it a shot. I pre-plan where I will go, where I will spend most of my time and whom I will see. I consider possible statements and questions people may ask.

"How are you?" "Good to see you!" "Are you okay?" From that point, I believe I can let them do most of the talking like the friends who visit the house. They know me. I am their friend, teaching cohort, physical education teacher and staff member. I don't know who I am other than my name. I know who I am supposed to be. They know more about me right now than I do. I will use other people's knowledge of me to my advantage until I get things figured out. I can give as little input as needed, yet be a part of conversations. Funny how that works. Many conversations really are surface and trivial.

As I approach the school, stress builds. Nearly a month has passed since I walked through those school doors in teaching mode. Oh, how much has changed since then. I fear a panic attack as I draw near the door. My breathing increases; my heart races. Allowing no time to reconsider my decision, I plaster a smile on my face and walk in. I am on a mission. I head directly to the main office where everyone congregates. The moment I enter, my evaluation begins. I stay nearby those I remember.

The event entails anticipated questions, concern, hugs and small talk. I feel somewhat normal again, even if just for a few moments. I perceive concern from the expressions on people's faces and the intensity of the hugs. Much of the assessment of my relationships with people correlates to those two things. I have little else to go on.

Endorphins flood my body. I decide I will stay as long as I feel capable, allowing the possibility for a quick exit. With the exception of Bonnie, this marks the first time I have engaged in direct conversation in person. Feeling confident and no longer fearful, I enjoy the interaction. In truth, though, I portray someone other than who I am, yet I still feel proud for making it through. On the flip-side, I find playing this poker face to be extremely stressful. The emotional pain runs deep, along with the insecurity of being discovered. I sigh in relief when I exit the school doors and silently replay the chorus of Lady GaGa's "Poker Face," which dominates my current existence. I head home and sleep from emotional fatigue much of the afternoon. I did it!

Feeling confident, I schedule a second visit to complete my end-of-year checkout. All of the students will be gone for the summer and I plan to encounter very few staff members. I imagine the visit to be easier than the first—until I arrive. I decide to complete only vital tasks: organizing the equipment, cleaning out essentials from my office and checking out grade books. This marks my first visit back to my office since going on medical leave.

The simplest tasks overwhelm me. My cognitive ability and memory are noticeably abated. Paperwork and file organization fall out of my realm. I cannot decipher important items from irrelevant ones. Time after time a panic attack runs through me. *How do I achieve what I need to accomplish not only for me, but the main office? What am I supposed to tell them?* I want to run again. I aspire to get as far away from the building as possible. *Where will I go, and what will I do?* No matter how long it takes, I need to finish. There will be questions if I don't. I bear down. My original goal was to get in and out as soon as possible. My focal point shifts to completion of tasks. Safe in my office, I close the locker room door, deterring people from entering.

After I finish in the refuge of the locker room, the main office navigation offers a new set of challenges. When around people, I feel far from myself. Incapable of hiding my inabilities, I go quiet. Other than a typical "hi" and "have a great summer," I nervously rush to check out. I recall the faces and names of the people I come across, but stand tongue-tied. I stare, unable to find words. I want to close up into a shell. *Push through! Push through! Push through!* This represents my biggest challenge in public thus far and a distant cry from the first visit. Relieved to be done, I make a quick escape and drive directly home. I refrain from outings for a couple of days.

8   No Turning Back Now

Never underestimate your problem or your ability to deal with it.
~Robert H. Schuller

With time to regroup after the school visit, a tougher challenge presents itself. Bonnie and I planned a trip to North Carolina a year in advance with a couple of friends. We have not discussed the vacation since my return from the hospital, as each day has been filled with its own obstacles to surpass. Now, six weeks past, the time has come to keep the commitment, or fold. Skeptical, I view it too demanding.

Vacation means living in close contact with other people. I still feel a loss of confidence from the second school visit; I view it a negative venture. Bonnie, the self-described Pollyanna, wants to push full steam ahead. My caretaker since the hospital, she regards the trip as a gift. My concern falls flat in swaying her. She fails to apprehend I combat panic attacks on the mere thought of going with her. I do not want to lead her on. I cannot distinguish our relationship from that of a regular friendship. It rips me apart inside. I can't tell her.

As we pack for the trip the night prior, no words exist to describe the torment inside me. I am to travel with someone who acts like my partner and utmost caretaker to a place far away from the house I consider my main refuge. I shall have no place to hide, no place to run to, and I dread the two-week challenge of my poker face façade. Panic attacks refuse to allow sleep. My and Bonnie's emotional responses to the trip sit at opposite ends of the spectrum.

Dawn breaks and we prepare for departure. Bonnie offers our traveling companions a brief and vague synopsis of my condition so there will be no surprises should something come up. She presumes that, as friends, they will understand the differences I exhibit from my normal self and will be agreeable if spontaneous alterations occur with our travel plans.

She told them I may not act like myself? What an understatement. I cannot act like myself when I don't know who I am. I don't know what I like, or what I don't. I possess no clue to my normal behavior.

Bonnie tells me our traveling companions are good friends. She describes highlights of our trip with them to Emerald Isle four years earlier. I hold no connection. I hope and pray I do not screw up their names at any point during our time together. I apprehensively wait for the moment we greet.

My worries alter as they approach us with smiling faces. Both of their faces and names register. Our road trip into uncertainty begins. Two vehicles caravan the entire way, making most of the same stops and staying over in the same hotels. Leaving Columbia and driving across the country turns into a blessing in disguise. I drive, scary as that may seem. This activity gives my confidence a shot in the arm. We stop at some places new to us all, and others that our traveling companions have visited before. I don't have to pretend to be anybody in these situations. No one holds a preconceived thought on what I should or should not know. Relief. When I feel overwhelmed, or symptoms hit, Bonnie drives or goes into tourist stops without me. I eventually make my way in or wait in the vehicle. I lower my guard one or two notches with the flexibility of travel and lack of questions by our friends.

Staying beachfront on the ocean translates into an awesome present. To quote a vacation buddy, "Life's too short to be second row!" We walk the beach daily, spending ample time looking for seashells and what turns into one of my favorites—olive shells. Something happens to me with the sound of waves crashing into shore. I can't explain it; the sound calms me. I walk in the water, sometimes up to my waist, waiting for the roll of an olive seashell to be visual. I stare out toward the horizon into the vastness. Dolphins beg for a picture with a near-daily trip across the oceanfront. For these moments in time, all I endure takes a backseat. I never want to leave and return to what is. Bonnie was right. This vacation serves as an emotional reprieve and exactly what we both needed.

On vacation, most of the work talk and daily life discussion fades for the splendor of the present. Focusing on the now makes topics easy to handle. Sleep heightens during this vacation, but waking always brings on a high tide of symptoms. Having our own bedroom allows me quiet time to pull myself together without inquiry. I wake with the wonder of where I am and whom I am with. Anxiety looms over me with the lack of connections to anyone or anything and bewilderment over my circumstances. My body shakes as a rude alarm. Feeling nauseous and dizzy, I fail to see properly due to blurred vision. My bed spins as does my entire world.

Once able, I open the patio doors for the sound of the ocean as the first point of business. I lie back in bed with sunlight flooding in to light the entire room, listening to the sounds of nature and of the tide rushing in. I hear talk from beach walkers and the occasional bark from their canine friends. In this manner, I achieve a sense of civility. After a couple of hours, I make my way out of my newly found refuge to once again hide behind my poker face.

After two days of apprehensiveness, I ease into the company of our friends, realizing no test of being exists. Any time I need to flee from people or hide my condition, the bedroom or the beach itself serve as my escape. I cannot stay in the bedroom all day without probing, or vanish every single time symptoms hit. I realize the necessity of fighting my symptoms in public to be the slightest bit functional. I privately struggle in my own skin, and the poker face I showcase. No one can possibly know the depths of my inner battle.

Finally, that dreaded day arrives—the day I am unable to compensate for my shortcomings. I am overwhelmed by the need to stay distant. As I gaze into the mirror in the rental house bathroom, depersonalization sets in at its worst. I stare into the mirror at a complete stranger. Once again, tracing each part of me fails to improve the perception. I feel nothing toward this person. Coldness sets in over my entire body. Emotional pain overpowers me.

Thoughts run amok without warning. *I want to shave my head. My hair means nothing to me. I don't recognize it as mine.* Any friend of mine knows I am vain with my hair. Growing up poorer, we bathed infrequently. My hair was straight and greasy. This day I hold no self-interest. With no razor to shave my hair, I improvise using thinning scissors. I cut a very healthy portion off and toss it in the trash. I then envision a tattoo on my body. I desire no certain design. I don't know or understand why. Maybe it gives me the sense of starting anew. I want to recognize some part of me—anything that will give me an indication of who I am.

Bonnie notices my hair when I exit the bathroom. She inspects the room and acknowledges the large mass left in the trash. I tell her my thick hair is driving me crazy. The thickness causes "big," uncontrollable hair on a windy beach. My explanation proves insufficient. She tells me point blank to leave the scissors alone, as well as my hair. I leave well enough alone to discourage dissent. Our two friends laugh at my and Bonnie's exchange. There is no way they could possibly understand the complexity of what just transpired. I expound on the hair-trimming incident later in the evening when Bonnie and I are alone. She offers reassuring words, unsure of how to help, and reiterates leaving the razor and scissors alone, asking if she should move them.

"No," I reply.

As a precautionary measure, she checks the bathroom the next two days to double-check I haven't done anything else. Not completely satisfied, I receive twenty questions as well.

I don't understand why I recognize certain people and not others. I cannot distinguish myself or many of my friends, yet I know who some celebrities are on the news as our group watches television with breakfast.

On one occasion, a report flashes on the TV screen to interrupt regular programming and report on an ambulance taking Michael Jackson to the hospital. As we discuss the news broadcast and the King of Pop himself, I realize Jackson's file remains intact as one of my favorite artists. I keep abreast of his status like I believe I normally would; however, I show little reaction to his death. The same thought holds true for Farrah Fawcett, who succumbs to cancer on the same day. *What makes me remember certain people and forget others? How can I remember them but not me? Is this a sign of recovery? Does this mean I will remember more people, places and events?*

Walking short distances daily, I overconfidently step beyond my bounds as Bonnie and I attempt to kayak. We thought kayaking the channels would be easy; neither of us considered the current. We stop frequently to rest. By the time we are finished, function collapses. I hurt all over. Fatigue overwhelms my body to the point of pure exhaustion. My brain shuts down, and I struggle to think. No thoughts present themselves to talk. My entire body switches to a protective mode. Within a few hours, the shield turns to rebellion as my body responds to the adventure. I pay for the mistake the remainder of the day and two to three thereafter. Dystonia and convulsions beat me silly. I exhibit a complete power failure. I cannot strong-will my way through this. Lesson learned.

Neither Bonnie nor I option packing up and heading for home. I enjoy the vacation. I never guessed I could appreciate something with all I bear. I play word games and, after initial trepidation, continue without tension. Busy competing, no one realizes my shortcomings. My confidence heightens. With each passing day, I try to converse on a more regular basis.

Over the span of the two-week vacation, it occurs to me that, while *I* don't know me, there is some part of me presently recognizable to others. I don't know what part that is. Our companions never question my behavior as different from the normal me, or at least they never say anything. Obviously, people grasp no idea of my internal torment, but they accept whatever I show at face value.

The drive home appears endless as I contemplate moving forward with hopeful recovery and healing. I hide so much inside me. *So far to go. How long could this take? Will I be ready for school in the fall?* Flashbacks of transpiring symptoms run through. My mind clutters with limitless questions as mile after mile pass by. I struggle with the concept of pushing through as hard as I can. It is what I have been doing. This strategy isn't working well.

I decide to invest more growth into the process of the journey delivered to me. Miley Cyrus' summer hit, "The Climb," rocks the airwaves and strikes a chord with me. As with any new hit, the song plays repeatedly the duration of the trip. The words bolster my spirit and perseverance. I fixate on the song as a source of motivation.

Upon arriving home, I glimpse my first real hope since April 27. Each day brings about a change for the better. I focus on preparing for the beginning of the school year, which is just more than a month away. I continue to work with math problems and memory games. I examine names of students and fellow teachers, props for aiding lesson planning and what I consider poker face skills until I no longer need them. Maybe I will not only be ready for school, but I will heal quickly now. All of my present dreams count on it.

On cloud nine, I improve rapidly during weeks eight to ten. It is too good to be true. I have made it. Bonnie and I celebrate with two close friends at the end of the two-week span. Believing the worst behind me, my sights set on getting back to normal life. I glance into the future with animated eyes. I do not know what the next 24 hours have in store for me, or us. Maybe it is best not to know what is around the corner.

9   Date With Destiny

You never know how strong you are until being strong is the only choice you have.
~Unknown

What is around the corner? Don't peek. A firestorm! Mid-July. Two and a half months have passed since my hospitalization for observation of the effects of the quick removal of Lorazepam from my body. I wake up to the floor falling out from beneath me, no walls or ceiling in sight. The two-week high vanishes into thin air. I free fall into a hell never known before. I lose the improvement and confidence I rallied for after my acute withdrawal phase. Far worse, my mind and body fall so far back no recognizable world presents itself. Bottom line—more than 70 symptoms bear down on me at different times, though often concurrently. I quit counting. Old symptoms rudely revisit from previous weeks, while new ones arrive as uninvited guests. Desperation.

If God never gives people more than they can handle, then God most assuredly made a hefty miscalculation with me. I occasionally sense myself pitted against Him, against my faith. Anger fills me. Each symptom represents additional weight anchored to my body. Thrown overboard, I sink speedily into the depths of obscurity.

My primary symptom—of tremors and body shaking—rebounds with a vengeance. I suffer dystonia and extended convulsive activity relentlessly after having been relieved of this shaking for three weeks. I thought it over; silly me. I cannot imagine, nor do I want to, my appearance as this occurs. It more than rivals a fish flipping around out of water. My body parts launch everywhere. The visualization is painful. Bonnie sits close in proximity, offering a means of support by her presence. She nervously keeps an eye on the shellacking. During the duration of body shaking, twisting and convulsing, she periodically removes her watchful eye, sneaking moments of respite.

The neurological antagonist submits many different faces. My body stiffens like a board, rocking back and forth in teeter-totter fashion, in rapid succession. All of my body parts form one lever, moving violently in unison. At its most brutal, a weird aura encompasses me and I shake side to side. I don't understand how my body can do that. Whenever this aura occurs, my brain contains a rotating fog sensation. Energy transfers back and forth between my shoulders, across my back. When the body abuse stops, I feel fatigue, dizziness and a dazed state with the inability for cognitive thought or communication.

Lying down with my trunk flat, my legs run in place. Bonnie and I burst into false laughter. Not funny, but better to laugh than cry. Periodically, my legs fly out to each side and return in sync, repeatedly slapping each other upon meeting in the middle. My arms singularly, or in unison, fly about. I possess no ability to control or rein them in. When I lie down, my arms move back and forth in front of me like chicken wings, or they fly back over my head. I cannot move them until the electrical charge in my body dissipates.

Sometimes, after minutes of waiting, I impatiently summon Bonnie to physically move them down. The forced retraction causes my arms to slam down onto the bed. Every so often, I take one of my own slaps or punches to the face. I incorporate the habit of locking my hands at the onset and crossing my arms across my chest to try to stabilize the movement. If that doesn't work, I put both hands into the bottom of the shirt I am wearing and wrap up my arms to lessen the force and damage.

I utterly hate moments when my body shakes so violently that the shirt used to help keep my arms down covers my face and head, with my arms locked and slamming the headboard. My flapping arms bother me more than most other body effects, second only to side-to-side movement. They only occur during very violent convulsive activity and they wig me out. I fail to understand how this body movement can happen.

My back arches to the point of locking my neck back underneath my head at awkward angles. When this happens, I cannot release the position until the force lessens, putting unbearable pressure and pain on my neck and the bulging disc found five years earlier. Pam, my masseuse, suggests I put two tennis balls in a sock and place them underneath my head where my skull meets my neck. In the cranial sacral world, this is called inducing the still point. The balls are placed under the occiput, putting the body in a relax point so it can heal. In Pam's words, opening the occiput also allows for better flow of spinal fluid.

After arching, my back sometimes goes down gradually with ease. Other times, an unknown force flings me down and I feel as though a bone-crushing World Wrestling Federation nemesis has thrown me from the top ropes and pinned me flat on the mat. *Count one, two, three, and get this over with, please. I give!*

Often, I fall asleep from exhaustion and struggle to open my eyes after waking. They do not open upon command. Seconds to minutes pass. Even then, one opens slightly while the other remains stuck shut in place. Both eyes blink uncontrollably, forcibly and quickly. Once open, they slam shut. I open them only to repeat the sequence. My left eye stays stuck centrally while the right moves about with normal visual intake. Bonnie hates that one, often turning her head away in repulsion. I make light of the situation by imitating the symptom, trying to keep one eye in place while the other moves. I can't; Bonnie prefers I don't.

My teeth chatter uncontrollably. Attempts to speak cease, with words being cut off or thrown. I vocalize words with a pitching effect, projecting them louder and forcefully. I struggle to get out anything as the attempts get caught or blocked. My words get slurred as though I have had too much to drink. Verbal communication evades me once again.

My head whips violently to one side repeatedly without notice or provocation, then switches to the other. The sheer force of movement gives the impression the next may snap my neck. Feeling exorcist-like, I wait for my head to spin.

The shaking and body movements seem bizarre. The total lack of body control and what the movements cause my body to do flusters me. So surreal. The movements, which hit two or three times a day for an hour, escalate until I am fending off three- to four-and-a-half-hour bouts. On alternate days, I shake ceaselessly. These endless varieties alternate between constant movement and tremors and a vicious mauling.

The 24/7 days frustrate me; I fear the three- to four-hour sessions. They are the scariest and most brutal. They beat the crap out of me with violent convulsive activity mixed with twisting, jerking, arching, arms and legs flying. The contender knocks me down for a ten-count, yet I continue to get kicked in my teeth and stomach. No let-up occurs except for seconds of pause for my body to recharge.

During the slight pauses, I cry many a tear, praying for a cease-fire. Crying "uncle" fails to stop the assailant. Pain eventually results from forced muscle contractions and the violent nature of the movements and duration. I scratch my itching scalp without relief afterward. The lengthiness drains me physically and emotionally. Feeling spent, I lie waiting and wondering when the next attack will come, knowing the probability, and if I shoulder the emotional capacity to handle it.

No matter what the day brings, I count on a little shake-and-bake at night. This serves as a regular occurrence upon lying down for bed and also occurs the moment my eyes open in the morning. My opened eyes function as a trigger. If Bonnie attempts to stop a movement or invokes the slightest pressure on any body part, the severity of the experience heightens. Electrical energy builds before surging into my body. The higher the electrical charge, the more brutal the beating.

Pain in my lower back, irritability and/or chills in my brain precede severe activity as well. Attempts to raise an arm, swing a body part, tap a finger or anything similar launch the body shaking. I try to remain perfectly still to minimalize the outcome, but find that difficult all day long. It never fails. Urgency for urination couples with the activity and sooner or later I need to make my way to the bathroom. My body revolts as if to say, "Who the hell told you to get up?"

When the initial tremors hit five years ago, I could maintain a standing position and hold them off for a short period of time to move to a safer area. Doing so, however, only served to charge them further, sending me into higher-intensity convulsive activity. Gradually, my body weakened over time and it became evident I must lie down immediately upon the emergence of symptoms.

When moving about the house, I pre-plan where I can lie down. The length and severity of body shaking holds me to one location. During one episode, fierce convulsive activity weakens me to the point of going down to the floor. I roll to my back and find my head bouncing off the hardwood floor. Wincing in pain, I attempt to grab my head. I have no control over my arms or any part of my body. I cannot protect my head, nor coil my body. Body enthralled with convulsions and dystonia, my head bounces again. The shaking tosses me toward one side. I manage to roll to that side and bring an arm up under my head for protection. Instead of my head, my arm and elbow now use the floor as a trampoline.

I hold on, waiting for a juncture to react. The instant the electricity dissipates, I crawl to the couch. I find myself bruised and hurting once the episode terminates. I never lie on the floor again. Whenever I feel the shaking developing, I move to the soft cushion of my bed or couch. I make certain a pillow is behind my head to absorb the impact. The few seconds of fighting the surge to move to safety can cause elevated activity, but far outweigh the negatives.

I experience increased respiration with the onset of this madness. Quickly forced pockets of air exude from my lungs without provocation. Attempting any simple movement, like putting my shoes on, can cause this heavy breathing as well as the harsh, long-lasting body shaking.

Shocks zap my body with no warning. Far worse than a mosquito bite, they remind me of the jolt I received from a cow prodder as a child on the farm where I was brought up. How would I know that? Five older brothers. The electricity running through me sporadically and inexplicably feels like it exits at the bottom of my feet. The burn at the exit point compares to someone poking me with a hot branding iron. From time to time, the electrical current flows from my head to my feet and returns, continually repeating the pattern.

I try to move my legs, but they get stuck in place. Breaches occur during the transfer of signals from brain to body and I become paralyzed. All falls on deaf ears as no degree of inner self-talk changes matters. Bonnie assists me to navigate the course. Without her, I stay glued to the floor or fall over to kiss it. Other times, my legs stiffen like thick boards, again causing immobility. The fierce, long-enduring and intense contraction causes pain. Until the muscles release, I remain painfully fused, whether I am standing, sitting or lying.

Body parts cramp excessively. Stomach constriction causes me to coil and the top of my feet cramp the entire day. Nothing relieves it. I must lie and take it. A charley horse is a good comparison. It wakes you up out of nowhere in the middle of the night and either causes you to lean away from the cramp or to cling to it. All you can do is bide your time until it lets up. This cramping never diminishes and lasts for days at a time. I cannot sleep from the pain and walking is excruciating. The degree of cramping when walking causes me to infer that every single bone in each foot is broken.

My body also displays physical numbness. I feel the presence of touch, but nothing more. Odd, considering I am touch-sensitive. Before I left school for medical leave in April, I participated in staff volleyball. Several times I dove to dig a ball from the floor with no painful effects whatsoever. The next day I would have multiple bruises on my hips and elbows; however, I barely felt the floor contact at the time. This is the same situation. I am numb to the core.

Balance becomes an obstacle of its own. Often, I find I have no clue what position my legs are in, whether I am lying in bed or standing up. My legs may be off to one side or turned in. I don't know the difference unless I look down at them. My body sways in different directions. Though standing perfectly still, I perceive movement. It periodically feels like someone has pulled the rug out from underneath me, causing me to pitch backward.

My body rocks continually as if masquerading as an oar-less rowboat that jostles side to side with each passing wave. I bobble whether I stand, sit or lie down. The feel of motion remains a constant in this ride on the stormy seas. I see no land in sight.

10 The Abyss

Crying is how your heart speaks when your lips can't explain the pain you feel.
~Unknown

For ten days I lie confined to my bed, hostage to an upstairs bedroom I neglect to see as my own. I receive a mauling from neurological misfires as my mind runs amok in each of its momentary breaches. I envision no escape.

I lie on my back and scrutinize every fragment of the backdrop. I observe pictures and try to remember when, where and why we acquired them. *What is their significance? Does Bonnie like them? Do I? Did we buy them together?* One of the frames contains a print of 1 Corinthians 13:4-8, which describes love. I lack the ability to comprehend or retain the words or meaning behind the verse and cannot possibly apply it to our relationship. I do not understand my association with Bonnie, who she is to me. I know she is my lifetime partner, yet I hold no feelings or attachment to the concept.

I canvass the layout along with the color of the bedroom wall and adjoining bathroom. I scrutinize the stroke where the paint trim on the wall meets the ceiling. Through my subconscious, my Type-A personality peeks through. I repeatedly count the five blades on the fan directly above the bed as if expecting a different outcome with each simple calculation. I eyeball the method by which each brown blade connects to the gold blade-holders. I inspect the simple decorative housing and light fixtures. Examining the dust on the blade sides when the fan sits still, I am cognizant of the sound of the loose blade when running. I repeat the counting sequence over and over again with no new insight.

The vision from the second-story bedroom mirrors that of a treehouse as I stare into the branches from the constricted view of a single framed window. Birds habitually perch on a limb, often eating a black oil sunflower seed as a favorite offering from the feeder a deck below. Squirrels chase one another in circles around the circumference of old oak trees. I occasionally hear tiny thumps and scurrying paws as the squirrels play a game of tag throughout the treetops onto the roof of the house and back again. When non-active, they stretch out atop a branch to bask in the sun. A greater sense of awareness never seen; not once did one stumble or fall from unsteadiness.

I, however, need assistance with everything. Each movement requires planning. First, I assess my body to see if the shaking and jerking has dissipated enough to move. This requires a mental check of the volume of electricity I feel in my body. If still present, my body will surge into a higher frequency attack or its presence will hold my body in a state of paralyzed check. A game of chance. I never know for sure until I initiate movement. Once I establish my state and determine it is safe to move, I sit up on the side of the bed and wait for the dizziness to pass so I can secure my balance. Bonnie then assists me to the restroom and back.

When electrical circuits soar, my body reacts with fury to physical movement during transfer and arrival at the destination. Walking ten steps to the bathroom, my body vacillates between an angry rag doll and a stiffened Barbie. My legs alternate between jelly and lead pipes. Bonnie takes hold of one arm and puts the other on the small of my back. I shuffle my feet, unsure of my strength and balance as my back jerks and my body quakes.

Bonnie occasionally assists me to the downstairs living area for a few hours of respite in another domain. Her presence and the sights of nature out of the bedroom window offer the only aspects of life seen. Isolation becomes a formidable adversary.

I do not possess the energy to stand for any length of time and fear my unruly body. In the shower, I become a punching bag for fixtures and walls, eventually plummeting to the floor. I cleanse in the bathtub—a bumper car's ride in itself. I need Epsom salt baths. Bonnie discovers how difficult assisting me in and out of the deep soaker can be. Once convulsive activity and dystonia occur, she cannot pull me from it. My body overtaken, no opportunities arise to rescue me. Limbs kick, arms flail, my head thrusts backward and water travels airborne. Bonnie hastily learns to keep a rolled up towel behind my head for protection. My body, however, lingers as fair game against the tub walls. Both helpless, we wait for the slightest break in shaking to make an escape, even if it means being plopped back into bed soaking wet with no time to dry off.

My human frailty comes to light. I cannot control movements with any part of my body and lose the ability to feed myself. This disability causes a major emotional reaction in having to rely so fully on another human being. Trust issues instigate rebellion like ill-treated prisoners. I quickly identify how I bank solely on myself in dire straits. No longer capable, the brick wall begins to crumble one block at a time, spoonful by spoonful.

Moments of anger and stubbornness have me crawling short distances without asking for or taking assistance, trying to fend off the onslaught.

My hand is forced—literally—if I want to eat. Tears emanate from my eyes as one small spoonful after another feeds me. I feel powerless; my heart breaks.

The strong-willed fighter in me accepts "feeding" only whenever absolutely necessary, even though my eyes have been opened to trust issues I am free to relinquish. I hold tightly to whatever level of functioning I possess whenever possible. In my fearful eyes, letting go means an admission of defeat. I am worse than I could ever imagine and refuse to question how much lower I can go.

After two weeks of living this way, relentless horror inundates me. I physically maneuver with constraints. Bonnie puts in a call to Lisa, my counselor, and offers me the phone. Lisa, concerned about the neurological symptoms, questions the need for further consultation with a neurologist to be on the safe side. My initiative to evade doctors and the medical field hits a roadblock.

I call Dr. Tyson's office—Dr. Tyson, the neurologist who hastily removed the Lorazepam and quickly sent me packing. I describe my situation, but he refuses to see me. His office secretary instructs me to see my primary physician. Morally and ethically, I fail to comprehend how this can happen, but then again, how can any of this be happening? Dr. Tyson removed the drug, not my primary, Dr. Baker. An internal medicine doctor does not specialize in tremors, dystonia and convulsive activity. Dr. Tyson is aware of these physical side effects from the drug. But it doesn't matter. He leaves me dangling for the second and final time. I never want to see him again. I feel repulsed by any words of his.

In disbelief, Bonnie and I visit with the school district's Human Resources Department to inform them of my situation and inquire about options. My dream of returning to teaching in August turns to nothing but a fantasy. Viewing my disability, the human resources director suggests early retirement. For me, that route mimics throwing in the towel and suggesting hopes of healing improbable. I postpone any discussion on future employment. I want to allow time to heal without making a rash decision. Decision-making is not a strong suit right now.

The director submits a medical leave request for the upcoming semester, with the entire year discretional. One pre-requisite, I need medical leave forms filled out and signed by my doctor before receiving approval from the school board. I return to Dr. Baker to request her signature and once again ask for her assistance. During the course of the appointment, we discuss my situation. I hand over my medical forms under the perception I retain her full support; she expresses nothing to the contrary and I plan to pick up the necessary papers at my next appointment, which is more than a month away.

Dr. Baker wants me to return to Dr. Clifford, the psychiatrist who had taken me off Zoloft nearly a year prior. I want to see a new doctor, but Dr. Baker informs me she believes a newly found doctor would seek to once again medicate my drug-related symptoms.

At my last druthers, I opt for a September appointment with Dr. Clifford. Quite frankly, I am shocked he booked it, since we parted on flawed terms. This means, nonetheless, that I must sustain myself for over a month before I receive any assistance. Bonnie supports me in all that I do; perseverance will be 100 percent me. *It is going to be one long month.*

I believed full healing would occur within a six-month timeline, which is the minimum number of months for recovery for protracted drug withdrawal. All focus turns to getting through each single day, minute by minute. The present moment demands my full concentration and renders me incapable of looking farther into the day. I exist in the here and now—that is all there is.

Formerly imprisoned by my body, my mind follows suit. Nowhere to run; nowhere to hide. This experience challenges the mere essence of my soul. I question my strength and the degree necessary to merely endure. *I know I'm strong, but am I strong enough?* I continue to wonder why God has let this happen to me.

11 Opening the Floodgates

We must build dikes of courage to hold back the flood of fear.
~Martin Luther King Jr.

A windfall of symptoms prepares to unleash. Already overwhelmed, I endure not only a survival test, but one for the will to live. Floodwaters continue to spill over the dam. My hair begins to fall out, leaving noticeable clumps in the sink, brush and towel whenever I wash my hair. Luckily, my thick hair saves any unusual looks; I have plenty to spare. On the plus side, I have no need to shave my legs, which at this point is highly impractical.

Sound turns into an issue, with every noise becoming a high-pitched scream in my ear. My favorite radio stations, which play mainstream Top 40 hits, are Y107 and Q106.1 on the FM dial. I am partial to pop, R&B and hip-hop with a mix of rap—all of them a far cry from the music of my nearly all-white, country, small-town upbringing.

However, hypersensitivity to sound prevents listening to any music to pass the time. Even played at the lowest volume, the sounds mesh together with jack-hammer vibrations rocking my head. My skull wants to burst. I keep the television at the lowest decibel possible, often muting it altogether.

The sound sensitivity reaches beyond television and music into everyday life. Even the meowing of Charlie, our white and gray rescue cat, sends me through the roof. I spend a good part of my day in complete silence.

Beyond hypersensitivity to sound, I experience tinnitus, a constant ringing in the ears. If my ears aren't ringing, my own personal concert plays in my head. No particular genre, but instead a blend of Sirius stations. Song lyrics play from the moment I wake until the time I fall asleep. Imagine no turn-off mechanism. In withdrawal, the sounds are not only earsplitting—they do not stop. The loud music rivals any thought. The same tune repeats itself all day long. I can't change the station.

My brain changes consist of more than disturbances with sound. It has rewired to play endless streams of malfunction. I, in turn, call the mental and emotional glitches "radio stations." They switch as quickly and easily as a tuner in scan mode. The normal stations I listen to are temporarily off the air. I possess no control over the dial. Some play singularly, but most play in combination. It is an all-day affair.

The "crazies" hold point as one of the scariest and most prominent stations. Bonnie would be the first to joke that my brain was originally like a hamster on a cage wheel, always thinking and planning. This symptom, however, is boundless. I do not retain the ability to calm or control my brain. My mind runs unbridled with intrusive thoughts, looping a negative thought pattern. Uncontrollable thoughts pass through at the speed of sound. My brain screams at me and I want to scream back.

I can't stand it. Envision the highest screeching sound of dial-up Internet and apply it tenfold. I want to cover my ears to stop all of the noise from entering, but it lies within. I find it difficult to deal with on many levels and perceive depression to be the only thing worse. Nothing makes sense. I exist in a state of total confusion; thoughts zip by so rapidly I am unaware of repeats. I cannot differentiate rational thoughts from irrational ones or process what I see, hear or read. I fear insanity.

During one of our sessions, Lisa informs me that "people with poor judgment don't realize they have poor judgment. You are *not* going crazy."

Lisa, always calm and matter of fact, assures me the symptom serves as another facet of withdrawal. Tough as it may be, it will go away at some point. She instructs me to change the negative term I attach to it so as not to be so antagonistic. She informs me that all of the symptoms I experience correlate to my body and brain healing. Turning a deaf ear, I never change the label and continue to call this station the "crazies." I cannot release the permeating fright with a name change.

Thoughts of permanent brain damage pervade my consciousness. I am totally cognizant of everything happening somewhere deep beneath the surface and it petrifies me. The constant fear of losing control and going mad hangs over me. In reality, no control exists. That fact is increasingly undeniable.

Bonnie asks me what I am thinking as I stare off into space. I shake my head. There is nothing here. Not one thought. Incapable of thinking in the present, I cannot plan for the future. Short-term memory fails me once again and my attention span disappears. Just when I perceived my memory and speech closer to normal, my mind betrays me one more time.

When people speak to me, I cannot keep up with the message they are delivering. I listen with intent, but it doesn't matter. They may as well talk to a brick wall. I suffer cog fog, a brain fog, or loss of cognitive ability. Thinking recedes out of my reality. If Bonnie talks to me about doing something, I must do it immediately or I will forget. Nothing triggers recall. When I start a simple task, I forget what and why I am doing it.

Household items puzzle me, holding no purpose. My ability to decipher statements or paragraphs plummets. Repeated attempts end up fruitless. In a dazed state, my mind pitches a shutout. I get to the point of telling Bonnie that it doesn't do any good to talk to me. I don't know what she is saying, making a meaningful dialogue impossible.

I question future capabilities. No abilities are apparent, physically or mentally. On a scheduled visit, Lisa assures me intelligence isn't the heart of the problem. Hard to imagine when forming words and sentences represents a chore in itself. I have lost the whole enchilada. *Why did I fall back farther into this state again?* Feeling like the scarecrow in the *Wizard of Oz*, I need reassurance I still foster an intellectual brain beneath the scope of withdrawal.

Sleep offers no escape. I dream vividly. Everything is up close and personal—every minute drama-filled and colorful. Dreams are highly detailed, extremely graphic and restless. Violent calamities permeate them. I feel like a character in a *Law & Order: SVU* saga as I endure persecuting dreams of choking, hitting, knife-slicing and bloodshed. I am portrayed as the victim, predator and onlooker. As a witness, I am never able to come to the aid of a person attacked. In predatory mode, I assault without remorse. With a victim status, I bear a persistent physical onslaught.

Even though I view sleep as a delicacy and important to my healing, I don't relish it. I live a nightmare during both waking and sleeping hours. I envision no means of retreat. When awake, I aspire to sleep and, when asleep, I desire to be awake. If all of my hair-raising dreams were taken away, I would have no dreams left. I crave something to transform my substandard dreams into congenial ones. I relish a dream catcher.

Visions haunt me with the mere act of closing my eyes—no sleep required. My eyelids function as the large screen of an IMAX theatre. At times an assortment of colors presents itself—seemingly beautiful. The splendor keeps me pleasantly engaged. Then suddenly, a flip-side appears. Spiders and insects crawl a short distance from my eyes as if I am lying down beside them. They gradually enlarge as they creep under and over each other, inching closer. Closer to what? My eyeballs. I retract when one gets close enough to poke at me. Not a spider lover, how ironic they dominate my visual experiences. I normally strain to keep my eyes open until overpowered by fatigue.

I view my brain as an enemy. It turned against me. *How can we become one again?* Until drug withdrawal, I believed my brain was me. I never understood anyone telling me different. It took getting hit with a lead pipe to realize my soul differs from my brain. I identified with the voice in my head. I realize now I am not that voice, but the one aware of it. These various brain symptoms cause a multitude of thoughts and feelings that are not me at all—just what is happening to me. A rich spiritual education slowly unravels.

My brain hurts. The origin of pain affirms it. I do not perceive the battling radio stations to be the cause. My brain runs a gamut of chills, vibrations, and pins and needles. Infrequently, a burning sensation strikes. The weirdest consists of the feel of something crawling around inside my brain. I refer to this as the "heebie-jeebies." Bizarre for sure. What part of this isn't?

My skull aches as if wounded. The feel of an ax puncturing the crown of my head returns, as does a tight band, which snugly circumferences it. At times, I feel as if someone has slammed a small football helmet down onto my head and I can't get the thing off. Pressure builds within my face and head with no means of emission. Sharp pains dagger my temples, with attempts to lessen the strikes useless. Grasping the sides of my head at the focal point of the pain serves as my only remedy.

Migraines knock me off my feet with an unyielding wrath for days at a time. Pain and pressure build on one side of my head, then move to the opposite side. I become nauseous and unable to use my eyes whatsoever. Nothing, no matter the size, appears visible. Any attempt to use my vision worsens the experience. Sound hypersensitivity elevates with the migraine and I stomach no appetite. I strive to lie motionless with hopes of imminent sleep.

My face rotates between feelings of contortion, numbness and pain. While obvious by sight and touch, my left side exists, though it often feels like it is missing. My perception flips back and forth between numbness and the sense that my head has been sliced in two. It feels like the left side hangs off to the side without purpose. Other times, I perceive my eyes to be at different levels. I believe my left eye to be midway down my face. My left side is always lower than my right during this misperception. I slide my fingers around my face for awareness. Surely someone has enrolled me into a version of Rod Serling's *Twilight Zone* without my permission or knowledge.

Inside my head, a decades-old television commercial plays. The ad depicts a man holding an egg, which represents someone's brain. He cracks the egg open and empties it into a heated frying pan, then tips the pan for display and says, "This is your brain on drugs. Get the picture?" I get it now. My brain is fried.

12 The Hardest Breath

"What is depression like," he whispered. "It's like drowning. Except you can see everyone around you breathing."
~Unknown

Through it all, I am told to breathe. Breathe. *How can I breathe? I am drowning.* I repeatedly try to explain to Bonnie how depression feels. The closest I can come is using the verse in Sara Bareilles' "Love Song." Many people suffer some level of natural depression throughout their lives. Previously, I had mourned the transition of loved ones and lamented the breakup of a long-term relationship. I thought I knew depression; I had no idea. What I experience now far exceeds my understanding.

Depression from drug withdrawal takes no captives, especially when suicidal thoughts are involved. It hits at the very core of my being. It drops me to my knees. Given my cognitive impairment and memory loss, it is no surprise I cannot think clearly. This is no "woe is me" funk. Lisa informs me the quick removal of the drug has caused a chain reaction of brain chemistry changes.

In shock, my brain attempts to adjust to functioning without the Lorazepam. Thoughts come in from nowhere. I don't know where they originate or when the next will infiltrate. I struggle to stop them—but it doesn't work. Nothing does. I hang on for dear life. Overwhelmed, I suffer emotional exhaustion on a daily basis. I never braved the depths of such emotional pain. I endure a moment-by-moment process of survival. Up to this point, I believed the death of family members represented the worst circumstances in life. *What could possibly happen to make me suffer more? Stupid question. There are no words. Only by the grace of God am I still here.*

My true self would not think of suicide. Slitting my wrists ranks last in methodology—it's so violent. Yet, for some unknown reason, this idea captivates my thoughts. Visually graphic scenes accompany the intrusive thoughts as if the thoughts alone aren't bad enough. The depiction parallels my first night home from the hospital. I turn my head to look away, but the imagery projects from my brain. My brain provides no exodus.

The combat lasts all day, every day. In this matter, I not only need to win the war, I must win each and every battle. I fear if I exhibit one moment of weakness the harmful thoughts may overtake me. I allow no breaks in focus—not even for a second. I can't catch my breath. I abort trust in myself. I possess an entity unknown to me. Either I survive or we both die.

A 24/7 event, I deem mornings the worst. Exhausted daily by noon, I remain alert and fighting. I fear any letdown or sleep, no matter how tired I surmise myself to be. If I sleep, I start from scratch—even from naps, which are usually toxic. Upon waking it appears my brain needs to readjust. It is morning all over again. Depression alone drains me. I have little left in me, yet I dread bedtime. I barely made it through today. *What will tomorrow bring? What if tomorrow is worse? Will I be strong enough to make it?*

During this dreadful time, I borrow a phrase from *The Biggest Loser*: "staying above the yellow line." I base this outcome on a different competition. Instead of weight loss, I rival my inner strength against my drug withdrawal mind. I wager my life. Often my life is a flicker of a candle in a sea of black night. I search for solid ground. I treasure anything that keeps my mind above suicidal thinking.

Another new experience arises—one that is depression-related, according to Lisa. With self-harm on the table, "cutting" emanates. While I sit in the deep-soak tub performing an Epsom salt bath, an incomprehensibly fierce impulse emerges. I aspire to cut myself. I do not wish to slit my wrists, but instead carve my legs. Luckily, no razor is available. Who knows what would happen if one were? I fear my mind. Thankfully, that ugly head shows itself only this once. Once is plenty. The thought took me by surprise, surfacing in a split-second flash. When I inform Lisa of the event, she instructs me to grab a handful of ice or stick my hands into an ice-filled sink as soon as possible if it ever happens again. She says the coldness of the ice ensures a sense of feeling once again and the impulse will cease. Ice supposedly dissipates panic attacks as well.

I search for coping mechanisms on the Internet, which suits me as an invaluable friend. The blue light depression therapy, effective with seasonal affective disorder, serves as a short-lived possibility. However, I toss the idea to the curb due to cost factors and the potential for eye problems. Without income for a year on medical leave, I decline investment in a method unsubstantiated.

I decide to pursue healthy and natural remedies, but locate few. Nutrition captures the forefront. I introduce bananas and nuts as household staples. I see no relief, but continue use. I alternate Body Calm pills and Body Calm Supreme every four hours to maintain a realm of balance. The Road Back, a drug withdrawal and recovery assistance program, advertises these products as aiding with stress, anxiety and insomnia. Body Calm Supreme is known as a clinically researched cherry powder and passion flower combination. More than anything, these products take the edge off. I keep whatever means I find beneficial. My life is at stake. Once suicidal thoughts subside, I can relinquish taking them as well.

Nothing scares me more than depression. Not one thing. I hold the utmost respect for people who suffer depression on a daily basis, their battles and journey as a whole. I hope to be free of it with healing and recovery. Other people carry it with them a lifetime. God bless and have mercy on them.

13 The Most Shameful

Shame should be reserved for the things we choose to do, not the circumstances that life puts on us.
~Ann Patchett, *Truth & Beauty*

Symptoms continue to manifest. Once they occur, they lodge in my memory bank. I may not remember much right now, but I always remember a symptom once it pops up. Unfortunately, I believe I always will. Beyond suicidal thoughts, my brain's other entity grows in numbers. I continually tell myself that I am not my brain. It does not help. My brain has acquired patterns and thoughts untrue to me. Even though these symptoms are withdrawal-induced, I must deal with them as my own. Unpleasant doesn't define it. It is far worse and makes me feel isolated, ugly and disgusting.

Being able to label my symptoms helps me feel better. If I can name them and know what they are, then at least I have awareness and feel I am not confronting an unknown demon. Once named, I come to realize others have experienced these same manifestations, not me alone. However, no improvement materializes, physically or emotionally, when I strain to ride out the fully evident effects of this drug withdrawal. Intrusive thoughts, urges and images are of inappropriate things at inappropriate times. They are unwanted, feel uncontrollable and often pertain to disturbing or distressing themes. These themes are often ones that the individual, in this case me, finds to be the most offensive and repugnant.

Going into sexual overdrive doesn't capture it and shows no relevance. There exists no thought or pre-determined interest in any of the people who appear in my intrusive thoughts. I have no prior or present attraction to any of these individuals. Without warning, a nearly uncontrollable desire comes over me with whoever happens to be in my presence. My environmental surroundings turn murky, nothing visually clear. Everything appears blurred, even the person in my line of vision. The yearning generates lust for the person near me. Once the intrusive thoughts begin, I cannot even tell you what the person looks like. My world turns fuzzy.

My first encounter with this manifestation occurred earlier in the summer when Bonnie and I were on vacation in North Carolina. One day, we pampered ourselves with a shopping excursion. The day was sunny and warm. We enjoyed a walk along the busy harbor. Boats of all sizes, but especially yachts, captivated our attention. Without forethought, my mind deviated. Sexual cravings filled my brainwaves as a lady approached on the sidewalk from the opposite direction. The quick and sharp digression of my thoughts led astray caught me off-guard. I fought to stop the spell. I dropped my head, staring at nothing other than the sidewalk. The phenomenon did not stop after passing her. Seconds seemed like minutes.

In shock, I could not think straight after my brain switched back. All I wanted to do was flee to the beach house before it happened again. I informed Bonnie I wished to head back to enjoy the beach. I could not describe the woman in my view. I do not know what happened. It scared me. It freaked me out. It is just one more aspect of withdrawal that holds no understanding. I do not know who I am, but I do know this is not me.

I pushed the incident deep down inside me, pretending it had never occurred. We spent the remainder of the vacation on the beach, where I felt safer and at peace. I hoped it would be a lone incident, yet I continue to repel intrusive thoughts frequently. Most deal with the urge to scream at Bonnie or family members in a hateful and hurtful manner. I fight to control my thoughts and the verbal explosions building in my mouth. The rage, I can deal with that. The sexual thoughts, however, are beyond disturbing. I never imagined something like this could happen. For that matter, I never imagined any of this experience possible.

I manage the rest of the summer without similar incident. Bonnie's family plans a visit prior to the start of the upcoming 2009-10 school year. She updates them on my progress, covering a limited number of facets regarding my condition. Bonnie and I decide to join them for a meal out. She assures me it will be short-lived and getting out of the house will be good for me. Our vacation in North Carolina worked out for the most part, so why not? I feel safe with family members present and a quick exit available with Bonnie if so desired.

Upon arriving at the restaurant, we sit at a table far removed from everyone. I place myself at the end of the table. Bonnie purposely sits next to me so she can remain alert for complications. I keep my head down to avoid eye contact with other people and to shun conversation. All is going well until the waitress approaches to offer coffee. I lift my head and give her direct eye contact to acknowledge her question. *Crap!* Once again, the intrusive desire fills my brain. As before, the restaurant appears nebulous. The waitress does as well.

I drop my head to remove her from my vision, as if that will stop it. In my mind, I yell, "Stop! Stop!" repeatedly trying to change the dial in my brain. An internal fight ensues to stop myself from crossing what I normally consider inappropriate lines, verbally and physically. I gather strength to control myself—that is all I can do. It stops eventually, seconds seeming like minutes, just as before. The time frame encompasses the most intense inner battle ever. Bonnie asks if I am okay. I nod my head, "yes." It is all I can manage. What else can I say or do?

When the emotional torture ceases, my own thought patterns of shame and dirtiness piggyback the event. I want to run and hide in whatever safe haven is present. Leaving is not always feasible without question. There is no way in hell I am telling anyone what happened. I feel agony over the experience and cannot find any solution except complete isolation, but isolation cannot last forever. That is not reality. *How long will I suffer from this?*

Tormented, I ask Bonnie to drive me to Lisa. During the appointment, I explain to both the nature of the symptom. I feel such disgust. I tell them my urge is such that I would go after a prostitute. I want them to understand the level of my disturbance. I sense no control. I sit in a slouch with droopy shoulders, a look of dejection plastered on my face. Bonnie and Lisa sit quietly. After a slight pause, Lisa explains that withdrawal makes you think and sometimes act differently than you otherwise would. She describes how a client began shoplifting during withdrawal. Obviously, this client lost the fight.

Lisa notes my strength and delivers words of encouragement. Feelings of despair supersede her reassurance. Labeling the episodes as intrusive thoughts, or something other, really doesn't matter. I feel utter shame. *This is not me. Who am I becoming? What have these drugs done to me?*

Up to this point, I have only skimmed over my sex-related symptoms with Lisa, but not talked in length about them. I don't know why sex talk is so hard. Maybe it is for most people. During one prior office visit, I threw out a sarcastic statement concerning my general sexual dysfunction as it related to neurological firestorms; I wanted no further discussion beyond that.

Clearly, I would have to deal with this issue and speak openly about it. The difficulty started several months prior to my hospitalization and was especially intense after my last intake of Zoloft. Afterward, exercise charged my body, causing shaking and often convulsions. Sex results in the same. Neurons flood my body and, within seconds, electrically charge my entire being. Intense convulsions kick in and I sustain a walloping. Afterward, I feel extremely nauseous and dizzy, often enduring bed spins. Thereafter, the slightest movement to scratch an itch or move an arm reignites my body to prolong the event. I suffer aftershocks nearly 100 percent of the time. *Oh, I'm doing slightly better today. It'll be okay.* Afterward, I lie demoralized. *Holy shit. It's not okay at all.* Bonnie always displays apprehension prior to the act and then feels regretful watching the consequences.

Since protracted withdrawal has hit, the ability to have sex has vanished, partly due to all of the other symptoms going on in my body. Worse than the fallbacks, the sexual dysfunction is not in synchronicity with other symptoms. It beats to its own drum—present more than absent.

My libido is non-existent. Whose wouldn't be with everything else going on? I struggle to get through a day, don't know who the hell I am and have little attachment to the majority of people or things around me. Days exist. I labor to walk or talk. Sex is not a high priority; in fact, it is not a priority at all. It goes beyond any loss of libido, which both Zoloft and Lorazepam can cause. At the time, the prescribing doctor told me the loss of libido presented no major alarm and would work itself out. Don't believe it. It can take a while—a long while—and extends far beyond lack of drive. My actual sexual ability and drive are not in alignment with the sexually intrusive thoughts that run through my brain. Intrusive thoughts are nothing but notions of my drug-withdrawal brain. They are not me.

14 Violent Ideations

Shame derives its power from being unspeakable.
~Brené Brown, *Daring Greatly: How the Courage to Be Vulnerable Transforms the Way We Live, Love, Parent, and Lead*

The pendulum continues to swing in the wrong direction. Violent, sometimes homicidal, ideations establish themselves under the intrusive thought umbrella. I aim the lion's share toward Bonnie, minimally at my mom. These two people represent those in closest contact with me, aside from Lisa and my natural healers.

Just like the sexually intrusive thoughts, my brain quickly focuses on someone near. A predatory-type fix develops as I stare with an unseen sneer. The typical gruesome plot that involves Bonnie consists of suffocating her during sleep with a pillow. Though I never move an inch, my visual mind places me overtop her. I witness her struggle to remove herself from my clutches. Her hands fiercely attempt to pry my hands from the grasp of the pillow. Her body contorts side to side in an endeavor to throw me off. My mind plays its own videogame, and a violent one at that. Lying at her side, I turn from her in disgust to stop the aggression, but my mind continues the track. I close my eyes, which only intensifies the visualization. I lie and wait for the ideation to conclude. My heart weeps.

The most painful ideation forms as Bonnie and I work on simple tasks in our garage. With many a tool nearby, I acquire the urge to take a hammer and hit Bonnie in the head repeatedly. I see the blood pouring down onto the side of her face. I never heed her scream, witness her falling or visualize anything beyond that. That is more than plenty. As with my own wrist-slitting visualizations, no consequential effects are noted. Beyond the blood, she appears unharmed. I move myself away to sit in a distant chair and gaze downward to remove her from my view. I put both my hands into my lap clasped together.

Bonnie walks over and smiles. "Are you all right? What are you doing?"

How can I possibly answer? "I just need to sit," I say. "I don't feel well."

Oh, my God! Oh, my God! Oh, my God! What's happening to me? What would she think? What the hell am I thinking?

I sit back in the chair and close my eyes while Bonnie continues to work on the other side of the garage. I anxiously wait for my brain to turn stations. *I don't care what station, just turn. Just get me off this one.* Just as the tide in my brain turns on this aura, the radio station auto-tunes back. Shame engulfs me. Disgust and torment of a whole other kind fill my being. I am emotionally spent and despise myself.

What kind of monster have I turned into? Do I need to kill myself so I don't harm another? I cannot bear the emotional pain caused by these occurrences. I will never allow anything to happen to anyone else. The knives in the kitchen drawer begin to look like a viable solution after all. Later, I inform Bonnie of the violent nature of my thoughts and how much they scare me. I give only general terms. The details are too revolting and chilling.

Even though it pertains to her, Bonnie responds, "I know you will never hurt me."

Her assuredness fails to convince me. She lacks comprehension of the shocking and hideous level of my thoughts. My forfeiture of details allows for her ignorance.

The tide periodically turns to my mother. Mom and I hold frequent phone conversations to discuss my progress. Thoughts of killing her run through my mind randomly without detail. The thoughts enter my head outside of our conversations, never during. Our dialogue is usually short. With Mom living in Wisconsin, I fail to directly experience my symptoms with her as I do with Bonnie. For this I am grateful.

When I inform Lisa of the depression, suicidal thoughts and homicidal ideation, she shockingly asks, "Why did you take so long to tell me?"

I offer the obvious answer. "I am ashamed."

"Depression is very natural during drug withdrawal," Lisa informs me with nonchalance. "Suicidal and homicidal ideation stem from that depression. As your brain heals and balances, these will disappear. They are nothing but intrusive thoughts. You don't need to worry, Pj. You will never do anything. You aren't the only one to go through it, nor are you capable of doing such a thing. "

"But how do you know for sure?" I ask.

"Because I can see your torment."

15 A Term Overused

There is no such thing as pure pleasure; some anxiety always goes with it.
~Ovid

Anxiety denotes a term often thrown around to indicate excessive worry surrounding stress. In my opinion, it is overused. I used to worry about certain outcomes on occasion, but I never saw myself as someone who could not handle anything that was thrown at them. Never meant there wouldn't be difficult moments, maybe even a learning curve, but I would get through and come out okay—usually better. I have always been driven by self-improvement.

To be told by doctors that all of my symptoms are anxiety-based, that this stems from something I failed to handle as a child, to be looked upon as a hypochondriac, well... that takes the cake. Every time I meet a new doctor, within minutes the doc is telling me he/she knows me better than I know myself. That is not very realistic on any level. Maybe it was good fortune the term "anxiety" was used often because the fighter in me came out, because I knew better.

With the cluster of symptoms that attack during drug withdrawal, anxiety is a natural combatant, just as depression. The one label I have been fighting to defeat turns into my reality. Anxiety is an immutable facet of my being, and finding methods to curb it are futile.

Lisa describes the situation best when she states how much benzos affect brain function and, when removed as such, put the brain in a state of shock. Benzodiazepines are central nervous system depressants that act on the brain by affecting neurotransmitter gamma-aminobutyric acid (GABA). Neurotransmitters are brain chemicals that facilitate communication between brain cells. GABA works by decreasing brain activity. Benzos boost GABA activity for a calming effect that results in sleepiness, a decrease in anxiety and relaxation of the muscles. In withdrawal, the opposite happens.

Lisa explains there are two types of stress. One consists of the thoughts or feelings I connect with what is happening to me and obsessing over them. I retain control over them. The second features my brain in distress. The symptoms I experience derive from the bombshell to my brain. In this case, time serves as my only healing agent. I have no way to control this type of stress. The weight of the load presents a burden. Lisa tells me my old methods for dealing with stressors will not work in this situation. I need to find new techniques.

I fight my brain on so many levels, making this task difficult. Chemical disturbances throw a number of curveballs at me. Lisa also reiterates my three and a half years of benzo use. Lorazepam emotionally numbed me to everyday stress. I operate on zero reserves. As such, minuscule life events may pack a punch.

Bonnie discusses hobbies and interests from the past. My old means of dealing with stress primarily focused on the physical aspects. I loved to work out and considered myself to be a health nut. I used our exercise equipment or attended the fitness center five days a week. Now, I experience days where crawling provides my only means of movement. I cannot always walk—and certainly not far. Not without assistance at least. Without Bonnie's aid, pieces of furniture or the wall itself work as my crutch to use from room to room.

Bonnie reminds me of my old loves: biking, hiking, fishing, working in the garden or on landscaping and toiling on house projects. They do not ring a bell and new methods of coping do not present themselves. My solution hinges on daily trial and error as days, weeks and months progress. I count on both Bonnie and Lisa for guidance with viable resolutions.

My anxiety soars. I cannot sit still, cannot concentrate. I view something wrong with each and every part of my world. Bonnie and I walk through each part of my life to discuss and uncover what I find unsettling. I grasp no understanding of it. Radio stations change so frequently I don't know what side is up. All I hold onto is the thought—*I am right here, right now. I will be okay. Everything will be okay. Now I just have to believe it.*

I battle constantly to slow down my chaotic brain as I bounce off the walls. I cling to this moment with all that I have. I try to survive each day and all thrown at me. I persevere one abominable day to make it into the next. That is a miracle in itself.

16 Box of Crayons

Life is about using the whole box of crayons.
~RuPaul

It has been four months since my hospital release in April. Emotional blunting has highlighted much of the summer months and endures into fall. Hard to decipher how I endure panic attacks when no positive or negative emotions present themselves whatsoever. Sixty-four colors in a crayon box and I get stuck with black—no mix of color whatsoever. Even with the latest setbacks in July, I feel numb on every level, yet emotional pain runs deep.

Lisa offers a nutshell explanation of how my lack of serotonin affects my mood and feelings. While a blank slate now, I will have feelings reappear with time and healing. With the relentless and overwhelming symptoms experienced from my distressed brain, irritability behaves as a natural. Other perceived negative feelings of depression, anxiety and rage follow suit. Definitely not a popular selection, but the dark colors represent a step up.

Lisa is right. Turmoil fills my days and nights with no ounce of joy to be found. Rage zips in without warning. My powerful fury creates difficulty with lashing out. I fight to hold my tongue. After one or two trials, I communicate my agitation to Bonnie to prevent direct verbal attacks on her. I express, due to anger, that I cannot have her near me. During these episodes she leaves me alone, offering frequent check-ins, until it passes. Bonnie says she can look at me and tell if all is well again. My eyes tell the whole story.

Plain and simple, I do not aspire to talk at all during these times. If I start to speak, something inappropriate might slip out. The ounce of control I feel pertains to keeping my lips sealed. I experience no forethought prior to the frenzy. Anger intrudes every crossing thought and deals with every facet of my life, no matter how trivial.

17 White Knuckles

If you can't fly then run,
if you can't run then walk,
if you can't walk then crawl,
but whatever you do you have
to keep moving forward.
~Martin Luther King, Jr.

Pinned down with body attacks, my mind vacillates from the "crazies" to depression, to cognitive fog. My brain's radio stations exhibit a life of their own. Life is a bitch at this point. Not very eloquently stated, but true nonetheless. Enslaved with horror, I find all options for help hopeless. I have never experienced anything as scary or painful, and cannot imagine I ever will again if I make it through this. I lie in the very midst of its clutches. I cannot supply adjectives to do it justice. No one can understand the agony unless you have lived it yourself. Hanging on until my knuckles lose all color, I brave the storm with all I have.

I believe death is upon me. On two occasions, I divulge to Bonnie my inability to withstand the calamity. Every part of my body appears to crash. The complexity lies with the multitude of symptoms and degree they hit simultaneously. *How much can my body take?* The thought of dying does not alarm me, though I consider dealing with the symptoms themselves horrific. Bonnie sits bedside and places a ring on my finger as a reminder of her love.

"I will always be beside you, now and always," she says. "You will get through this. We will get through this. Any time you feel alone, look at and feel the ring on your finger. It's okay you don't understand our relationship. Just know I'm right here."

While I cannot grasp our connection, I am fully aware of her support.

August takes forever as symptoms continually mount. My internal temperature gauge is erratic. One moment I cook on the inside and the next I freeze.

The furnace comes and goes for hours at a time, but the fridge frequently stays a few days. The fridge hauls baggage—a sign of things to come. The coattails contain some of the most intense symptoms that send me reeling for days and weeks to come. Smash-mouth dystonia and convulsive activity jump first in line and are last to say goodbye.

The "freezing" episodes also bring symptoms reminiscent of the flu. Sick daily, I cannot distinguish between flu and virus or withdrawal symptoms. Vertigo and nausea are ceaseless. I want to puke. Maybe I would feel better. I never do. I deem adequate nutrition impossible. I drink liquid forms easier than digesting solids—mainly protein shakes. I sip on one all day, though I rarely finish it.

A metallic taste poses a matter of contention. Nothing tastes good. Additionally, nothing settles in my stomach during digestion. Bonnie keeps small bagels stocked, especially blueberry. I tear small pieces off to steady my bitter stomach. While food intake remains questionable, my thirst runs off the charts. I keep two things at my side—water and ginger ale. As a priority, ginger ale counteracts the acid in my stomach, even though it lacks nutritional value.

Midway through August, I rally to spend half of my day on the main level of the house. The tremors, jerking and shaking brutally hit first thing each morning, periods in the afternoon and extend into the evenings. Minor breaks, however, allow me to move with Bonnie's assistance, and sometimes without. We view my ability to function independently critical with Bonnie in the education field. School starts soon. I cannot rely on her for my mobility, or constant support. We devise a plan for check-ins by phone, or for her to stop when her schedule allows it. I owe gratitude to her school district bosses for allowing her versatility. We both feel unsettled as the first day of independent living approaches.

"Are you sure you'll be okay?" Bonnie asks.

"I have to be," I respond.

The choices are limited. Bonnie cannot stay home with me all day, every day. Neither of us knows how long withdrawal and recovery will take. I awaken to her alarm, which sends a shockwave throughout my body. The abrupt arousal fires neurons in every direction, resulting in an immediate invasion of tremors, jerking and convulsive activity. Beaten senseless, I lie in bed until my body settles to where I feel confident enough to physically manage.

The body attacks halt. The electricity in my body dissipates. The bed spins cease. Nausea and dizziness settle enough to allow sufficient vision. Intrusive thoughts and crazy thought patterns convert into fizzling memories as I wait for the chemical changes to take place in my brain. I often sense the wave slowly cross my brain as my mind adjusts. The time differential varies day to day. At a minimum, it takes about an hour for everything to settle. I undergo the same vigorous, predictable occurrence each morning. Now I can attempt rising.

Bonnie escorts me downstairs if she is still home. If not, she sets things up the best she can so I can cope on my own. Walls provide boundaries of support. I walk when I can, crawl when I have to. Stairs become my first challenge. Better days see me navigating my way using the railing, one foot then the other on the same step before transferring myself to the next. Worse days put me in a seated position, moving down one step at a time on my butt. I go back upstairs only when absolutely necessary.

My legs refuse to bend in attempts to walk up the steps. My stiffened legs feel like lead pipes. A blast of air forcefully exerts itself from my lungs to mimic the sound of a freight engine with each step. I reach the top of those six steps with a paramount triumph equal to climbing Mount Everest. Bent over with hands on knees, I pause to catch my breath. I just spent my energy. Not worth it. I choose to navigate the steps in a seated position.

When I move down to the main level, I can use the computer. I search for assistance online when my brain bids rational thinking. I have never been in the position to beg for help—until now. I will do anything to relieve this torture. *How could everything have gone so wrong?* In a fearful state, I hold tight to the belief I need to reinstate Lorazepam, or Diazepam. I want to try removing the drug from my system again, only this time slowly, and properly taper off. I ignore Lisa's judgment from June when she advised me it was too late. I am desperate for any level of sustenance. I ponder use of a joint to calm my brain. I don't know how to attain one. I am not saying it is a wise choice, but one I assess. I mull over each and every option. *I am scared. I am desperate.*

Finally, September's appointment with Dr. Clifford arrives. Bonnie and I hesitantly walk into his office. I sense his annoyance in seeing me. His demeanor is cold. His eyes look directly into mine with zero facial expression. He proceeds with the appointment as if I have never been his patient and shows his intent not to hold any discussion. I ask for his assistance with this Lorazepam withdrawal; he offers none. He plays dumb, acting like he does not know any of my history or problems with Lorazepam before he abandoned me. *Why did he bother to see me again in the first place?* My short appointment turns into a waste of time—no shock. As with my neurologist, he abandons me for the second and last time. This is getting redundant.

I turn the Internet into an ally. I search for drug rehabilitation facilities and peruse alternative healing sites. I explore traveling out of state if the need arises. The drug facilities deal with counseling people in recovery, revolving around the issues that caused the drug dependency. Okay, that's not me. I discover the alternative healing locales as mostly out of state and costly. Bonnie and I cannot financially afford any of these places. I am on medical leave with no pay for a semester to a year and have to foot insurance premiums as well.

I search for support groups in the area. I locate Alcoholics Anonymous and Narcotics Anonymous. I regard neither harmonious to my situation. I search and I search and I search.

I fall into a state of agony. Bonnie lugs me to see Lisa. Barely able to speak and sorely beaten from neurological attacks, I offer few words. I feel defeated and have nowhere to turn. Bonnie tries her best to be a substantial means of support, yet I feel very alone in my struggle. I cannot fathom any more happening to me. The mounting symptoms render me hopeless. I inform Lisa of my inability to find doctors or support groups to help me.

Seeing my gloom-and-doom nature, she changes my sentiment with a few simple words. "You can do this," she proclaims.

Questioning my own foundation, I inquire. "I can?"

She nods her head. "Yes."

Still uncertain, I ask, "Are you sure?"

With unwavering confidence and a modest smile, she replies, "Yes. It will be incredibly hard, but yes. You can do this on your own."

Prior to seeing Lisa that day, I had reached a place of wishing it all to end. Engulfed in pain, I wanted it all over. I would never intentionally harm myself. I professed to Bonnie several times that I wished someone would put a gun to my head and pull the trigger. I was not joking. Lisa's sentiment transformed my condemned disposition into one of wavering optimism. I cannot determine what made the difference. Maybe I required someone with background knowledge and experience expressing their belief in my ability to succeed. Lisa's confidence in me sparked the flickering match of survival into a continual hope for life flame.

After visiting with her, I conclude that a successful recovery will be accomplished through my own individual work. Bonnie remains a source of emotional support, but I am the one dealing with the perpetual symptoms. She can walk the path with me, but not for me. She can hold my hand. She can hold me up. She can support me. I am the one who has to do the work to get through. Bonnie, feeling helpless, often observes me as she waits for adverse effects to subside.

Frequently, she asks, "What can I do to help you? I don't know what to do. I feel so helpless."

"I don't know," I say. "Nothing. I don't even know what to do to help myself."

Bonnie's powerless situation produces discomfort with her inability to fix the problem. She conjures up reading to me at bedtime. I concur, knowing the act allows her to feel of assistance. What comes out? *Harry Potter and the Deathly Hallows*. She cradles the book, bound and determined to make the most out of my endorsement. I cannot keep characters straight or understand the plot. Some nights I take in bits and pieces; other nights, I simply observe her as she beams, summarizing each occurrence. Her face glows; therefore, my purpose is served. It functions as the tiny morsel I can give to her.

18 Did You Ever Really Know Me?

There are some things in this world you rely on, like a sure bet. And when they let you down, shifting from where you've carefully placed them, it shakes your faith, right where you stand.
~Sarah Dessen, *Someone Like You*

I return to Dr. Baker's office expecting to pick up my signed medical leave papers. On the last visit, I perceived no hesitation, but a change in tone has ensued. Apprehension settles in the room. During the appointment, she never volunteers the paperwork, so I request it. She performs a complete about-face, acting as if she never agreed to the documentation in the first place. Now, I'm frantic.

Unsure of what to say, I implore her to sign the paperwork.

"I didn't realize there was a problem," I say. "School has already started. You know how bad I am. You know my situation." The visit turns uncomfortable as Dr. Baker redirects the conversation away from the paperwork issue. In shock, I am at a loss. Abandoned by my own doctor now?

Prior to school starting in August, I conveyed to the Human Resources Department that I would furnish the proper, signed medical leave papers. Paralyzed, I concern myself with the consequences of a forfeited signature. I return to human resources. To my relief, the school district backs me without hesitation. The director assures me of my high regard within the district and the value of my teaching ability. She confirms the district's knowledge of my ongoing health status and realizes the legal ramifications of a doctor's signature in this situation. Frustrated herself, she further guarantees the school district's protection from allowing this situation to jeopardize my career.

The director provides me with substitute information to obtain from Dr. Baker. I need to schedule follow-up visits for my condition to show I am under a doctor's care. In addition, I must gather a list of symptoms causing the inability to work. I contact Dr. Baker and this time she signs without quarrel. Now I have a semester, a year if needed. Surely that is all it will take.

The entire deliberation with Dr. Baker upsets me. I feel as if it is the breakup of a long-term relationship—a long-standing, seventeen-year, doctor-patient relationship. This raises trust concerns and I begin to doubt how well she knows me. She had advocated for me in the past. Our doctor-patient relationship has always been positive. What happened between those two visits? Did she converse with Dr. Tyson or Dr. Clifford? I may never know, but she had a change in heart. Maybe she did not want to chance a legal suit, which could pit doctor against doctor. Her signature on the medical form held the possibility of opening a can of worms.

In a state of anger, I once mentioned to Lisa the option of pursuing medical negligence. She conveyed the enormous finances a legal suit requires and that drug company monies would not run dry. She also hypothesized ruthless medical and drug company lawyers running every personal item about me through the wringer trying to theorize psychological issues to cover their neglect. Lisa foresaw a no-win situation. In her mind, my recovery constituted the number one priority and required every last ounce of my energy. Additional stress to my already fragile health implied delayed healing. My healing target converts to reaching the highest functioning level possible without guarantee of 100 percent recovery.

I plan on attending the scheduled appointments with Dr. Baker. I consider their primary purpose to validate my imperfect health status and monitor progress. Bonnie and I ponder the thought of dismissing her in search of a new doctor. I agonize over the perceived betrayal. After deliberation, Bonnie discerns it best to table the discussion in lieu of complications regarding immediate action—me learning how to function with my dysfunction.

Lisa speaks to me about post-traumatic stress disorder (PTSD). Like many of the other symptoms, I view it as merely another label. I tried to erase April 27 from my memory. I sought to do the same with the bizarre attacks to my mind and body. Somewhere along the path, I progressed into protective mode. Maybe it started when convulsions worsened a year or two ago. If not then, I know day one of the hospital stay is a likely starting place. I terminate visuals of myself with a head full of electrodes. I cannot think back on that day. My brain shuts off, forbidding reference to it.

Denial. I stubbornly believed that fighting my way through translated into eventual healing. Denial tolerates an operative capacity, but not emotional healing. I carry a heavy emotional load. I cannot fight my way through, nor can I outrun myself. Withdrawal is happening here and now. It is not going anywhere any time soon.

Lisa's voice serves as a constant reminder: "As you go emotionally, so does your body."

To relieve post-traumatic stress, I strive to find answers and a means of coping. I feel broken and opt for more than surviving my days. Bonnie hauls me into Barnes & Noble. What better place to look than the self-help section? We stumble upon a godsend, *Finding Life Beyond Trauma: Using Acceptance and Commitment Therapy to Heal From Post-Traumatic Stress and Trauma-Related Problems*. The book, by Victoria Follette and Jacqueline Pistorello, turns into a building block for changing my thought process. The workbook contains short chapters, which work great for my inattentive brain. A series of questions ending each chapter enables me to delve in deeper.

Many of the effects of PTSD parallel drug withdrawal, making differentiation difficult. One thing sticks out, though—avoidance. I dissociated from the events in the hospital and thereafter. I also learned over the course of four years to put my mind elsewhere once body jerking and convulsing begin. I sought refuge outside of my mind and body from all of the pain. Never for a second did I think it would be detrimental to my emotional health down the road. It was self-preservation at best.

As an athlete, I often put my mind elsewhere, into music or a zone, when conditioning intensely. The concept does not work here. The intensity of the all-encompassing pain makes me think of my mind and body as "it"—completely abstract entities. I feel far from whole and will need to change my thinking.

19 Holy Grail

We work on ourselves in order to help others, but we also help others in order to work on ourselves.
~Pema Chodron

How much emotional pain can I withstand? I crave a Lorazepam pill! *How is this happening? Why is this happening?* My brain cries out for the pill I longed to rid my body of. My head spins in circles trying to stop it. Initially, I deemed the drug craving the night I came home from the hospital a freak occurrence. I don't know how to get any Lorazepam pills. I discount intentions of trying. *Oh, how I want that drug back!* It is all I think of. The obsession induces restlessness. I want to bang my head on the wall.

During one of my sessions, Lisa sits across from me, conveying a more serious demeanor than normal. Once the discussion begins, I understand why. She does not regard the drug craving as unusual. She looks me squarely in the eyes and informs me I have a drug addiction.

"What?" I say. No way.

She explains to me my brain has become accustomed to functioning under the presence of the drug, which had been in my system three and a half years. My now-addicted brain flops in attempts to function normally in its absence. She continues by labeling me a drug addict.

"What?" I hate the term used on me. My posture collapses. "Don't call me that," I say. "I didn't do anything wrong."

The term signifies something far different to me. I think of a drug addict as someone who abuses cocaine or meth. I did not abuse anything. I depict a drug addict as someone who struggles with life circumstances and turns to drugs as a reprieve from them. I have heard of issues with prescription pain killers, but not this, and certainly not me. This could not be *me*! Lisa tells me Lorazepam will forever resonate in my life. I fail to understand that concept. She does her best to explain it to me. I close off. I cannot listen to any more of this. This is not me. I believe I am stronger than any of this happening to me. Once I recover, in no way will this be a part of my life.

With no obvious means of support in sight, I spend an increasing amount of time surfing the Internet. Home alone and feeling isolated, I seek to connect with someone who shares my experience. Is there anyone out there like me? Lisa says there is. She says there are tons of people like me. I need to find them.

I finally scroll upon benzowithdrawal.com. Several websites catch my eye, but benzowithdrawal.com abounds with thousands of members from across the globe. The vast number of members and differences in time zones create the ability to communicate any time of day or night. Misery loves company. I read over bits and pieces of drug withdrawal and recovery information on the site's main page. The information is extensive. All of my questions can be answered right here.

Membership is not open. I answer website questions and submit my inquiry. I impatiently anticipate my admittance, incessantly checking the computer. I receive confirmation of my membership within two days. Upon approval, I transform into a sponge as a "newbie." Longer-term members welcome me into the group and direct me to various site locations based on my circumstances and questions. At first, I yield to an overwhelming sensitivity to the multitude of people and amount of information. I spend numerous days reading select information and several more digesting it. I wish I had unearthed this place sooner. Things start to make sense. My eyes widen reading the information and its relevance to me.

I quickly appreciate the mass of people in my boat—thousands. Not that I want to see anyone suffer, but I recognize solidarity. The awareness offers a sense of relief. People offer insight into my circumstances, and I gain a great deal of knowledge about drugs, tapering, withdrawal and symptoms. A bountiful number of cases depict the never-ending ignorance of the medical field. Unlike society's popular belief, many people endure drug addiction and withdrawal due to their doctor's ignorance.

Yes, I said it—addiction. I now suffer drug addiction and now fully understand what Lisa was telling me. I can no longer turn a deaf ear to it or bury my head in the sand. I can say the word, but only for my ears and Bonnie's ears—and mostly in a whisper. I do not know how long acceptance of that fact will take. I am in shock. I am angry. I refuse to call myself an addict. It seems so harsh. *How can I be a drug addict if I didn't do this to myself?*

Many people come to benzowithdrawal.com in a panic, ignorant of their plight. Once they arrive, fear smacks them in the face, just as it did me. The length, intensity and duration of symptoms involved in tapering and withdrawal is unnoted. It does not take me long to understand that we are all unified by our quandary. We would rely on the tragedy of similar paths more than anything else, second to ourselves.

Other people's journeys provide hope and experience in dealing with my plight. I quickly note the lengthy, tenacious road through hell everyone has traveled. There is no way to go around it. No short cuts. The only road is straight through, no matter how long it takes. I hold to my one-year recovery deadline with blinders on, grateful I am no longer alone in my trek. Next to Bonnie and Lisa, benzowithdrawal.com becomes an indirect lifeline.

I recognize early on several sincerely helpful people and those I click with behaviorally. Some members get caught in endless quagmires, and too much of my invaluable energy drains in their self-defeating, fearful and negative thought patterns. I then have no energy left for me. I need to drop the weight to keep my own head above water or I will drown with them.

I gravitate toward people who have their heads on their shoulders even though tormented by their circumstances. I don't do drama. Within a short period of time, I learn it enriches me to be of service to others. Writing in support of other people on their posts enables me to find my voice in the chaos. Somewhere deep down inside I am present. My words instill a sense of hope and peace with various people. Some tell me my words of support comfort them. When I extend myself to assist someone else, my woes take a back seat no matter how extreme.

I fill my days with the purpose of searching for others to help and each friendship, respectively, turns more meaningful. The more I write to reach out, the more I enjoy it. I look forward to it. I find more peace in my service to other people than can be found anywhere else. Right now I consider the site a godsend.

I find no greater education than learning from other people's experiences. People share information on the symptoms they experience and their methods of dealing with them. I gather insight on use of vitamin supplements, the question of medical care from surgery to dental to flu shots, allergies and use of over-the-counter medications.

I realize the interaction of length of time on a drug, use of multiple drugs, age and individual body chemistry as it pertains to the circumstances of one's own withdrawal. The method of taper or cold turkey also plays a key role. Cold turkey, unless a medical emergency, is never an option.

Benzowithdrawal.com serves as a social hub as well. The outside world cannot grasp the complexity of this condition. Those of us afflicted aren't always capable either. The website serves as a shelter for discussion of all of life's topics inside and outside of drug withdrawal and recovery. Drug addiction and withdrawal affect every facet of one's existence. Nothing is spared.

Initially, Bonnie concerns herself with the amount of time I spend on the site. She strives to keep my environment positive and questions putting all of my energy into it. I share information and solicit her to read my findings daily. We both demand insight into this calamity, which neither of us signed up for. Once Bonnie recognizes the wealth of information and level of support Benzowithdrawal.com offers me, she gives her full endorsement. Sadly, it is the only place I feel at home. Everyone can relate to what I am going through, and I to them. It is the only real world I know.

The outside world is a world of its own. I don't understand it or my place in it. Doctors live in that world. Unless presented with a dire emergency, benzo-withdrawal sufferers urge everyone to stay away from the medical community. Ignorant doctors may perceive a person crazy due to the bizarre nature of symptoms. Fear lies in the fact that ill-informed medical professionals may incorrectly diagnose the symptoms, which mimic other disease. Doctors who choose to prescribe another line of medication for an incorrect diagnosis or side effects of a drug would only serve to worsen the situation. They prescribe drugs quickly. Everyone on the benzo site knows that.

The site did not condone use of any aids to recovery, like the ones I chose from the Road Back. I believe each person is different. What works for one may not work for another. Some people maintain a stronger mindset than others. The philosophy steers clear of dependency on any pill. I understand it, but do not fully buy into it. This assumption may bode true for people who choose drug use as a means of coping. I see myself differently. I know I can take what I need to help me through and have the ability to stop with transpired healing. We don't all fit into one nice tiny knit box. I know what I am doing. I know my strength. I resent the inference.

I inquire into another benzo-withdrawal site. I figure if one site is good, two is better. Within a short time, though, I detect the poor match and learn quality is better than quantity. One of the administrative helpers on the site rudely probes my use of the supplemental products Body Calm and Body Calm Supreme from said Road Back. The questioning comes along the lines of, "How in the world could you possibly go back and depend upon another pill to get through this, when that is what had gotten you here in the first place? Do you want that kind of dependency?"

Excuse me? What? Needless to say, rage sets in. Before a moment's breath, I write back: "You don't know me from Adam and have never corresponded with me before. You throw me in the mix as if everyone with drug addiction is the same. I never had dependency on a pill for my existence. I never will. I know what I am capable of. Body Calm and Body Calm Supreme did not get me here. Furthermore, all I care about is staying above the yellow line. I don't want to kill myself, but fear I may. I need to maintain a level of sustenance to keep me above that line so I can concentrate on methods of recovery.

"Drug addiction will not define me. Doctors caused this and I plan on rectifying it as best I can. How dare you talk down to me! How dare you judge me! You are one of the first persons people come to for help on this site and this is your response? Great source of help! Your quick judgment of me is no better than the doctors who put me here. My inquiry into this site was a mistake. Thank you for helping me appreciate I will be okay on my own."

I hit send and terminate my membership. This experience marks the first time I have been judged on the basis of drug addiction—by someone I perceived as an advocate. *What will happen when people with no knowledge of drug addiction realize I have one? How will I be judged by them? How will I respond?*

20 Protracted Withdrawal

The most painful tears are not the ones that fall from your eyes and cover your face. They're the ones that fall from your heart and cover your soul.
~Unknown

On the benzowithdrawal.com site, I investigate Lorazepam. It was introduced in 1977 and marketed under the brand name Ativan. It is a benzodiazepine and mild tranquilizer, sedative and central nervous system depressant. Lorazepam acts on the central nervous system and affects the way chemicals are produced in the brain.

In 2007, the FDA devised labeling changes for its oral use in a report titled "FDA Safety Changes: Ativan, Femara, Invirase." The safety label revisions were instituted to underscore the risks for exacerbation of depression, dependency, withdrawal effects and drug interactions in patients receiving Lorazepam oral therapy.

In the report, the FDA noted that use of benzodiazepines can lead to potentially fatal respiratory depression and that this risk may be increased with the concurrent use of other central nervous system depressants such as alcohol, barbiturates, anti-psychotics, sedative/hypnotics, narcotic analgesics, sedative antihistamines, anti-convulsants, anesthetics and anti-depressants. I was prescribed the anti-depressant Zoloft for the same duration of time as the Lorazepam. I also was not advised against alcohol use.

According to the FDA, use of benzodiazepines can also lead to physical and psychological dependence. This risk is dose- and duration-dependent. Benzodiazepines, in their words, "should therefore only be prescribed for short periods (i.e. two to four weeks) and therapy extended only after a patient has been re-evaluated. Because withdrawal symptoms can occur with discontinuation of therapy after only one week, treatment should be gradually tapered after extended therapy." The doctor at the time instructed me to take Lorazepam as needed after two years of use on three milligrams a day. My prescription lasted three and a half years!

As I read the FDA report, I feel … Relief? Anger? Validation?

The report includes a long list of withdrawal symptoms associated with abrupt discontinuation: headache, anxiety, tension, depression, insomnia, restlessness, confusion, irritability, sweating, rebound phenomenon, dysphoria, dizziness, derealization, depersonalization, hyperacusis and numbness/tingling in the extremities.

Wow, I think. It was like my body read the list of symptoms and decided to act on them all.

Hypersensitivity to light, noise and/or physical contact/perceptual changes had also been reported, as well as involuntary movements, nausea, vomiting, diarrhea, loss of appetite, hallucinations/delirium, convulsions/seizure, tremor, abdominal cramps, myalgias (muscle pain), agitation, palpitations, tachycardia, panic attacks, vertigo, hyperreflexia (twitching or spastic tendencies), short-term memory loss and hyperthermia.

After reading up on Lorazepam, I decide to investigate addiction with regards to the drug. I search several websites—from medical to drug recovery programs to drug abuse hotlines. All state the same information as the FDA. Pick any one of them. If all of the websites have the information on Lorazepam and the FDA-endorsed safety labeling, why isn't the medical community educated? They are the so-called professionals. Why aren't they aware of the drug addiction and withdrawal they impose?

I stumble upon ativanabusehelp.com and find physical dependence can develop after only two weeks of use. Within three months of beginning regular benzodiazepine use, nearly one third of patients develop full addiction. On top of that, Lorazepam generally loses its effectiveness after four to six months, which the site notes is evidence of extensive brain adaptations in users.

Wow! I guess my doctors never received the memo, or never took the time to look over the FDA report or any other concerning Lorazepam. Bonnie and I always felt like the doctors looked at me as if I were crazy as I described my symptoms. Who is the crazy one? I would say it is the one who prescribes medication without full knowledge of its adverse effects. It is the one who daily causes patients to become addicted to prescription medications. Prescription drug addiction is rising through ill-informed practitioners who prescribe addictive drugs for longer than their intended use periods.

Upon entering the benzowithdrawal.com network, I realize I fall into the category of a protracted withdrawal candidate because of my duration on this highly addictive drug, and the rapid taper. Protracted withdrawal means the possibility of symptoms lasting months into years. Aside from learning of my drug addiction, protracted withdrawal functions as an "a-ha" moment.

The acute stage of withdrawal lasts four to six weeks. I thought I was healing rapidly after that point until the jolt at the two-and-a-half-month mark. Getting nailed near the three- to six-month mark in withdrawal is very common when anyone is removed quickly and/or has extended use.

The event serves as a prominent sign of protracted withdrawal. In readings associated with benzowithdrawal.com, I discover recovery can take six to 36 months, with eighteen the norm. *Shit! I am screwed! How can this be?* The thought of this lasting 36 months seems insane to me. The jolt of this awareness lasts for weeks. Additional insight into my crisis fuels the post-traumatic stress I have been dealing with.

Lisa and I refer to my quick taper as a "cold turkey," though not technically correct. Three days is close enough. She emphasizes the difficulty in trying to get through a withdrawal on either a cold turkey or rapid taper method. The majority of people reinstate due to the intensity of the symptoms that become too difficult to handle. At each appointment, Lisa challenges me to make it through, frequently reminding me of my strength and to take pride in how far I have come. I feel no pride; I feel nothing except fear and pain.

I research *The Ashton Manual*, which is the primary source of information on the benzowithdrawal.com site. The book's author, Heather Ashton, is a retired clinical pharmacologist. She spent years researching benzodiazepines at a benzo-withdrawal clinic. I spend a great deal of time researching her findings on the website and seeking resources to help deal with symptoms. I hope more understanding of my situation leads to more peace of mind.

During my next monthly checkup with Dr. Baker, I provide information from the FDA and other resources on the highly addictive nature of Lorazepam. I discuss my length of time on the drug and the recommended method of tapering. I highlight the consequences of not tapering. I am thrown by the fact that roles in this dialogue should be reversed.

Dr. Baker tells me that doctors have differing theories on rates of taper. Some will taper one pill a day, while others proceed with a slower rate. She then asks to look over the information I uncovered.

I ask how there could be differing viewpoints on such a potent drug with such high addictive risks.

"Shouldn't there be a standard? A pill a day is not a slow taper, especially after years of use." I pause, awaiting a reaction or comment. Dr. Baker is quiet, so I continue. "All of the websites linking Lorazepam and addiction express a constant theme. Why don't doctors know and follow the guidelines?"

I tell her about the numerous drug recovery sites I have unearthed and the benzowithdrawal.com site I joined. When I joined there were 6,000 registered members. The number has now hit 11,000. This is just one site. Think of all the people who do not know what is wrong with them, do not know where to turn, or do not have access to the Internet.

Dr. Baker offers no comment, just a shrug. I put her in a hard spot. She cannot speak for other doctors. For self-assurance, I ask her if my medical chart highlights the fact I am to take NO benzodiazepines—as Dr. Tyson mentioned after my hospital stay. It does not.

Really? Glad I asked. I consciously watch her note my vulnerability to benzos on my medical history. I perceive no prior designation on my chart as her lack of discernment. *What would happen to me if medical personnel gave me a benzodiazepine again? I may as well be dead.* Before I leave, Dr. Baker asks to keep the drug information I researched. I leave it with her, but never hear another word about it again.

While I covered myself with regards to my medical chart, I begin to wonder about what would happen in case of an accident. Some people on the benzowithdrawal.com site wear medical bracelets depicting the affliction. I cannot. I refuse to wear something that labels me. I cannot digest the concept of my drug addiction to that level.

21 Rape

Resentment is like drinking poison and then hoping it will kill your enemies.
~Nelson Mandela

I am beside myself. Reality hits. I am not only addicted, I am in protracted withdrawal. Self-blame fills my being. I feel shame and guilt for allowing myself to be in this situation in the first place—for not listening to my instinct. For not telling Dr. Tyson, "No, this is not what I want!" and making him listen. For not pushing harder to transition to Diazepam and properly taper off the Lorazepam. For not walking out of the hospital when he refused to meet my demands.

I bear responsibility. I knew Dr. Tyson's method was unsound, yet I didn't stop him. Even after the first day, I let the steamroller continue on, fully aware of his ignorance. I clung to his words, hungering for the drug to be out of my system. I beat myself up one side and down the other. I regress back to the day Dr. Reynolds prescribed both Lorazepam and Zoloft. Anger boils over, thinking I should have investigated the drugs farther before ingesting them. I was desperate. I sickly reflect over checking into tapering methods instead of listening to his instructions to take Lorazepam as needed. I trusted him. I trusted all of them. I malign myself for trusting the medical practitioners.

Raped! That is what I have been. Stripped of all dignity. I maintain no memory, no emotional attachments to relationships and places, or myself, for that matter. Permanent brain damage poses a real possibility from where I stand. Yet, through it all, I stand here as my own worst enemy. I blame myself for poor judgment. The "if only" echoes in my regrets.

Mixed with the self-blame, utter rage at Dr. Tyson ensues. I express no shortness of vulgarity with reference to him, or Dr. Clifford for that matter. Hate immobilizes me. I declare them my enemies.

I repeatedly tell Bonnie, "I would shoot the sons of bitches if I had a gun."

I anguish to pay them back for what they did to me and what they will continue to do to others. I wish upon them the same traumatization I endure. More so, I wish it upon one of their family members, knowing only then will they fully appreciate their handiwork. I view my "eye for an eye" mentality for the sake of it happening to someone the world might listen to. The medical community needs to wake up. There needs to be someone with a voice loud enough to be heard. Drug companies need to be stripped of their greed and self-indulgent behaviors, becoming more humanitarian. People need to be put first. *How do we go about that?*

I do not seek death for their family members. Dead people can't talk. If a doctor's son or daughter acquired accidental drug addiction, attentiveness and empathy would reign. No prejudgment or misguided priorities. In this matter, they would not brush off their findings because of some poor experimental soul whose only purpose is to become a data point for their premeditated findings.

If medical institutions cared more about their patients, the doctors would take the time to get to know each patient. A production-style line for insurance and financial purposes would not exist. Instead of physicians asking preliminary questions for insurance codes, they would improve their bedside manners and get to know their individual patients before diagnosing them.

I believe all methods of supporting the patient should be utilized before a drug is even mentioned in a conversation, let alone prescribed. If they aren't knowledgeable about a specific drug, they should guarantee access to a full list of adverse effects, tolerance, addiction, tapering, withdrawal and recovery. If they are not versed, they should not be allowed to prescribe. Drug education should not come from drug manufacturers.

As for tapering off the drug, the benzowithdrawal.com site recommends a ten percent reduction every two to four weeks, depending upon how one's body responds. A person usually needs to go slower toward the end of the prescription to the final taper. It is also suggested a person taper one drug at a time. The second drug taper should not begin until the body has a chance to adapt to the first. Amazing how not one of my doctors utilized any of this. Not one doctor mentioned switching to a longer-lasting drug to aid tapering, or trying water titration. In benzo circles, titration is a procedure where milk or water is used to make a liquid from benzodiazepine tablets. Liquidizing benzo tablets allows for very small, very accurate cuts to the dose.

Bonnie, being a peacemaker, tries to calm my fury. She tells me my doctors are probably good people, just ill-informed. She believes they are doing the best they can with what they know.

"Good people my ass! They are uneducated assholes!" I rage. "These so-called 'good people' abandoned me after visually observing my symptoms. Is that for self-protection? These good people were so self-absorbed they never once listened to me as a patient. Do you think one of them has thought about me since? Do you think they ever wonder how I am doing? They haven't given one thought about me and you know it. Look at me!"

Silence ensues. I fancy screaming at the jerks who did this to me, but doubt they would care, or if they would even understand.

22 Take My Breath Away

Just breathing can be a luxury sometimes.
~Walter Kirn

The thread continues to unravel with a new symptom that confiscates my attention. Ire with the doctors moves to the back burner. *I cannot breathe! I cannot breathe! I cannot breathe!* Trepidation fills me with the inability to take in air.

I have been punched in the stomach. There is no pain; I cannot inhale. The wind is knocked out of me. I feel as if I am suffocating. This symptom generates a childhood memory of running on the farm from the barn to the house and falling. As a child, I lay motionless, gasping for air. Initially, nothing came and I felt like I might die. Moments later, the air returned and the panic dissipated. I would stand and carry on with my business wondering what had just happened. But not this time. My ribs cannot expand, nor can my lungs. *Has a lung collapsed? Have they both collapsed? Why can't I breathe?*

My chest constricts, as does my neck. Choked off, I cough from the constriction. Swallowing becomes difficult; at times, I forget to even do it. During some episodes, I leave liquids in my mouth for minutes at a time before I remember to swallow. I often wake up gasping for air. I raise the question of sleep apnea. My airway seems swollen in my chest, neck and nose. Nothing improves the condition. Whenever I sleep, on the couch or in bed, I prop pillows behind me, discarding comfort for the ability to keep the passages open. Sometimes, I sleep sitting up. I am apprehensive of sleep no matter how exhausted I feel. *What if I stop breathing while I sleep and don't wake up?* Experimenting with new methods, I perform variations of the child pose in yoga to elongate my breathing apparatus. Nothing works.

My respiration slows to breathlessness. Several seconds pass before an involuntary breath ensues. I wait, paralyzed by the moment and trying not to unhinge. I find it extremely difficult to stay calm when I cannot breathe. These episodes scare me. If I don't keep track of my breath, my breath may not come. *How can I forget to breathe?* I count a slow pace of one breath, two breaths, three breaths and repeat. The breaths do not come quickly or easily. I never use larger digits, keeping my focus on breathing instead of remembering numbers.

To top it off, a sinus infection follows with a low-grade fever. I refuse to introduce any kind of antibiotic into my system in fear of aggravating a horrid situation. Life has already dished out a disproportionate share for me to manage. Who knows how these drugs would mix? I negate asking for a doctor's opinion. Pam ultimately convinces me to obtain a prescription. She alleges no healing can take place during this time period.

In her mind, seven weeks with a low-grade fever behaves as a stumbling block. I sample saline wash with sea salt, but it acts as a very small temporary aid—definitely not a cure-all. I throw in the towel and summon Dr. Baker. Two rounds of antibiotics seem to do the trick. With a sigh of relief, I place those worries to rest.

Bonnie and I ponder the longevity of my breathing difficulties as I display a struggle to suck in air. She reprimands me for searching for a diagnosis on the computer when we both know the guilty party—withdrawal. As with other symptoms, I search the benzowithdrawal.com site for victims of this dreadful exhibit. Victims rapidly surface. I distrust my similarity with their respiration difficulties by the intensity of my symptom.

I so badly want the symptoms to be from something else. Or do I? I am supposed to heal from all of this. Do I really want another ailment instead? Fear consumes me. Fleeting thoughts of the emergency room briefly pacify me. I can't go. I fear a misdiagnosis of asthma or chronic obstructive pulmonary disease or God knows what. I hold tight, citing the motto of many benzo-withdrawal sufferers, "Stay away from doctors unless an absolute emergency." I sweat it out. Choices are scarce.

23 My Toolbox

Don't let what you can't do interfere with what you can do.
~John Wooden

Anger-stricken and feeling defeated, I sit on our lake dock as a storm approaches. The grumble heard in the distance now looms overhead. Streaks of lightning illuminate the sky over our lake and neighborhood. I taunt nature's electrical eruption to strike me. Trying to defy death? No. Enraged, I challenge God to deal me one more card. *Give me something else. I'm standing right here. Surely there is something else you can throw at me. Come on. Do it!* I stand strong, accosting my circumstances until drenched with rainfall and stomaching the fullness of my platter.

On occasion, I linger outside as ominous clouds approach. The whirlwinds that circle my being parallel the animation in my body. My strained breath labors further as I walk out onto the upper deck and down the eighteen steps to the landing. I sit in a black iron deck chair in the middle of the concrete patio with my eyes closed in the middle of it all. I champion a sense of peace and comfort amidst nature's fury. No fear here. I acknowledge oneness with the storms and envision being carried away by the blustery winds.

I grieve moments of sheer hopelessness and wish my heart would have forsaken me in the hospital. Yet here I abide. Feeling shattered, my wish for death intersects the assertion I am not going anywhere any time soon. Slowly, I get through my head that staying stuck in anger and blame is useless. The pain is too much. I do not abandon my anger. Oh, no. It isn't that easy. I elect to use anger to fuel my recovery. Lisa once told me I could recover on my own. I commit to resolving how, though I possess a mind ill-equipped for strategizing; therefore, small steps must be taken in everything. Fluctuation and deviation behave as the norm in all I pursue.

I understand only one way through exists. Straight through. Oh, how I envy a shortcut. I beg and plead to the universe for another route. Nothing develops. The time has come to move forward. I require frequent redirects, sometimes by Bonnie or Lisa and, after enough irritation, my own awakening. Bonnie allows me to do what I feel I need without any preconceived notions on how to manage me or the situation. She offers suggestions. I heed some, decline others. No guidelines prevail. No prescription for recovery. No medical assistance. We find ourselves trekking in new ungoverned territory, both searching for answers and a means of rehabilitating my health, our relationship and our lives.

I lack patience and struggle internally. To my advantage, cognitive thought re-emerges in thin layers—nothing deep. When my brain allows introspection, I prepare coping tools to use when each symptom thrives at its worst. I must devise a plan prior to symptoms hitting. Once they do, it is too late. I need a counter tactic ready to go. My methods are not magical. Most are actually quite simple. If the trick works, I use the approach the next time the symptom arises or to help ward it off. It is all about trial and error. I turn to the benzowithdrawal.com site to read about other people's hit-or-miss attempts to stave off symptoms. I now have a plan of action. Before, I was more like a housefly stuck on a fly stick.

I focus on the circumstances surrounding me when symptoms hit the hardest. If I manage to circumvent an episode, I pay attention to what happened. I stay mindful of everything—from what I eat to what I drink. I know my body well, but this adds another layer. I develop attentiveness to anything and everything going on within the framework of my mind and body.

I afford myself a minuscule and deceptive sense of control where none reigns. I envision actions I can accomplish, even if modest, without a wasteful sense of energy on things I cannot attain. *Where do I begin? The negatives far outweigh the positives.* I work feverishly on staying in the present moment. I distract myself from the continual melee and plug away without contemplation on where I position myself on the recovery ladder.

I activate the scheme immediately, though not all at one time. Sometimes, all I can manage is to sit in front of a computer screen, anxiously anticipating release from the neurological issues and lack of breath that cause comprehensive inactivity. There is no formula. I pick and choose with flexibility depending upon what each day allows. My goal is to sharpen or add one tool at a time until I own a full toolbox.

24 My Physical Tools

If Plan A didn't work, the alphabet has 25 more letters!
~Claire Cook, *Seven Year Switch*

After a time, I see patterns emerging within the tools that help me. Some days, my body copes well with physical activities; at other times, I push myself to improve my mental agility. The variety helps make each day tolerable, though my memory is so bad at times I cannot be sure I am not reliving Groundhog Day.

Get Busy Quick: Anxiety strikes, the instant my eyes open in the morning, propelling a gamut of symptoms. I cannot retrieve any realm of calmness. My body and brain exude emissions of bottled-up electricity waiting to explode like a sprinter holding a set position on the starting blocks. First order of business: get out of the house. My frantic energy radiates off the walls that confine me.

Water: Pam advises me to utilize water as a primary instrument for recovery. As luck would have it, we live on a lake, or I can access the local fitness center five minutes away. To afford the luxury of driving, I limit all of my activities to a one- to two-mile radius.

Pam instructs me to float on my back so water covers my ears. I am to do nothing but listen to my breath. This process enables me to focus on myself in the present moment—a form of centering. I starve the distractions by removing other senses to focus on breath alone. The breath is believed to be the bridge between the conscious and the unconscious.

On the lake, I stay shallow enough to touch and keep a floating device with me at all times. Bonnie is never far away. When I move to my back, feet on the raft, my body shakes with reckless abandon. I permit the body movement until I reach my emotional ceiling.

At the gym, I feel extremely self-conscious and evade social interaction. I arrive at various times to check on availability of pool use. I want to be alone but, at the least, desire the lanes sparsely occupied to eliminate conversation or questions. I don't want anyone to question my act of constant floating or observe my body's version of water aerobics. I observe other gym members as they swim laps effortlessly. Water, especially over my head, represented a past fear. Drowning posed my number one phobia. I recall this immediately upon entering the water;

however, no hang-ups surface. I float, and I float, and I float. It is the best I have.

I last fifteen to twenty minutes afloat. I debate the worthiness of such short endeavors. Putting my one-piece suit on along with shorts, T-shirt, white no-show socks and tennis shoes entails work. The subsequent procedure involves more. I towel off and put my clothes on over my wet swimsuit. I drive home with my towel on my seat, shower when I can and lie down to recover. I expend a great deal of time and energy on the before and after sequence. As I look for distractions and beneficial activities, however, floating serves both purposes. Time is meaningless. I have the entire day. In later weeks, I possess the energy to shower off and dress at the gym. I make floating an immediate near-daily habit. The activity balances me to the degree I never question the yellow line for two to three hours afterward.

The experience calms me so much I want to remain in the water all day. These minutes border the only all-embracing tranquility I achieve in a 24-hour period. I inhale oxygen through my nose and open my mouth to expel it. I listen attentively to each and every breath. No counting. No concern over the amount of air taken in or released. I close my eyes and simply breathe. This phase is colossal following my hampered breathing. I stand up to take breaks as needed and then continue. Somewhere, deep down, I comprehend that life still resides inside me.

Pam informs me my body will do what it needs to do to heal when in the water. I tilt my head, mystified. She said when situated back down, my body may contort into different positions. My body shaking has been seen by a couple of my alternative healers as two things: neurological misfires in my brain and a means of release for the body. Not accustomed to this theory of practice, I discount her viewpoint. I am proven wrong. When I support my lower legs with a raft or boogie board, my body shakes and jerks repeatedly. I learn to keep an open mind.

Pam and Lisa both suggest I use the whirlpool to help with circulation and moving toxins in my body. The hot tub provides an alternative to deep tissue massage. It bodes well as I increase my time at the gym by sitting in either the steam room or whirlpool after floating.

With the good comes the bad. Intrusive thoughts spoil the day, no matter the duration. One day after using the gym pool, I decide to sit in the jacuzzi for a little rest and relaxation. I seat myself in front of the jets for ten to fifteen minutes. The instant I step out of the hot tub, the urge to strip my bathing suit and go butt naked overruns me. *Oh Lord! Stop! Stop! Stop!* As with all other intrusive thought episodes, I become ignorant of the environment around me as the people and place slip into a blurred fog as if I am in some other medium.

I back myself up to the brick wall of the raised whirlpool and place myself on top. My head lowers as if to hide my presence. I sit on the edge with my hands, clinging for dear life in hopes the hot tub will somehow restrain me. I battle to protect my dignity. *I must not move. Hang on. Just hang on. Please. Please. Hang on.* Not trusting myself, I dread attempts to exit into the locker room. Just sit and fight it. I feel as if everyone notices my struggle. I wonder if they know my thoughts.

Once the urge releases me, I beeline for home. Forget the shower. Forget toweling off before dressing. I put my clothes on over my wet bathing suit in the locker room and rush straight home where I hold fort the remainder of the day. I suffer embarrassment for having the thought as if it had occurred in reality. *What would I have done if I removed my suit? What would I have done? I would have been so humiliated.* Losing my gym membership would have been the least of my worries. I burrow into the safe haven of our house for more than a week until I resume confidence from the failure of more intrusive thoughts to occur. Thereafter, I surmise the only practical choice to return to the gym and my program, limited as it may be.

More upsetting thoughts sit on the horizon. After floating on my next visit, I decide to use the whirlpool, followed by the steam room. I favor the steam room and the wet heat, which produces a sweat on my body. With my internal temperature gauge altered, this is the only time I sweat. I consider it very cleansing.

I attempt to settle in, but all of the foreseen benefits are overrun by another sexually intrusive thought. Several people position themselves in standing positions near the steam nozzles; others sit atop the benches. I seat myself close to the jets and directly across from the door to allow for a quick exit if needed. As the steam flows out, figures recede one by one. One person remains standing closest to the steam jet and directly in front of me. In an instant, I am overcome with inappropriate sexual thoughts focused on this person. Seconds seem like minutes; minutes like hours. I don't know the length of time. It doesn't matter. The blur of the world turns into the fog of the steam room.

Soon, the steam fills the entire room and the person disappears. I want out, but cannot run. The thickened steam makes vision unmanageable. I cannot see the door. I keep my head down, waiting for the steam to dissipate enough to see light coming through the glass door. I feel such ungodly emotional pain for the thought. Secondly, I hate that the person is a man. It disturbs me tremendously. I am gay, not bi. That is, and never was, a question. The first chance I get, I leave as quickly as possible and make tail for home.

After all of the on-again, off-again floating attempts, I progress to treading water. In time, I move to short-distance swimming in the gym pool, using only my legs for propulsion. The next step progresses to the addition of arms with side movements, my arms remaining in the water. Gradually, I work my way up to overhead arm movements as well. My interval work consists of swimming a half length, float to recover, swim the other half distance, float to recover and repeat. By the time I can swim a full length I feel so proud. *I am improving. This turtle has skills.* Water was once a trepidation for me. Now, I have developed a newfound respect for water and all of its attributes.

Exercise: I crave exercise. It is in my DNA. I once considered the gym to be my second home. I took pride in keeping a fit body and enjoyed the look of defined muscle on me as well as other people. I loved the attire of shorts and a T-back shirt with colorful matching tennis shoes. I enjoyed the sound of weights clanking when placed back on their racks. The motivation I experienced from loud, background, pump-up music excited me. Running made me feel I could travel to eternity and back. I didn't run long; I ran intense. Staying in good physical shape gave me the impression my body was capable of anything. I felt alive. Exercise was my number one stress-coping tool.

Drug withdrawal plays havoc with this prevailing personality trait. Limited movement governs withdrawal and recovery. Therefore, it is no surprise that I behold this problematic on both a physical and emotional scale. Aside from swimming, I aspire to incorporate more activity. Walking itself is an adventure. I cannot decipher what will happen during the walk, or afterward. I stroll off-balance as if a drunkard trying to walk a police line. I habitually venture off to my left. The slightest weariness underlines it and fatigue is but a breath away. My exercise plan begins with attempts to walk down the street and back—a mere 0.2 miles. I keep home close by. Friendly neighbors and a curb to sit on offer security. After only a week, I progress to the 0.6-mile block.

Bonnie accompanies me on my initial walks. I find it impossible to stay within the confines of the sidewalk. On one trip, I move into the street, unable to maneuver the constraints the sidewalk and incline pose. Bonnie is worried about the traffic. She is worried about me.

"Get out of the street and back onto the sidewalk," she beckons. Bonnie knows my emotional status and protects me from the possibility of an intrusive thought popping up causing me to jump in front of a car.

"I can't walk on the sidewalk," I tell her. "I need a larger area. If a car hits me head on I won't feel it. It won't hurt. I don't feel anything. I don't care what happens."

"That's why I want you out of the street," she says. I heed her request and move back up to the sidewalk to her presumption of safety.

After a month, I independently walk sessions totaling 20 to 30 minutes. Buster, our 110-pound, laid-back snow Labrador, walks by my side. He is my constant companion, always in proximity, but not under my feet. His daily need for exercise instills motivation to walk whether I want to or not. He persuades me to push myself. There is something to be said for the ability of a dog to get his way by his stare and persistence alone.

My body determines whether or not I float, swim, walk or "couch it" each day. Fatigue and withdrawal symptoms serve as key factors. I hope to accomplish one activity daily. Two is a perk.

Nature: Whether or not I exercise, I consider getting out into nature a must. It affords me a glimmer of comfort, even if I have to be inactive and just sit or lie. I discover another way to distract my brain for short periods of time. Nature imparts a sense of stillness, a small essence of peace, by just "being."

I relish sunlight. A hands-on approach with gardening, landscaping, weeding or planting flowers places me in the "now." I welcome tasks I can start and stop whenever time or health demand. Bonnie helps me arrange potted plants on the lower deck to make my own serene area in which to flee—a refuge during periods of heavy depression. We hang two Boston ferns on each side with colorful blooms strung across the frontal western side for sunlight. Covered by an upper deck and surrounding vegetation, the enclosure offers me the security of a dog in a kennel.

The open upper deck allows me to gaze into the treetops full of leaves and overhead into the blue sky to view the clouds. Lounge chairs offer me the opportunity to catch some sun and seize a better view of our lake, yet remain secluded. I turn these two areas into a focal point. They provide my only sense of ownership with the entire house.

Realizing the increasing importance of nature, I cherish walks on trails instead of around the block. I drive to Stephens Lake, the Katy Trail or Capen Park to make for lengthier and more enjoyable outings. Buster treasures them, too, for the increased length and chance to socialize with other dogs. I ask him, "Want to go for a walk?" and he prances around the house, showing his pleasure with a smile turned into a sneezing frenzy. His smile is so wide people often think he is showing his teeth. Aside from symptoms, my biggest hurdle is my ability to drive on any given day.

I savor foliage on the trees—something I once paid little attention to unless during the change of colors in autumn. I now notice the kind of bird perched in the tree, its markings, the kind of food stemming from its beak and the choice melody it sings. I am more observant of animals and rodents of all shapes and sizes and catch myself softening to their needs. I no longer scold Bonnie for abruptly stopping or swerving to miss a squirrel in the road, instead slowing myself. I witness the stunning color of each butterfly that flutters about me. My eyes are opening to all dimensions of life that surround me. Nature's pull provides a second home—one I desperately need with the loss of my definition of exercise.

Baking/Cooking: Bonnie informs me that, previously, I didn't like to cook. Weirdly, I spend afternoons standing over the kitchen counter making breads, cookies and salsas. I guess I have turned over a new leaf.

I start simple, making foods that require the fewest ingredients. Bonnie checks to make sure we have all of the ingredients and places them on the countertop the night before. I have difficulty searching for ingredients. By the time I read one on the recipe and begin my search, I forget what I am seeking and often do not know where to look.

I need help opening containers. My clumsy hands lack the grip strength to open items. I know the frustration of seniors who attempt to open sealed food bags and "kids safe" containers. I struggle with the can opener as well.

Grocery shopping is a nightmare. First task—making a grocery list. I lean on Bonnie to identify what items we house and those needed. She then drives me to the store. Like an apprehensive mother watching her toddler learn to climb the ladder to the slide, Bonnie hungers to assist me. I want to do it alone, so she sits in our Honda Pilot and anticipates my first test. I fail miserably and walk back to her in a confused state to ask for service. No need to test farther.

Once I step inside the store, I neglect to remember what I went for, even if only for one item. I purposely do not write it down. I want to remember. Self-harassment ensues. *One thing. One damn thing.* I try to force myself to do something I am not yet capable of. I do not remember the aisles of the store I have frequented for five years. I stand in one aisle and forget what I am searching for by the time I step one aisle over. Some days, I stand frozen when I forget what store I am in. Initially, Bonnie and I must shop together for my success. She exercises a vast amount of patience in my undertakings and cheers on future attempts without noticeable hesitation.

Some days, small hallucinations distract my shopping. The worst is the large rats in the store. Big, gray, furry rats with beady eyes and long bony tails. They eat from boxes on the uppermost shelves, run atop the units from item to item and scamper across the floors. They are everywhere. My decision is made quickly no matter what is or is not in hand. Time to go home. Now. I bolt for safety, unsure of the aftermath. Hallucinations are commonplace—just another day in my life.

Once we have the ingredients, I can work through the recipe. I continually re-read the preparation. Hours are needed to make the simplest of things; however, I proclaim the time factor to be an excellent diversion.

All of my thoughts amplify the silence held captive in the house. My sound hypersensitivity prohibits music or talk radio. I stand over the counter, repeating recipe lists and directions in attempts to distract myself from the irrational thoughts present. My mind chatters insanely. Attention to detail is a luxury I do not yet retain.

I lack comprehension and memory. *Did I put in the baking soda? Did I put in one cup of sugar or did I already put in one and a half? Is this spoon one tablespoon or one teaspoon? Did I decide to double the recipe or keep it single? How much flour did I put in?* I need to scoop it back into my measuring cups to make sure. After several stabs, Bonnie hints to mark off the steps I complete. I keep tallies on each measurement so I can tell amounts added and quantify what is left. I think she is relieved each day she returns home to find the house still standing and that I did not burn it down.

Another big obstacle presents itself in food preparation—knives. Remember the knife and the wrist-slitting suicidal thoughts? I must use a knife as a tool to cut meats, vegetables and fruits. I never make anything when I am below the yellow line or suffer major depressive episodes.

I learn to adapt and continue stepping forward, even when symptoms present themselves. With cooking, once I reach the ability to make a dinner, I feel a sense of satisfaction and self-assurance. The task is monumental and the time frame which it takes does not matter. It is the accomplishment. I can contribute now. Bonnie has been taking care of me, and on some small level, I can reciprocate.

I gauge improvement by independence and the ability to read and understand the recipe, identify the items needed, find my own ingredients, write down the grocery list, drive myself to and from the store, remember where I am and which aisles items are in, maintain composure and finish the task, hold mild conversation and check out with a cashier, carry groceries, put them away, follow baking directions, make sure preparation is completed and the item made. Big sigh. Overwhelming. It is exhausting.

Step Out Once Daily: Once a day I force myself to get out of the house and around people. The main derivative involves people. I suspect something other than agoraphobia—I do not fear a panic attack. I suffer undefinable symptoms that the common person would fail to understand. Often without proper memory or the ability to speak, my impairment appears prominently. People provide comfort, but from a distance. I keep interactions minimal, which allows me to align myself to feel a part of the world, but safely off to the side.

I avoid interaction except for situations guaranteeing short, surface-level conversations. The instant I begin to speak, I know the depth of conversation I can handle. I know if my brain is fogged over or capable of marginal dialogue. My files are either in place or they are lost. Words come out normal, or they are chopped. There is no in between. The grocery store, fitness club, parks and trails afford the most comfortable exchanges because the people I meet have no preconceived ideas about who I am.

Church, however, is problematic. Our minister and members look directly into my somber eyes upon greeting. As Bonnie states, my eyes tell it all. As we hug, they hold the embrace or tighten the grip of the handshake, always moving their gaze directly back into my eyes. I feel they can sense something wrong. Maybe it's my paranoia. They do not relinquish the stare until I remove eye contact and take my seat. I divert attention from discussion of any kind. I am not ready for their help. I cannot talk about this with anyone else yet. I view myself in another domain intersecting with theirs. I sit in the pew hoping for a mere glimpse of hope during the service. Something I can take away with me. A word, a phrase, a moment, something.

25 My Mental Tools

If you forget you have to struggle for improvement you go backward.
~Geoffrey Hickson

The emotional turmoil I agonize over leads me to believe I am becoming this person my brain plays out. Withdrawal causes me to see myself as an out-of-control suicidal nut, a perverted sexual being, a homicidal fruitcake and, due to brain damage, a non-intelligent shell of a being. Not true but, when in the midst of it, no one can tell me any different. I cannot detect my true essence at all. My focus turns to the cerebral elements within my toolbox.

Brain Work: The *Finding Life Beyond Trauma* book discusses how we get confused, thinking our thoughts and feelings are us. We are to base things on experience, nothing other. The farther I read into the workbook, the more I realize this read needs to be a daily occurrence.

The self-protective mode of not informing others of my true state causes additional suffering. I have been ashamed for having the event and damage thereafter happen, overly concerned about what others think and do not want anyone to see me so mentally, emotionally and physically disabled. I fear not recovering. I am afraid of new symptoms or old ones returning. I wonder if I will ever be able to work again, if my thoughts are the new me or the drug? I don't know which end is up. I bash myself when I find it impossible to stop symptoms from occurring. It does not help.

The power of the mind blows me away. Up to this point, withdrawal has shown illuminating negative dominance in its symptoms. When I calculate the mind's capacity from these symptoms I experience, I regard a positive mindset instrumental in my resurgence. To reap what I sow, I must plant positive seeds. Before withdrawal, I could always find a negative side, or something to question. Some people would see it as a glass half empty, but I saw it as looking at all possibilities and being realistic. My parents raised me in terms of everything being black or white, good or bad. Lisa taught me that, in reality, most everything is gray. Our perception of events determines what we call it.

I want to change my mindset. I need a lot of practice and small steps. I place a gratitude journal by my bedside and use it before retiring each night. It is simple. It is a start. I indicate such things as Bonnie for being my caretaker, the house I stay in, the decorations, the lake, anything I am able to accomplish in that day, sometimes just surviving the day. While I do not feel true gratitude, I sense being on the right path.

Get Growing: The journey is mine. No one else's. Bonnie can travel it with me, we will both learn from it, but it is mine to get through. I consider the enormous task of dealing with this misdealt hand. I try to learn from each step I face. I discover my strength, both physical and mental, and ability to persevere. I observe challenges to cope with dysfunction, my emotional response to failure or success of such attempts, and contemplate ways to proceed.

I attempt to center myself on days I take an emotional, mental and/or physical beating. I practice the concept to just "be" on days the couch calls my name. Feeling like a victim of circumstance, I struggle to reach my goal—a positive frame of mind. I lack control over my thoughts and my brain as a whole. I inhabit 24/7 physical, mental and emotional confrontation and exhaustion.

The hardest undertaking is self-love—not beating myself up for not doing any better. For realizing in each moment I am doing the best I can, whether I fight to stay above the yellow line, float at the gym or stay in bed all day. I counsel myself as well as through Lisa. I will suffer moments, days and even months of despair, but I want to live. Saying such is a step in itself. I hold no answer except to continue what seems like trivial baby steps to move forward.

I plan for full recovery and living my life to its fullest again. Time can take what it needs. Aside from the internal struggle, I infuse a mindset to win. Triumph means finding me, a life and joy. I do not know what it means to be happy or joyful right now. No idea whatsoever. I do not possess enough crayons in the coloring box yet.

A luxury exists in not knowing my interests. Holding no inhibitions, I take a stab at anything and everything. I begin at ground zero. It doesn't matter what I am told about prior likes or dislikes. I don't know the difference. Lisa told me to establish who I want to be, not concern myself with who I was. The sky is the limit. I welcome new experiences and memories. No doubt this prototype will slant toward some unrecognizable features. This journey bids the start of a self-understanding and discovery I have never known before.

Bonnie's mouth is watering. While we supposedly had many similar interests in the past, she imagines a try-all disposition may increase them. Always ready for an adventure, she plots to attend more theatrical productions and concerts, general outings and church classes. That's just the start. I gain security knowing Bonnie always keeps an exit door available if symptoms get out of hand so I oblige her offers. With attendance, I still possess the inability to show interest in an event or activity. My mind switches stations continuously, thus forbidding full attention. Nothing triggers feeling or attachment. As long as I show no displeasure in an activity, Bonnie considers it a success and possible future hobby. I do all of these for the sake of growth, a possible spark, for Bonnie. I figure all that I partake in will serve for my betterment. Nothing is destructive.

Memory: I understand who I am supposed to be, but have zero connection to this identity. People have interacted with me on the basis of that person, but I have no idea who is returning. I retain little knowledge of my old character and believe that person has vanished forever.

My poker face façade has made the grade. I pass inspection with the hedging methods I employ. For the first time, however, my ability to dodge questions and in-depth conversation evades me. In need of borrowing landscaping tools, I tag along with Bonnie to visit one of our best friends at her home. Upon arrival, I recognize Mug's face and hold my own in minimal surface conversation. Discussion quickly turns to catching up with her and her partner and mention of relatives and other friends. As each person is named, I irrepressibly inquire about their identity. Bonnie subtly coaches me but, unable to hold back, I shake my head—oblivious to who these individuals are. I have known all of the aforementioned people for several years. Mug's face goes expressionless, realizing my lack of memory.

She and Bonnie then banter about all of us getting together to play games. It is a standing joke how much they enjoy any and every opportunity to play games, especially "Encore," and I always dart whenever possible. I have no recollection of the game, the teasing, or the fact that Mugs loves playing games. In fact, I don't remember anything about her. It is obvious to us all. I have stepped in too deep to climb out. *Abort. Abort. Abort.* I finally reach the control panel to shut my mouth. Mugs stares in silence. Bonnie tries her best to cover as we part ways and head for home.

On the ride home, I express my frustration. "I don't know who any of those people are," I tell Bonnie.

Bonnie nods her head. "I know."

"I don't remember anything about Mugs or playing games either."

"I know."

We ride the remainder of the way home in silence.

Regaining memory takes on a whole new urgency after that experience. Without thinking, I stepped outside the comfort of my poker face and flopped. I decide once again to pull out the photo albums secured in the antique chest. I turn my focus to albums of friends. *This can't happen again. It just can't.* As I view the pictures, I search for anything to trigger my memory.

I continue game-playing, predominantly word games, to exercise my brain. While I still pull back from adults, I find it tough to say no to our friend's kids. The puppy dog look in their eyes can still get me even in this state, not to mention their persistence or the fact that Bonnie sets me up. She also instigates puzzle competitions for me with them. I speak of the 25-piece set, some with the outlines on the board to match the puzzle piece to contour. I serve as no competition and they win every time.

They are always surprised to beat an adult. "You didn't do puzzles as a kid, did you?"

"No," I answer. "No, I didn't."

But it's more than just my lack of experience with puzzles. I cannot coordinate the shape of the puzzle piece to its matching figure. I take one puzzle piece and slide it around on the board to pair it. It takes forever for each and every one. Frustrated, the kids actually help me finish when they are done with theirs. I don't last long.

I think it easier to play with kids than adults. I can be me as I am now with all of my dysfunctional attributes. They do not question or examine me. It is precisely what I need. Errors in most games look as if I am throwing the game or joking with them instead of what it truly is. They don't think any deeper than that. The kids only seek my attention and participation.

In Scrabble games with Bonnie now, I take longer turns with attempts to put down larger words. Instead of making three- or four-letter easy words, I study the board in attempts to maximize my letters—a basic strategy of the game I was incapable of using before. Bonnie takes the opportunity to once again revel in a glass of dry red wine and encourages me to take my time. In our two-handed games of Bananagrams, I work on both, quickly building words and larger word development. Other people focus on winning the game. I focus on developing my brain.

I expand my game-playing with the introduction of Sudoku. On the easy level alone, I stink. I make mistake after mistake, never completing the game. I cannot make associations. I cannot figure out moves even when possible numbers are placed inside the boxes. Surely the persistence in the activity will pay off. Maybe the continual dysfunction and number of mistakes in attempts to trigger my brain can assist me in the removal of perfectionism.

Bonnie and Lisa remind me frequently how hard I am on myself. At this point, I have no reaction to error. I have no reaction in general. I use Sudoku as a gauge. I continue playing each game until I lose all possible solutions and in my terms "lose." I cross out the individual game, put the book down and move onto another version another day. New page, new day. I do not look back at my errors. My goal emphasizes my brain figuring out the game and one day successfully completing it. After a month of trial and error I give up. I am getting nowhere. I set it aside for a later date. I will get back to it.

No Rash Decisions: My mind runs in all different directions, which makes decisions hard to come by. I find it difficult to make a decision without the ability to have a feeling to back it up. My sense of direction is lost without emotional attachment to a thought or concept. I rouse no instinct. When I do possess a thought or feeling, many are irrational or rage-filled. After extensive emotional torment, I decide to hold off decisions of any magnitude for a minimum of a day. Questions of a thought's relevance are often answered by its absence the following day. No need for a coin toss. The only truly important decisions revolve around getting me through a day. Stacked up against that, nothing else really matters.

Meditation: I read several endorsements on the benefits of meditation and decide to give it a shot. As I sit in the church service, I shut my eyes and follow the lead with the beginning of meditation. Within a few minutes, my mind short-circuits with a series of intrusive thoughts. I hear a voice I initially depict as God telling me, "Kill thyself!" My eyes shoot wide open. *Who is that?* I listen to hear that or something else again. I collect myself, realizing my brain is playing tricks on me. Meditation will not be a part of my handy book, at least not any time soon. Intrusive thoughts rule my psyche.

Writing: Lisa discusses the benefits of journaling. She considers the act of putting pen to paper an effective tool in vacating deep emotions out of the pit of the stomach.

Insomnia plagues me. Lying in bed endless hours waiting for sleep to occur frustrates me. I introduce a new tactic. If not asleep after one hour's wait, I move downstairs and take advantage of journaling. *Writing to Heal* by James Pennebaker describes the benefits of writing for twenty minutes each day, for at least four days in a row. Twenty minutes eventually turns into hours. The tranquil quiet of the night alters an otherwise frustrating lack of sleep into impetus.

Because I am concerned about my future, my journaling turns to thoughts and feelings around anger. My anger derives from pain and fear. I steer away from emphasis on sentence structure or spelling. My drafts convey simple statements. My initial writing style parallels writing a sentence 100 times over as a means of punishment for some ill-advised maneuver in elementary school. The idea, however, is to write no matter what the pen crafts. To open the floodgate. To trigger the brain's thought and memory. To voice my anger, my pain, my fear. *No one will view my writing. No one will judge me. Whatever I script is okay.*

I discover writing to be very useful during periods of depression. To my surprise, I can attain the depths of my soul and apply my exact thoughts to paper much more easily than I can convey them verbally. Even though I struggle for emotional survival, all seems crystal clear to me during these spells. My soul speaks. Not the chatter in my head, but my spirit. Thoughts begin to pour out onto not just one, but several pages. My only hitch consists of infrequent tremors in my hand and fingers.

I write more and more frequently on the benzowithdrawal.com site. As people respond positively to my style of writing and means of support, I look forward to spending hours a day searching statuses and being of service. The more I write, the more efficient my brain translates thoughts onto the screen. I appreciate evidence of a functioning brain.

Reading: I want more information on people dealing with drug withdrawal and how they survived the journey. While I aspire to flourish, I grapple to move beyond survival mode. I locate *Read Between My Lines* about Stevie Nicks. The book helps me understand the severity and length of drug withdrawal but, due to my doctor-induced problem, it holds no answers. Discouraged, I ask Bonnie to escort me to the library where I hunt for exoneration. Selections are few. I stumble upon a book of profound meaning—one that will be the eventual turning point in my recovery and spiritual awakening.

Moments of Clarity: *Voices from the Front Lines of Addiction and Recovery* by Christopher Kennedy Lawford is a collection of stories from a diverse population. The book chronicles several people's stories, from their descent into addiction to their road back from the brink. Over the course of several readings, I recognize each person's individual road to addiction and how all differed from mine. Many were self-induced, which puzzles me. How can any of these people's experiences help me?

Then it hits me. Each story included one similarity. Each person had a turning point from an "a-ha" moment, their moment of clarity. Understanding what each of them needed to do turned into my own "a-ha" moment.

26 Moment of Surrender

Sometimes God lets you hit rock bottom so that you discover that He is the rock at the bottom.
~Dr. Tony Evans

I do not know where withdrawal ends and recovery begins. Healing during recovery is marked by a step forward and two steps backward. I inch my way onward. Abounding symptoms are present daily with the addition of hideous waves that knock me off my feet. Often staggering, I pull myself back up, dust myself off and pause to rally. Confusion sets in as if hit with a concussion.

Drug-withdrawal recovery differs from other health crises in that it is not linear. Recovery is marked by repeated fallbacks of varying intensity. Symptoms in the recovery phase actually mean healing is occurring. One fallback can rank as a two out of ten in severity, while the next is a ten out of ten, followed by a six out of ten and so on. Unfortunately, most at this early stage are on the upper quadrant. Withdrawal manifestations spare me a few days. I seldom find strength or balance between.

Even with all of my planning and steps to move forward, improvement is minute. I strive to take matters into my own hands, not allowing deep faith in anyone or anything. I require more than just my own plan of action.

This journey is not going to be over with the snap of a finger, my strong will or anything else. Believe me, I fight with it in every sense of the word. I lie in bed, pulling every ounce of concentration to stop the onslaught of symptoms that strike me, mortified afterward with ill-effect. I assume no power over this. The experience will be done with me in its own time. I am being schooled—lesson after lesson. The only satisfaction I find exists in the pride of sluggishly moving one step farther. I've shot the last bow in my quiver. I have nothing left to fight with.

I cannot do this alone. The ultimate test in my faith lies before me. As with each person I read about in overcoming drug dependency in *Moment of Clarity*, I need to completely give of myself. I need to let go of the struggle and surrender to what happened to me. This is the biggest "a-ha" of all. I always conceived letting go as giving up. Of weakness. I acknowledge myself as a fighter and this goes against all of me. I must surrender my struggle to God. I embrace faith that God will provide strength and guidance to carry me through this trial. I pray for help. A self-realization phase begins.

I painted myself as if living in a densely populated black forest since the removal of Lorazepam. The coppice reigned so thick no shimmer of light presented itself except for the flicker of my spirit. The dense and barbed vegetation made maneuverability appear impractical. A quagmire of hopelessness existed. Weights fall from my shoulders the moment the epiphany of surrender emerges. The slightest twinkle of sunshine now shines through a newly found orifice. That light in the darkness embodies God and my newfound faith.

I wish for a speedier process. It may not happen. Finding true faith does not imply the marathon converts into a sprint. My faith gets tested several times a day, every day. Surrender comes after a daylong dogfight. Letting go does not come easy to me. I do so begrudgingly, only after my futile attempts fail time and time again. My passage entails some relearning.

The more I practice faith, the more I work in the light to move the surrounding brush. I spend weeks clearing clutter, gradually moving my way forward. Each push forward brings extreme exhaustion, which makes me feel stuck once again. Growth occurs most during these difficult times as I sit with myself in internal chaos. It feels as if months may need to pass before chaos turns into intermittent glimpses of peace.

27 The Dark Horse

Another world is not only possible, she is on her way. On a quiet day, I can hear her breathing.
~Arundhati Roy

By September's end, two realizations set in. The first involves dealing with my mom's forthcoming visit from Wisconsin. She remains distinctly in my memory. Who can forget her mother? While I have spoken to her several times over the phone, I have not seen her since my major fallback in July. Neither Bonnie nor I can keep her at bay any longer. We concern ourselves with my symptoms and capabilities during her stay.

Mom once joked during a weeklong visit, "If you don't have things to keep me busy, I'll go back home."

Alrighty then. She was only partially kidding.

We joked with her about the comment for some time. She always smiled and, yes, we always managed to keep her busy—a difficult task. After discussion, we decide to be upfront with her over my symptoms as they occur. We do our best to prepare ourselves for an impatient busybody. To our relief, Mom settles into whatever my condition dictates upon arrival. At 86, age has stripped a few gears. Bottom line, she wanted a face to face with me. She sought to see me in person to give me the once-over and offer support.

The second realization generates unrest as the decision on teaching approaches. The deadline for the resolution to return for the second semester rests in November. Medical leave remains unpaid and we consider insurance a must. I ask the school business office about short-term disability; I never hear back. Bonnie carries the load, for which I carry guilt. Failure to return will kick us in the butt financially. Savings dwindle fast. I display no power over the circumstances, but feel liable nonetheless. I hope to make big strides this next month so I can return to work. Deep down, I know reality. *I can't face it. I haven't been symptom free one day.* Conversely, the symptoms bog me down. At times I still occupy the couch all day long. Nevertheless, I apply pressure as if I can somehow will myself to get better.

The thoughts come to the forefront one day in the kitchen. Over a countertop discussion, I bring up the gloomy prospects with Bonnie. I do not foresee daylight in the near future. Not in finances, not in my health and, most important, not in my ability to feel and hold attachments to her or anyone else.

"It's okay if you leave me. I would totally understand."

Bonnie walks closer, brushing up against me. "I know you are in there."

I shake my head. "I don't know who I am. I don't have any attachment to our relationship. It isn't fair to you and I know it has to be hard. I have no feelings at all. I'm just here."

Bonnie repeats her previous response. "I know you are in there." She gently presses her fingers over my heart. "I'm not going anywhere."

"I don't know who is in here or who is returning," I say. "I can't guarantee anything, including our relationship."

Bonnie softens her voice. "I am staying right here."

Emotionally tormented, I respond. "I don't know how long it will take for me to get well. Or if I ever will." *I am damaged. It will be a miracle for me to come out of this fully functioning.*

Bonnie presses her fingers a touch harder against my chest to acknowledge it does not matter. "Let's focus on right here, right now."

It is the first of several such discussions over the next few days. Each time, Bonnie does not waver.

Handling our relationship and any kind of stress bears great complexity. I dislike being around people because I strain to handle the angst that comes with it. Friends comment I look healthier, I appear to be doing better and seem to be handling things well. *My God, you have no idea.* From the outside, maybe I do look more able. My outside appearance gives false indicators. In reality, I feel extremely tormented by what I fiercely wrestle to hold in. I work so intensely to get through each day, I lack time or energy to deal with my emotions surrounding the hardship. I struggle with each shadow of existence.

Exhaustion overwhelms me. Sometimes, I have to stop and lie down—immediately. Within seconds, I fall cold asleep, nearly passed out. Awakening from this type of sleep is not pleasant. My mind auto-searches at a fast pace and the "crazies" settle in. An hour may pass before I get my wits about me again.

In comes October. One of the biggest eye-openers ever smacks me in the face. B vitamins supercharge me. They make me anxious, irritable and send intrusive thoughts rushing through within a short time frame of taking them. The Biotin I have been taking to aid with my mood and depression has been sending me over the yellow line. Several health websites suggested that Biotin, a B-complex vitamin, is effective with treating mild depression. I suffer the opposite effect, which typically occurs during drug withdrawal and during the early stages of recovery.

All of these months I have been taking this vitamin for help and it turns out to be the offender.

I discontinue Biotin and evaluate other supplements. Stopping it does not end the depression, but the yellow line no longer exists, nor do the atrocious mood swings. I feel sad knowing I dug a deeper hellhole for myself. However, I am so relieved my suicidal thoughts have ceased I do not dwell on my blooper. The act of allowing myself a break is in itself a reprieve.

Since my discovery, symptoms are not as acute on a daily basis and I do not deal with such a massive number at one time. My body shaking and tremors seem to near their end by the beginning of September, only to return in October. I had been free a month and twenty days, but who is counting? Although the shakes occur frequently, the duration lasts an hour tops, averaging 30 minutes. Fallback days are usually the only days of never-ending body attacks. It's a far cry from the daily three- to four-hour ass kicking of the past.

Many of the other physical symptoms seem to be slightly waning. At month three, I contemplated a wide range of things to end the pain that engulfed me. I wished someone would put a bullet in my head, pleaded for reinstatement of Lorazepam for proper taper, contemplated smoking pot and searched whatever was available within my reasoning. At this point, no way. Why? Windows appear.

Windows establish a view into my future. They are periods of time symptom free, or close to it. Normalcy returns; daily functioning is possible and painless. While most days I continue to handle several symptoms, I experience eight full-day windows of relief during October. Additionally, a sprinkle of days I enjoy several hours of freedom from my plight. I mark symptoms on a calendar, checking the symptom-free days to help me gauge progress.

Relief sets in each morning as I awaken to a homecoming of memories. Not wanting to stifle them, I often lie in bed to treasure the flow. Memories often rebound very raw, as if the circumstances happened yesterday. It makes me very sensitive. Good memories = good feelings. Bad memories = upset feelings. Lisa once told me major memories would come back due to the deep connection I hold to the person or event involved. She also told me I don't need to try and remember everything. At any rate, my brain has taken another step forward in healing with the gradual return of retrospection.

Lisa insists I keep my sights set on making new memories. She stresses the importance of the present day, with a big emphasis on moving forward. While not always easy, it makes sense to forge ahead with hopes of the return of my core self. Lisa hints that, after all I have been through and continue to go through, it's impossible to be the same person.

To aid my memory for the prospect of returning to school, Lisa suggests I match student names to the physical education squad pictures I took prior to leaving. I look up names on the school's teacher attendance page and begin quizzing myself twice a week, playing my own version of Concentration while seated on the carpeted, computer room floor. I pick ten to fifteen names. I write them on small pieces of paper and place them to my left side. I place the pictures on the right. I switch out students as I memorize them. I also review staff on the school website. I do not know anything about 95 percent of them, but I learn to match names to faces. Maybe I can manage second semester. Miracles do happen.

My feelings shine through a peephole, stamina shows improvement and my memory slowly makes a comeback. The cog fog holds ground, but depression graciously begins to fade. This lower-level cog fog keeps me focused on the present moment. My debilitating brain stymie exists to the degree I cannot think about the past or stress about the future. I have to focus on this exact moment or I forget what I am thinking about in a heartbeat.

Anxiety still throws me off track even though strides have been made. Mornings are the worst. I now exude confidence I can survive anything a day brings. Easy yet? Nope, but I have made it through everything up to this point. I focus on the present day with the newfound attitude I can handle whatever tomorrow brings, tomorrow. To say I am prepared to handle another day of depression to get through this is a statement in itself. While my road remains long, I feel I have managed the worst part of withdrawal. With that said, anger fills me. Coping with the ever-shifting symptoms exhausts me on all levels. I am still not me.

Out of the madness, a revelation arises. My true self—it whispers. The first time, shock follows. *Oh my God, what was that?* I stop movement and get as quiet as possible to listen further. *What was that?* I search yet again, but only glimpses appear. Bewilderment sets back in as radio stations fly about my consciousness. By the second and third murmur of my original self, I distinguish the difference and cling to those periods of time. When I experience a fallback again, I know all of the intrusive and irrational thoughts and feelings are not really me. They are just thoughts—nothing more.

I long for my true self to reappear, but get caught up in the daily self-preservation of recovery. Long spells dwell in between, but snapshots ultimately return. During true-self moments, I notice a slight difference in how I fare. Radio stations pause, the world comes in more clear, rational thoughts present themselves, life suggests meaning and my inner dimension reflects on the outside world.

Out of the depths, new hope develops. I often push forward bull-headedly, never knowing my chances with recovery. Fear drives me. Fear of remaining like this. Anyone who observes my disabilities may question my power to heal with such a handicap. I am down, but I am not out of this chase.

28 Reaching Out

Sometimes we need someone to simply be there. Not to fix anything, or to do anything in particular but just to let us feel that we are cared for and supported.
~Unknown

With the re-emergence of memories, I attempt more reconnections with friends. I desire to rejoin the real world and overcome my sense of loneliness. Except for Bonnie and a few close friends, I have been alone—alone in the house, alone with my chaotic brain, alone with several facets of the recovery process. It will not be warm and fuzzy. I am not yet capable of such an affair. I sense good friends surrounding me will make for a smoother ride. My problem remains the difficulty in deciphering relationships. Lack of feelings, attachment and cognitive thought take a bow.

Most people appreciate numerous friends—the more the better. Sometimes, they provide a sense of security; other times, an elusive confidence. I have come to realize some of my individual friendships comprise a very false sense of both. True colors shine bright.

Near the end of August, I tried to reach out to a couple of school friends who remained in my memory bank. Free-falling without the security of a parachute, I sought something or someone to grab hold of. Feeling completely out of control, I extended myself for moral support. Desperate failed to describe my emotional state, which lacked attachment to anyone or anything. I made vigilant attempts to connect and grasp for any relative sense of life. Communication consisted primarily of email to allow for me to take whatever amount of time I needed to write them.

I unconsciously put myself out on a limb describing the horrors I endured. The result: little sentiment shown of any kind—no life lines thrown. No ongoing support, call or card. Maybe they were blown away and didn't know how to relate. Maybe I scared them. The predominant response I received was a "make sure to stay in touch" email. *Really! I don't have a fucking hangnail. Obviously, you don't understand how difficult it is for me to communicate at all.*

What makes a good friend? Do you recognize your true friends? Do you have friends who will be there for you no matter what? This odyssey grows into a painful awareness that many of the friends surrounding me prior to the traumatic event were far from what I had envisioned in my mind. It is heart-wrenching and oppressively hard to swallow.

Friendships come into question during drug withdrawal, as I'm sure they do during any trying time. Who is there for you? Who never is? A picture is developing quite clearly to me beyond the brain trauma I experience. Some people keep silent and distant, too busy for whatever reason, or just plain lacking concern. Maybe they didn't know what to do, but inaction is an action in itself. Some say they didn't know how bad I was, yet they never bothered to check.

Worse yet are the friends who have known me for years, but discount my condition. They point to me as if this entire event serves as a figment of my imagination. In their minds, I inexplicably developed a psychological issue in my forties. I have never seen or heard from them once, nor has Bonnie. I fail to understand why they couldn't at least be a support for Bonnie, no matter what they thought of my circumstances. The lightbulb eventually turns on. I would rather lose people now than carry them with me throughout life not knowing the difference.

Drug addiction and withdrawal are very difficult to understand, adding to lack of support. People can't comprehend the magnitude of suffering. Symptoms present themselves—symptoms that impersonate everything from fibromyalgia, asthma and multiple sclerosis to Parkinson's disease, panic disorders, Alzheimer's disease and chronic fatigue syndrome. Symptoms occur simultaneously. Every part of the body can be affected and, in my case, every system needs to go through healing stages. If someone acquires a labeled disease, a flock of people would organize to advocate for them. This is not the case in drug withdrawal. There isn't a rank-order process for disease or suffering. People do not understand it or take the time to do so. Instead, they place unsympathetic judgment without any kind of knowledge or experience to back it up—a reflection of society today.

I spend the entire day trying to find my sanity, experiencing symptom after symptom in what can only be described as a living hell. Every essence of my being is torn apart and no one understands the never-ending pain of surviving each and every day. Saying I feel alone doesn't explain it. I feel abandoned on so many levels. The hurt goes deep.

Life Beyond Trauma explains how uncomfortable society is as a whole talking about pain and suffering. People think if it isn't talked about, maybe it won't happen to them. Maybe if I talk about my pain and suffering, it brings their swept-under-the-carpet pain to the surface level. This probably isn't even personal, rather it has to do with people's inability to deal with their life's circumstances. One of *The Four Agreements* by Don Miguel Ruiz is not taking anything personally. Hmmm. I will be a slow learner.

Without walking in another person's shoes, there is no way one can fully comprehend another's journey. I just want someone to try. No need to say or do anything for me other than be present. I want friends to walk beside me while I travel down the treacherous path to health. That is all. I may struggle with memory and attachment, but I can see who is nearby. With that being said, I look over and see Bonnie with me each step of the way. I do have someone.

By informing only a few close friends of the hospital stay, we compromised our support system. Bonnie says we have several good mutual friends but, after the storm hit, we failed to contact them. We did not know things would turn out this way. According to Dr. Tyson, the hospital stay required one week. Thereafter, he declared I would be on the road to recovery. After leaving the hospital, however, I moved to "La La Land" and Bonnie had her hands full with her job and my caretaking.

We kept most of my prior problems with removal of the prescribed medications under the table. Few understood and we felt like discussions were a revolving door. This present scenario exceeds all others. Additionally, a number of our closest friends suffer health crises with a partner or family member. Right or wrong, we decided to not keep them in the loop so we would not add onto their share. Mistake. What are good friends for if not there for you in your time of need?

The lasting effect isolates us both. My psychological status prevents habitual visits, but Bonnie's status poses otherwise. The 24/7 emotional toll carries heavy on her shoulders. She confides in a couple of closer friends; it isn't always enough. I see the strain in her face and hear the pain in her voice. Work provides her only respite. She needs a break— from my drug withdrawal and recovery, and sometimes from the current me. Bonnie needs a hiatus to take care of her own needs. This journey is a long way from over for both of us.

Friendships comprise a major learning curve for me. Good friends aren't always the people you frequent Happy Hours with, or the ones you joke with throughout the day, every day. Sometimes the ones you think will be there for you aren't, and the ones you never expected show up. Surely with healing time my relationship with closer friends will be obvious to me. Bonnie can assist with reconnecting with our mutual friends as I heal. While hurt by lack of support, I discover areas where I can be more supportive of others. It isn't a one-edged sword. Even without the ability to feel for others, I can understand the need to help them. My eyes have been opened by the brutal beatings and dysfunction I face.

Bonnie and I both appraise our part in standing friendships. People, including myself, often get so caught up in their own lives and travesties that they are not active in anyone else's life. I acknowledge a gradual change in my priorities and uncover a softer approach with people. Fearing judgment, and often being judged, I absorb the need to appreciate people for who they are, without condemnation. I recognize the need to practice this philosophy with the present anger and hurt.

Having said that, not everyone will remain in my life. I can already see the changing of the guard with some current relationships. People come into our lives for a reason; most are seasonal. Lessons appear to come at me one after another. I need to continue forward on my journey and allow relationships that will not be in my future to fade away. A lengthy lesson approaches in the forgiveness of people I perceive as having treated me poorly or who were not present when I needed them most. Some lessons take longer than others.

My family members try to understand, but nurturing is not a strong suit. Our parents showed strict discipline with little to no communication of feelings. They looked down upon shedding tears, unless someone had died. Change occurred over time with age, but our childhood memories remain engrained. The resounding idea fixated on not getting knocked down in the first place. If you got knocked down, you stood without attention or complaint to what put you there. Learn from your mistakes and carry on—that was the message of my childhood.

My symptoms are difficult for my family to comprehend. I get that. They are for me, too. While I want and need support, I don't benefit from lengthy conversations. I live here. They live in Wisconsin. My lack of attention span and the ever-changing radio station in my brain just won't allow long dialogues over the phone. It would be difficult for them to hear. I know we are blood, but feelings and emotions connecting us are unavailable to me. They periodically desire more communication to reinforce the bond.

Conversation in itself, however, will not reinvent my feelings. I am numb to everything and feel family persistence as pressure. One more thing added to the cart, which causes increased isolation on my part. Not one part of this process can be rushed. Already tried that more than once. It doesn't work. I don't want to keep explaining myself. I endure different symptoms changing my circumstances every few minutes to every few hours. I just want to get through it. I do not have the energy for any more, which makes family dynamics awkward.

My mom tries her best to be a good means of support. She agonizes over it. Mom is the only family member who has seen me undergo turbulent and uncontrollable body shaking and jerking.

"That is awful!" she said, the first time she witnessed it. She stood frozen, stammering to speak another word. Bonnie sent her off to run an errand so neither of us had to be concerned with further reaction, thinking it would be terminated by the time she returned. It was. There also resides a part of me that is embarrassed to have anyone see me this out of control—physically, mentally and emotionally.

Since that day, Mom holds an image in her head of my nightmare, even though she strains to understand the emotional and mental side of it. My pain turned into her sorrow. At times, she acts as if she fears losing another child. She waits impatiently between calls, often glad to hear my voice, but shying away from deep health conversations. She opts for a visit to be near me, but her aging frailty is increasingly evident. Mom struggles with emotional support, but quickly aids with unsolicited financial assistance and other means of subsistence she deems important. She frequently asks what she can do to help. I respond to her the same as I do to Bonnie. "I don't know. I just need time. Until I heal, I need to surf the waves as best I can."

As with friendships, family concerns will remain a work in progress for some time to come. The more my brain heals, the better my attachment. How long that will take, I do not know.

29 Phoenix Rising

In the scented evening air, let living water flow
Bathe my many fears and cares, I release and I let go
Pour over me Holy Spirit, cleanse my heart and comfort me
Pour over me Holy Spirit, help me know how to let go
Pour over me Holy Spirit, cleanse my heart and comfort me
Pour over me Holy Spirit, help me know how to let go
Baptism of tears, clear my vision
Bathe me in peace, reveal my mission
~Sue Riley, "Pour Over Me, Holy Spirit"

The pendulum continues to shift. As quickly as the sun offers a beacon of light, withdrawal clouds out the sky. Another big wall hits in mid-October, second only to the one in July. Symptoms make me grossly dysfunctional on all levels. While I manage for a few hours on given days, most days are troublesome.

Fallbacks are inevitable. I know this and yet, when a backward shift occurs, I forget all about my progress. I get to the point where I think I am beyond a symptom, only to have it hit with a harsh degree once again. Each and every time, I tell myself I won't get carried away with that line of thinking, yet it happens again and again. *What a sucker.* It is never just one symptom, not even a handful. It is a basketful.

One day I feel closer and closer to myself only to have the floor dropped from underneath me by a wave of symptoms. In a heartbeat, I move from a diminutive sense of confidence to battling for each moment of life. Symptoms never stay for a day or two, most often lasting two weeks into a month, if not longer. The fallbacks alternate. Sometimes the symptoms are primarily physical, with minor mental glitches. Other times, they are primarily mental, with minor physical hitches. There exist times, however, when both hit simultaneously.

I discuss these setbacks with Lisa, who advises me that both physical and mental symptoms heal at approximately the same rate, one not getting far ahead of the other. After a fallback, noticeable advances transpire and I come to realize that fallbacks are a natural and necessary part of the road to recovery. The body does what it needs to do to heal itself. I foresee a profuse number of loud hiccups along this path.

With this month's fallback, my previous improvement disappears and I collapse into despair. Relentless and unbearable pain occupy the entire day with little chance of reprieve. The bed and couch call my name once more. Nerve pain radiates body-wide, head to toe. I suffer complete numbness to skin touch. Underneath my soft shell, an unimaginable fireworks exhibition displays itself as nerve endings ignite. Sometimes, I am numb; other times, an inferno of heat ferments my body and my skin brandishes the feel of a second-degree burn as if I have been lying on the beach all day in the scorching sun. I cannot stand to be touched. It hurts to lie or sit on anything. I hurt all over. When that colossal parade ends, I incessantly itch with the sense of bugs groveling over my entire body. Gross. I scratch endlessly to no avail. Makes my skin crawl.

Intrusive and obsessive thoughts ravage my brain daily. Tired of the upheaval, I get overwhelmed and frustrated, not caring about the damn lesson and growth. I tire of hearing how much stronger I will be by getting through this and how much my faith will manifest good things. Right now, all of that talk nauseates me. Constant, intrusive thoughts exhaust me. I top all of it off with a heavy dose of shame. What a vicious cycle.

During my next meeting with Lisa, I talk over these obsessive thought patterns. I misinterpreted the healing process, believing that, once the drugs clear my system, I will heal and all of the excessive, anxious and repetitive thoughts will automatically cease. Apparently, that is not the case. My brain is damaged. I will have to work my way out of it. Lisa instructs me to alleviate thought patterns by not attaching any emotion to them. The key consists of practice, practice, practice. I think it foolish of me not to have grasped the concept sooner with my other "plan of action" steps. However, my multifaceted daily focus on so many symptoms means little is clear to me.

As we continue our discussion, one area confuses me—intrusive thoughts. I consider this extremely difficult concerning the content and intensity of them. "How can I not associate emotional pain with sexual intrusive thoughts? Or homicidal ideation? Or any of the other crap my mind puts in front of me?"

"They aren't you," Lisa says. "Let the thought pass through without stopping it for consideration. Don't dwell on it or attach a feeling to it."

I sit, expressionless, as I reflect on her directive. After much contemplation, I sense relief as I embrace ownership of the power to stop this turmoil in my brain.

"Okay. Okay," I say. "It will be hard. I can barely handle my emotional pain. This has to help."

For days to come, I spend a countless amount of time talking to myself. Irrational thoughts and fears stream through. I initially catch myself attaching shame and pain, then remember to let the thoughts flow without hesitation to stop and think about them. *I am not my thoughts. I am not my thoughts.* This process is a battle within itself.

Few crayons highlight my box except dark colors of anger, rage and depression. Emotional pain indicates a profound color as well. I cannot even fake a smile with the inability to feel or express joy. So, what's next? Crying. Continuous crying. No reason for it. I am not crying for me. No emotional pain attachment. No sad movie being shown. I just cry. Some of my natural healers depict crying as a natural release.

Three weeks. This cruel fallback lasts three long weeks. I pick myself up to greet another day, another week and another month. Working with my thoughts and emotions becomes a daily task. I find it difficult to look fondly upon the earlier windows I exhibited, as if they never existed.

I make my way back to Lisa for one of our bi-monthly sessions. I think she waited for me to pick myself up again before exposing another revelation. She warns me that, within the next few months, there is the possibility of another major fallback.

Son of a bitch. Respites of fresh air are extinguished by the return of asphyxiation. Concern is an understatement. Shackles and chains appear all over again.

"How can I possibly endure another major fallback? I don't know how I survived the one in July, and I don't know if I can again."

Lisa models confidence. I shimmer with fear.

She wants me to understand what could possibly come, but not be fearful of it. Her philosophy rests on living each day without focusing on when, or if, it will hit. She asks me to take pride in how far I have come and use that as a focal point.

Lisa asks, "How have you gotten this far?"

My response is timid. "I don't know. One day at a time. One moment at a time. Using anything and everything I can."

Lisa continues with a set-up question. "What will tomorrow bring and how will you deal with it?"

"I don't know. I will deal with it when it gets here. I can't afford to worry about it today."

Nodding her head, she replies, "And that is what you will do if and when another major fallback occurs."

I leave her office with the intent to live each day accordingly. The possibility of the upcoming hurdle lays heavy in the back of my mind. With all that has taken place, my thoughts turn to a different stressful situation. It appears the continual fallbacks and the possibility of a larger one in the near future have made a decision for me. I cannot return to teaching second semester. It requires so much on so many levels for a healthy person. I spot myself far from fully recovered, far from feeling whole. Physically, mentally and emotionally I cannot manage part-time teaching either. I set aside trying to ready myself. I let the stressor go. I have until the next school year to heal and prepare myself. I put school on the back burner to concentrate more fully on healing each day; however, I struggle to rid my mind of the financial burden the decision places on us.

Bonnie and I frequent church activities whenever possible. One evening, she persuades me to attend a PosiPalooza concert, which features New Thought musicians. She considers it a good source of distraction. There are several singers. Sue K. Riley performs a number of songs that strike a chord with me, two in particular. I swear she wrote "Pour Over Me, Holy Spirit" and "When My Moment Comes" entirely for me. *Does she know what I'm going through?*

Tears stream down my face, my emotion uncontained. I sit with Kleenex in hand. It is probably the first time I do not have a negative reaction to my very visible sentiment in public. All of the anguish from the physical, mental and emotional struggle flows freely from my eyes. Bonnie reaches for my hand and squeezes tight. I take in the lyrics and profess to be the phoenix rising from the ashes in Riley's ballad. I let down my guard for the duration of the concert and acknowledge the toll this hell has taken on me. Tomorrow, I bid to clothe in armor to fight another day.

30 Belief System

It's the repetition of affirmations that leads to belief. And once that belief becomes a conviction, things begin to happen.
~Muhammad Ali

Up to this point, I have exhausted every positive quote, cliché and success story at my disposal to further my development. Of them all, I discover colossal meaning in the term "phoenix." A phoenix obtains new life from regenerating itself from the ashes of its predecessor. Dying by the fire of withdrawal, I, too, am reborn.

Branding myself a phoenix, I evaluate my current plan of action and concede I lack a major tool. My strategy comprises physical and mental aspects, but I invite more spiritual and emotional connection. Much of my original scheme surrounds distraction and measures to trigger forward progress. In times of immobility, however, I find myself stuck between a rock and an emotional hard place. In the fight or flight stress response, I herald the fight reaction. My mind shifts to flight when denied success. I look for a means of redirecting my attention—of looking inward instead of outward—of obtaining the capability to just "be" without any response, to sit peacefully in the space.

Whether faced with a series of convulsions with dystonia or a barrage of physical symptoms, I attempt to slow—and, when possible, stop—my thoughts during the chaos. *Stay present. Stay calm. I am okay. I am okay. It will be okay. Just relax.* One moment I fly off-course, the next I wind myself back in, grateful for periods of reprieve. *Practice. Practice. Practice.* This is no easy feat. I hate what happens to my mind and body. During lengthy episodes, my mind digresses. *I hate this. Stop! Stop! I hate this. When will this ever stop? Please stop!* Pain overtakes my emotional state and tears flow generously. They automatically flow following extensive body shaking, whether painful emotion mounts or not. My aim—better awareness of my inner self and finding peace, no matter how nasty my symptoms.

On the flip-side, mental symptoms comprise a whole new ballgame. I exude no control over the ever-changing radio stations of my brain. I wait for a pause, regroup, center as best I can and ready myself for the next round. I detest it—all of it. I concentrate on increasing the amount of time

I spend in an unflustered state during the assaults. I long for a juncture of time without the incessant melee.

I quarrel with myself incessantly. Brené Brown, a well-known scholar, author and public speaker, states that "a perfectionist is such because they believe that if they do everything right, they will not be judged for it." I am harder on myself than anyone. I grew up trying to please my parents and family. Nothing ever seemed good enough; I never felt good enough. I began an ongoing trend of internally bashing myself every time I perceived my performance lower than their standard, which was all the time. Real or imagined, I felt scrutinized in all I did. I feared stepping out of a tightly-knit box into something spectacular in case I failed. My parents perceived failure negatively, not as a means to individual growth. They were critical, which made me critical.

Don't get me wrong. I love both my parents and blame no one. They taught what they knew. Both put heavy stock in saving money, spending wisely and taking few chances. They embedded the importance of honesty, hard work and good character in doing whatever necessary to get by without complaint.

The self-compassion I lacked growing up weighs heavily on me now. Every time I fall, I kick myself for the inability to pull myself out of it. When I stand back up, I discount myself for the length of time taken. Bonnie and Lisa frequently note how hard I am on myself. I sit and stare with little to no feedback. The passion and drive I exhaust to endure each day often tops any foreseen emotional need. In both of their minds, however, full emotional recovery requires me to raise self-compassion to a pinnacle theme.

Okay. Okay. Self-compassion. More lessons—more learning. I work tirelessly each day, often frustrated by the outcome.

Bonnie frequently asks, "Are you doing the best you can?" to help me take the pressure off myself.

My first response is always, "Yes, but it isn't good enough. I can't rid myself of this."

I emphasize my lack of control over my healing and slow progress instead of success in making it through the horrors of another day.

Lisa quickly reminds me of my success. "Many people wouldn't have made it this far without reinstating, Pj. Most don't. Take pride in where you are and cut yourself a break. A rapid recovery would not equal full healing."

After a prolonged period of time, I finally understand their lecture and the pendulum shifts direction. When asked if I am doing the best I can, my response changes to "yes," without exception. It is all anyone can do. I direct my focus to the present moment—not yesterday, nor tomorrow. Easy to say, but hard to do. I realign in a quest to show myself love, patience and understanding. I work to discard self-judgments on the trauma, recovery and diffuse self-evaluations. I am a work in progress. When a symptom appears, I tell myself, *I suffer symptom* du jour. *I'm dealing with it as best I can. Stop.* No further thought or feeling is needed unless it involves self-love and compassion.

I begin using "I AM" statements as a means of expressing positive growth. The "I" is for intention, the "A" is for attention to, and the "M" is for manifestation. I initiate morning and evening rituals of reciting mantras and sometimes throw them into the middle of my day. "I AM strong." "I AM whole." "I AM fully healed." "I AM loved." "I AM calm." "I AM at peace."

I also mix in the occasional, "God loves me." "I AM a child of God." Do I automatically believe all I say? No. Not initially. Far from it. Negative thoughts interfere often. I feel far from whole and full healing. My mind pesters me. *Pause—redirect—keep it positive. Repeat.* I sift through the crayon box, eradicating dark colors in search of lighter ones.

With practice, I awaken each morning and switch from the habitual toxic tailspins to a calmer demeanor. I practice saying affirmations periodically throughout the day. I notice a slight difference within a few short days. I'm hooked!

I want to take my power back—to love, accept and embrace myself in all circumstances, especially these. By doing affirmations, I acknowledge my influence in the present moment. The more I practice affirmations, the more I realize the importance of positive self-talk and the power of the brain. I hope that, as I say these affirmations repetitively over time, I will portray faith in the statements I say and the negative intrusions will cease. Affirmations work when they are something you know to be true, not merely statements one wishes to be true. Once again, it is all about faith.

31 Boogeyman Cometh

Monsters don't sleep under your bed, they sleep inside your head.
~Unknown

No matter how many affirmations I repeat or how much I sharpen my tools, my symptoms continually find ways to shock me. A never-ending need for the next coping measure, or a new tool, always presents itself.

I have dealt with hallucinations—an adverse effect of the drug itself and its withdrawal. I considered them a mere nuisance—a symptom commonplace and usually insignificant. Every so often, however, an all-too-real hallucination leaves me frightened and momentarily terrorized when it wields itself too graphically.

I awaken one November evening to find a shadow, which frequents the bedroom lately, transformed into the living head of a beast-like creature. A replica of a *Star Wars* Chewbacca introduces himself. His head is covered in long, coarse-looking hair. He stands hulky and menacing. The creature's breathing is not only audible—each breath visible. The room temperature appears to rest below freezing; each exhale produces a stream of vapor. The nostrils flare with each deep-sounding breath. The scowling eyes appear jet black as do the nose and mouth.

I lie as still as possible, holding the covers up to my chest, as if this offers protection. I stare at the figure, fearful to glimpse away. I am afraid to blink, lest he move. I never once think of turning the side table lamp on. I dread stirs of any kind. Reaching for the light mimics the thought of peeking under the bed for monsters as a child. For what strikes me as hours, I await the return of dawn. At some point, fatigue takes me and I awake later to find the covers draped over me in the same manner. Rational and sane people know this visualization to be untrue. Included in those categories, I know the same. By nightfall, reality becomes obscure. Reality and dream-like states mesh together. It is a nightmare of utmost proportions.

With the recent history of my vivid hallucinations, I know I will again rendezvous with this creature or something like it. *What will I do? What will I do? What will I do? I know he will come again. This isn't over. I need to be ready.*

I require darkness to sleep, so the light must be left off. I don't want to shift rooms. Bonnie doesn't want me to, either. Changing rooms won't alter my circumstances. Something else will pop up. *What can I possibly do?* One thing comes to mind and one thing only. I have to name him—like a friendly pet. The gorilla-sized head lacks the impression of a domesticated animal. The name Tark comes to mind. It is short for Tarkenton, the famed quarterback of the Minnesota Vikings. *Okay. Wow. Where did that come from?* I don't know where files pop up from in my mind. I search to evaluate other names, but find none more suitable. Tark soon turns to a more animal-like Turk. The encounter stays fresh on my mind the entire day as I wait for nightfall to approach. I go to bed with the simple approach fixed in my brain. Sure enough, I fall asleep only to awaken to the sight of him beyond the end of the bed.

Alarmed, I lie still, remembering earlier tactics from the day, but making no attempts to follow through. I find the lifelike illusion credible. Once able to think more clearly, I begin talking to him, addressing him with my new pet nickname. *Do I feel crazy? God, no. I'm too damned scared.*

The next step is to reach across the end of the bed and use my trembling hand to stroke the crown of Turk's head and long mane. Fear runs rampant through my body. I am fretful he will tear my hand off on approach. Finally, I make my move. I stroke his long hair like I would a horse, making sure I never engage his eyes. After several minutes, I withdraw my hand and lie back in bed, never removing my eyes from the apparition. I return the covers to my chest and stare down Turk into the night, until sleep overtakes me.

I wake up, visually searching the room. All is well. Another night down. A smidgeon of hope readies me for the subsequent days and nights to come. *Is this the worst of the hallucinations or will there be more?* I ready myself for what the next night may bring.

Turk appears the next few evenings but, with each appearance, I find myself increasingly calmer. I immediately call him by name without need for action. The delusion runs its course. I start to think of him as a friendly protector instead of an ogre. I roll over and fall back asleep without apprehension. For weeks to come, the creature returns to the residual shadow on the wall before finally disappearing into oblivion.

32 Baby Steps

The journey of a thousand miles begins with a single step.
~Lao Tzu

Hallucinations aside, I display more awareness as mid-November greets me. I understand I no longer share a relationship with my ex, instead having been united with Bonnie the past seventeen years. The awareness exists in concept only. Thoughts and concepts remain detached from feelings, but it is a start.

During the past few months, I have transitioned from my anorexic look to feeling bloated and robust. Clothes that once hung off me are now skin tight. I shy away from the overindulgence of bad calories though my diet may not be the healthiest. I feel nauseous; eating poses a great complexity. Nothing looks, smells or tastes good until early afternoon. As the day passes, my appetite increases, with dinner serving as my only regular meal. Bready foods, especially the blueberry bagels, are still prevalent. Not sure where my weight and size come from, but I resemble a puff pastry. I can't do anything about it.

I try to walk 20 to 30 minutes on a daily basis. My body accepts the activity with little question. I have slacked off with swimming. My body needs more exercise to rid itself of this weight, but it isn't possible right now. I believe the swollen features point to another symptom of withdrawal and not overeating.

I have stretched my massages out with Pam to bi-monthly. Savings have slowly dwindled, but she affords me treatment without full payment.

"I know the determination you have to recover and I want to do whatever I can to help," she tells me. "Pay what you can. I don't want money to be a stressor or deterrent."

I am not used to asking for help or having someone offer assistance without concern for payment. I accept Pam's offer, disturbed I cannot pay in full. After a few sessions, my emotional concern wanes as I learn to accept generosity. Self-growth sometimes comes in atypical situations.

With memory recall, I feel the need to reconnect with my past. Once a teacher, I believe that facet of me must still be trapped deep inside. An opportunity arises to volunteer at a local elementary school two days a week for an hour each morning. My job entails support of the fourth-grade teacher in individual and small-group reading. I consider the set-up perfect.

To start, the teacher is a friend. The school sits blocks from the house and each hour-long session offers a chance to gain some much-needed confidence without overexerting myself. The thought of stepping back into a school brings apprehension as I have yet to stretch myself under these conditions. I beckon the real world and need to know if I can function with abounding symptoms. I think it important to appraise other people's attention to them and means of dealing with them.

I judge it safest to experiment with younger kids before moving to youth and adults. My symptoms hit worse in the morning, but I need the test. The position requires a few weeks of work until Christmas break. The stint allows ample time to gauge my ability and possible progression from that point. The arrangement also allows flexibility in case symptoms prompt my absence.

As predicted, walking through the school doors presents fear. Not just with the task at hand, but with the assortment of people I must meet and greet.

How "normal" can I behave? Is fear written on my face? Can people see the confusion and torment in my eyes? Will I be able to speak okay? Will files pull up without hesitation?

I am a little nervous because, to make this work, I must attend to an assortment of simple tasks without focusing on restraining my symptoms. I talk with office secretaries and familiar teachers before I ever hit the classroom door. Once I enter, I speak with the fourth-grade teacher about her style of teaching, daily classroom routine, order of tasks and her version of classroom management. I listen, allowing her to do most of the talking. Next, I begin the process of learning students' names. The teacher states she wants me to work individually with every student in the classroom at some point. I like the idea.

I stay reserved, constantly balancing the intake of my surroundings, evaluating my own status and preparation for work with each student. After a couple of sessions, I walk into the school with ease. The fear of this unknown has disappeared. I bring home student books and future assignments to adjust for my present intake, comprehension and memory. After a couple of weeks, my brain kicks in. I find no difficulty. Once I realize my brain triggers, my nature relaxes. Of utter importance, I realize, I not only enjoy working with the students, I enjoy being around them.

With continued improvement and volunteer work off to a good start, I decide to take another step—a bigger step. Thanksgiving sits on the horizon. Why not drive myself home to Wisconsin? It is a seven-and-a-half-hour jaunt and I have not driven myself home independently in two years. I missed last Thanksgiving, as well as many other holidays, because of withdrawal and complications. Travel, even when Bonnie drove, always fatigued me, creating an incursion of symptoms. Bonnie and I both notice a newfound spunk to move myself forward. Success with volunteer work and noticeable healing and improvement provide a long-awaited shot in the arm. I want to do this.

My family and friends worry through silence, but support my endeavor. Bonnie realizes it is something I need to do and yields to my mindset without attempts to talk me out of it. Did I mention my stubbornness? I do my best to prepare for the drive and any complications that may arise along the way. Bonnie insists I stay in contact with her as she realizes this trip is something I must do for myself. Time will tell if the step is too big. I prepare to pull over at any point, staying in a hotel if needed. The trip is all I can think about. The day arrives and I ready myself to leave. I feel nervous about the distance, yet excited about the opportunity.

I drive much of the trip with the music at low volume. November marks the first time I have been able to listen to something other than classical or talk radio. I can listen to my music now—pop and R&B, mixed with a little rap. I am grateful for this change. My enthusiasm carries me much of the route. I reach the halfway point without a hitch. When it begins to rain, I worry about the possibility of fatigue. Nothing noticeable happens for over half an hour. Then, the sky opens and it rains cats and dogs. The sound of the rain hitting my windshield and the fast twitch of the wipers crossing in front of me send me into a rage.

My brain changes stations—just like that. I pull off onto an exit ramp to deliberate my next move. It makes no sense to turn around and go back. I search my iPod for a soothing tune, something I can concentrate on that will perhaps drown out the sound of the rain. I find "Hallelujad" by Shiva's Quintessance on the album *Cosmic Surfer*. I play it repetitively, hoping to center myself, and decide to continue on my journey. Once the rain stops, I switch to complete silence. I know sound hypersensitivity pre-empts more symptoms. It is just a matter of time. I make fewer pit stops as my arrival in Wisconsin becomes time sensitive.

It is evident from the faces and hugs that my family is happy to set eyes on me. Since the hospital, only my mom has seen me. The sparks and joy I expected to find never surface. Sadness sets in instead. My family members know me, their feelings visible, but it activates nothing in me. I feel very out of place as they share memories, expecting me to remember as well. I do not. I resemble a visitor and want to return to my safe-haven home in Columbia. I attempt to release the feelings as I have only just arrived. I have a couple more days to reap the benefits.

By late evening, my energy deteriorates and I look forward to bedtime. The setback I suspected would follow after the drive raises its ugly head as I lay my head to sleep. Months prior, I endured periods of paralysis, but they only lasted five to ten minutes. This time it's different, with the intensity upped to an all-time new level. Up to the ten-minute mark, I show no concern, having experienced this before. Once paralysis carries into fifteen minutes, butterflies flock in my stomach. I lie on my back, completely numb and motionless from the neck down. The weight of my body exaggerates. The familiarity reminds me of a spinal block I once received before surgery.

For a few short minutes, my neck follows suit as I succumb to merely blinking, swallowing and breathing. I repeat my mantras and wait impatiently to be liberated as I try to focus myself and maintain composure. Nearly 30 minutes pass before the anguish frees itself. My head is unbound first, with my body slowly following suit. I offer a sigh of relief as tears roll sideways off my face onto the pillowcase. I fail to sleep until the emotional pain dissipates.

A restful night of sleep follows. Waking on Thanksgiving, I set aside the night's disruption and again rest my hopes on restored connections. I search my heart and mind with each family member, pressuring myself to remember. Brother, sister, brother-in-law, sister-in-law, niece, nephew. I understand the relationships, but that's the extent. Mom realizes my disconnect. Maybe they all do. My heart ruptures. I can't do this anymore right now, but I hesitate to shorten the visit. My body cannot handle a quick turnaround drive back to Columbia.

Slumber the second night produces its own malaise. I sustain violently dramatic dreams around the clock, one after another. A taxing nightmare wakes me. In the vision, I am crouched over a woman, hands around her neck, choking her. Her head turned sideways, long hair partially covers her face. I don't want to know her identity. As an angst-riddled onlooker, I want nothing more than to wake myself from this perdition. When my eyes finally open, tears roll down my face from the emotionally disturbing incubus. I lie in bed for an hour, silently crying from the inner pain that engulfs me.

Homicidal ideations in my sleep now? I do not want to awaken or upset my mother who sleeps two doors down. How could I possibly explain my misery? Once I gather myself, I look in the mirror to make sure my eyes aren't red and swollen. I hasten the commencement of the day to distract myself from the ghastly visions that interrupted my sleep.

I resign myself to condensed visits with family members to keep expectations for myself restrained. I keep Mom by my side to direct conversations. With her along, I am no longer the central figure, which allows me to join conversations when I can—not when I feel I must.

The short trip nears its end. Family members bid farewell, pending a Christmas visit. I sleep like a log my final night and rise for an early departure. I travel back to Columbia like a horse heading to the barn. While I did not succeed in reorienting myself, I independently made the trip. That in itself denotes a big accomplishment. With each achievement, I explore my capability to conquer increasingly larger steps even though I stumble along the way.

33 Tug of War

Strength does not come from physical capacity. It comes from an indomitable will.
~Mahatma Gandhi

I find myself in an emotional stupor. While I strive for grander steps, my anesthetized body hasn't improved like I wished.

I mull over recent efforts to lift weights or do cardio work. My aspirations are short-lived. I lose balance easily. I shake as I stand on one leg, eyes open, for ten to fifteen seconds, and then attempt the opposite leg. A headache ensues along with unusual pain in my head, which catapults into dystonia or convulsions. Bending over unleashes the same. I need to keep my head upright.

My arms remain pain-filled, inoperable swinging levers. To gain minimal strength, I raise both arms laterally and hold for fifteen seconds. I perform two sets of fifteen and wait 24 hours to appraise my body's response. Fifteen works so I extend the time to 30 seconds. Anything more sends electricity into my spine and disperses it into my body which converts to fair game from that point.

My body cannot build muscular and cardiovascular strength and endurance on top of essential healing. Cardio work sparks neurons to fire in all directions like explosives. Stubbornly, I try to force the issue, only to be pulled down into dystonia and convulsive activity. After repeated hour-long beatings, I conclude I cannot push it. It is not worth it. Once the body activity starts, a chain reaction ensues.

My body plays tug of war in relationship to exercise. Physically, it waxes and wanes, as do I mentally and emotionally. I take a few steps in a victorious direction, only to be ferociously thrown off-balance and pulled back down again.

My body baffles me when allowing me to do an activity, only to punish me later. My reprimand may come during the activity, a half hour later, or 24 hours later. I try to listen to my body, but I never assess it correctly.

Bittersweetly, I have progressed to the point where I can walk two to three miles at a time, though I cannot do it consistently. My overall goal consists of the ability to run. Anything less just isn't significant enough. All I can do is walk, walk and did I say walk? *I want more.* Bonnie advises me to concentrate on where I came from a few months ago when I was immobile in bed.

I am downtrodden at the next appointment. Lisa tries to pick me up. "There are many healthy people who aren't able to walk the distances you do. I don't walk that far."

"That's my point," I retort. "My version of healthy is different. I want to run again. Running means freedom—freedom from restraints, freedom from all of this body dysfunction and pain."

Running symbolizes the end of this nightmare. Running means I will be able to lift weights and push my body aerobically, and because physical and emotional attributes heal evenly, my brain will be mine again. I will be able to think without confusion. My memory intact, I will know not only who people are, I will know who the hell *I* am. I will feel attachment to people, places and things. *Am I pigheaded? Okay. Maybe.* At some point, my tenaciousness is going to get me through all of this.

I focus on the end goal of running while a majority of my symptoms remain discreet. I count on them to continue as such. Bonnie and I pre-plan a half-marathon trip to Disneyworld for the following Christmas. We check the dates and look at the possibility of staying with her relatives. I want something life-sized to look forward to. *Surely I will be able to run soon and begin training?* I see no obstacles to participating in the event, nor do I have any reason to believe I will not be healed in this time frame. I reference the timeline and event to Lisa.

In response, she offers modest eye contact. "It's always good to set goals," she says. Unusual for her, Lisa fails to offer further dialogue.

I take notice but keep my mind set. I continue the one-sided conversation, paying little attention to the significance behind Lisa's short-winded comment. I believe my running goal keeps me moving on the continuum in the opposite direction of one of my biggest fears. Aside from a fear of drowning, another big trepidation I have always harbored is the fear I will end up in a wheelchair. From a young age, I counted on my physical prowess in sports to help with socializing—to fit in, to aid with self-confidence and to be noticed.

I also relied on sports and fitness activities as a means to cope with stress. I was always fearful of how I would handle life should it be taken away. I regarded my athletic ability as crucial to my existence but, over the past few years, it has gradually faded into a shadow. Recovery forces me to sit with myself and the circumstances without using it to lean on. To say I am uncomfortable is an understatement.

34 Christmas: Waiting on a Gift

A wonderful gift may not be wrapped as you expect.
~Jonathan Lockwood Huie

How can I stay positive every moment of the day? A positive outlook helps, but the weight of withdrawal gets burdensome. I hit peaks and valleys emotionally without allowing myself to glow in my successes. I fear the depth of the fall from the ladder of success with each rung I climb. I have spent several days in Lisa's office throughout these past few months, trying to muster the willpower to fight another day. My body uses an exceptional amount of energy during recovery, leaving little for anything else. No reservoir. I fall back, pick myself up, only to fall back again ruthlessly repeating the sequence. The magnitude of each storm withers me helpless. Some days I feel completely depleted and melancholy and wonder how much longer I can continue.

I lug myself into Lisa's office once more. I have nothing left to give myself.

Lisa listens to my quandary and asks, "What are your options?"

"I'll try to pick myself up when my body allows me to again. I'll try to move forward. I am so sick and tired of this. Sometimes, I don't know what to do. There isn't much choice."

"There is always a choice," Lisa says. "There are people who would not make that choice. Some would choose to remain stuck." She informs me full recovery is not guaranteed, but I possess a good chance from all I do to stay positive and move myself forward. She tells me recovery normally lies between 90 to 100 percent of original capacity, with possible mild impairments in cognitive ability and memory. The question, thus, becomes length of recovery time.

The Ashton Manual says many symptoms recede after a year; some take several years for full healing. Gastrointestinal, motor and sensory symptoms—along with memory and cognition—fall under the latter category, and some are occasionally permanent. I refuse to hear anything less than 100 percent. Lisa never once mentions any time frame for recovery. I realize I consider myself a victim instead of a survivor. I feel beaten down. I return home, allowing myself a couple of days of couch time to re-energize.

I return to the benzowithdrawal.com site to read about long-term sufferers. These people failed to heal within the average 18 months, or protracted three-year period. Multiple drugs and improper removal, cold turkey or quick tapers are a common thread in these cases. I cannot fathom this. Most people seem to leave the site after a year or so, whether fully healed or not, because they want to leave this world behind them; therefore, few long-term sufferers remain to seek guidance and support from one another. I bond with some of the longer-term users and try to offer solace and motivation. I notice similarities with myself concerning drug complexities and means of drug removal, and warehouse this information in the back of my mind. The "what ifs" remain stored there, with focus residing on my own continual improvement. I vow not to freak out unless I do not notice visible growth for an extended period of time. Each body has its own timetable. Each person differs. It isn't over until it's over.

I consider my memory by this point more intact, and the notion of my former life present. I have a better handle on my former identity and life, minus the connection to it. Who I am presently remains a mystery. I feel tortured by the inability to connect with family, but especially Bonnie. Hearing "I love you" causes frustration to the point of anger. I must identify with myself before I can enjoy a partnership. I do not have the capacity for reciprocation or attachment of any kind to anyone or anything. Future planning invokes pressure as I cannot predict forthcoming scenarios.

While both of us have upped our game with communication in all other issues, I find it increasingly difficult to talk about my lack of affection. That crayon color does not exist yet. Who knows when it will? Confused myself by this inability, I doubt Bonnie will understand this far down the road. I cannot tell if she exerts pressure or if I do. I think the latter.

To make matters worse, I feel paranoid. Maybe it has been there all along. Due to the horde of other symptoms, I may not have spotted it before. I convey a shortage of trust with everyone, including myself. I write lengthy updates on the benzowithdrawal.com forum, hoping for answers from other members. Many suffer the same symptoms with lack of attachment, numbness, paranoia and relationship issues in general.

I read one story after another, but numbers offer no consolation. It helps to read of other people going through similar battles but, away from the computer screen, I am on my own. Internally, my indifference tears me apart and I desire nothing more than to wake from this abomination.

My own paranoia and confusion bring about an obsession to maintain a tight hold onto my past role of teacher. That glimpse of my life represents all I have to hold onto; it does not matter that I feel no correlation with it. Absence of human connection entices me to grasp the position I once held, as if it was, and is, mine. Lack of control with my situation causes me to focus on returning to the school I went on medical leave from without looking at other opportunities. With that derives the additional need to visit and evaluate my circumstances with the position and friendships. In my angst, I overlook the incapacity to interpret either.

Moving into mid-December, I fall into some sort of middle ground as symptoms appear sparsely. Quite out of the blue, this shocks me. *Where did everything go? Is this it? Am I done or is my body synchronizing for another major fallback?* The "crazies," intrusive thoughts, constant anxiety and depression have been laid to rest, at least temporarily. If nothing else, my brain welcomes a much-needed breather. I no longer hang on by a thread, nor cling to someone or something for dear life. I am alive!

I taper myself off the Body Calm supplements suggested in the Road Back Program as my anxiety and depression lessen. I trash all of the remaining Road Back pills. The only supplements I use involve probiotics. Used for my immune system, they also ground the somersaults my stomach performs.

Two relentless symptoms are insomnia and body shaking—the shaking consisting of twitches, tremors and nasty dystonia and convulsions.

Like clockwork, each night reflects the same. Physically and emotionally bruised and beaten, I lie in bed waiting for the electricity to dissipate. I find it difficult to remain psychologically present under such conditions, wanting instead to let my mind wander elsewhere into some distant fantasyland. I learn to keep my headphones bedside to listen to relaxing music. Beyoncé and Lionel Richie serve as regulars. Melodies offer a temporary retreat as energy in my body maintains control hours past my selections. Lying as still as possible, I am unable to move a muscle without reigniting the electricity that instantaneously causes further body motion. I cannot read or write, my brain foggy and dizzy from convulsions, my vision blurred and stomach nauseated.

I attempt deep breathing exercises to calm body and mind. I position one hand on my stomach and breathe in through my nose for five seconds. I release through my mouth for seven. *It's too long.* I switch to three seconds in and five out. *Nope, my breath remains shallow.* With my breathing incapacitated from withdrawal, relaxation efforts bestow no tranquility.

I lie in bed, Bonnie out cold, and stare at the rotating fan over the bed or beyond the single window into the night sky. Through the small lens and darkened tree limbs, the stars appear so far away. *How I wish the window was doubled. Better yet, I wish the entire side was a glass wall.*

Nights drag on forever. My body offers a handful of snooze hours around 3 a.m., sometimes as late as 5 a.m., and then my day begins.

I take advantage of a good day to pay a social call to school. In a nutshell, my visit causes more confusion than it gives answers. I meet with the new principal to introduce myself and make him aware of my interest in returning. Anxiousness with my impairments causes me to stumble throughout the discussion. Difficulty speaking upsets me. I leave his office unable to read if he is the slightest bit interested in having me back. I am unable to ascertain if it is his personality, indifference or my inability to read him.

As I circulate, several teachers ask me to play in the annual faculty vs. student basketball team game. I never missed playing in a game since joining the school staff. There comes a first time for everything, I guess.

"What? Really? No, I can't play," I say. "I'm on medical leave. Besides, I truly am not able."

The last thing I want to do is explain my circumstances. But it never ends with "no." They continue to bring it up.

I must appear okay. I can't believe this shit. It shows how much people go by an outward image.

Staff members look at me and talk as if I have only been away a short time frame—like it is no big deal. I'm walking and talking so I must be okay. They may not view a few months as significant; to me, these months seem like years. People I deemed closer friends acted excited to pick right back up even though I never heard "boo" from them in my absence. *What the hell? I wasn't playing hooky.* Though I may struggle to fully understand my past friendships, I definitely recognize who has been supportive. I don't know how I feel about any relationships right now. In my confusion, everything comes up mixed messages. I plan to schedule future trips to reorient myself with people and my position throughout the remainder of the school year.

As I yearn for more connection, I benefit from the use of Facebook. I send "friend" requests to family members, people present the past few months of recovery and school staff. I watch who answers quickly and take note of those who never respond. While there are many reasons some people may not respond—such as minimal Facebook use—a simplistic measurement presents itself. I signify a quick response with friendship. Having nothing to do with concern over feelings, I want to gain perspective as I prepare to return. I don't remember everything and seek to understand areas that bewilder me.

Facebook turns into an indirect route to refresh and gauge relationships with people. I observe posts to gain a better understanding of personalities and life circumstances, which brings me up to speed with people who have been, or will be, frequenting my life. I watch for mutually perceived friendships or one-sidedness. Easily confused and absent of instinct, I deem communication extremely important. I am incapable of reading between the lines but can differentiate words and actions. While I attempt to find an indication with relationships, I feel anxious concerning my own lack of personal understanding. I tirelessly search to find a trigger to reintroduce my past into my consciousness.

I consider Facebook use safe no matter my state of being. I can respond to someone's post coming from a place of high spirits when in fact I type with limited mobility from a bed I have dwelled in all day. No one knows my true-life circumstances. In reality, I don't know theirs either. Maybe we all hide behind a monitor. Maybe we all find ourselves reaching out at some point in our lives, unbeknownst to others.

Luckily, my reprieve of symptoms lasts through the Christmas break, leaving me able to function on a daily basis. Bonnie and I travel to both family homes for our Christmas gatherings. As with Thanksgiving, I am oblivious to connections, even calling people by wrong names within my immediate family. I detect it the instant it comes out of my mouth, but out it comes again. I try to reel it back in before family members hear, but it's too late. Bonnie and my family correct me, but I can't close the trap door.

The only daylight I appreciate is my mom's house filled with laughter—deep belly laughter with watering eyes and maybe even a few snorts. I come from a family of jokesters. My siblings reveal one thing after another to tease each other about. As I look around the crowded living room, I observe their faces contorted with expressions of joy. Their humor carries me. I don't notice until readying myself for bed but, for the first time, I had set everything aside and was laughing too. My once bleached-out emotions perhaps reveal a new crayon color. If only I could feel our family closeness.

During the stay, family members reflect on a local chiropractic doctor who aids healing without physical manipulation by working with a person's energy. My mom and brother call him a "voodoo" doctor and explain how much he has enhanced their health. He supposedly works with a small wand, performing different movements around the body. *What the heck—why not?* I am game for anything with potential to aid my healing. I won't know unless I try.

I set up an appointment. As I enter the room, I notice him scanning my body by sight alone. Without a machine of any kind, he somehow senses various ailments without mention from me. Before beginning treatment, Dr. Best and I discuss my situation and how I arrived at this place in time. I immediately notice his listening skills. Not only polite and easy to talk to, he intently listens. *Wow! I'm not used to this.* He doesn't try to insinuate what I am feeling or pretend to know what I am going through. He isn't concerned with rushing me, clearly not worrying about the money he could make on me or filling out insurance company codes. Quite the opposite. He allows ample time for discussion and treatment and offers an economical rate to reach more people so everyone needing assistance gets it. Dr. Best genuinely cares about people. I find him quite refreshing.

He and I discuss his non-traditional methods. He says he combines Reiki with other alternative treatments in his approach. "I don't know if I could put one name on it," he tells me.

He begins the treatment with powder, a wand and several raking hand movements which barely, if ever, skim my body. Upon leaving, I immediately feel the need to crash—like now, right now. Something obviously happened. One treatment will not fix what ails me so I decide that, each time I travel home to Wisconsin, I will call him. I realize I discovered another trusted holistic healer and ally.

As for my Christmas trip home, instead of being eager to leave like at Thanksgiving, I yearn for more. I take the added emotion as the slightest notion of healing—a small gift in itself. I must seize what I can get and be grateful for the tiniest of progressions to get me through psychologically.

35 A New Year

I dwell in possibility.
~Emily Dickinson

Happy New Year! My resolution: full recovery. Two months earlier, I set December 31 as the trial date for caffeine, sugar and alcohol. I considered them to be a no-no up to this point. *Why always the good stuff?*

I crave all three. My body wants a substitute for the addictive drug no longer coursing through its system. I tried a few swigs of Diet Mountain Dew a couple of months earlier, which was all it took. Zero to bonkers in fifteen seconds flat.

I read blogs about people on the benzowithdrawal.com site who have tried alcohol. Nearly everyone suffered detrimental effects. Some were bothered for a couple of days, others a few weeks. My nervous system already runs on shock mode, so why throttle it up more?

In low amounts, solid forms of sugar fail to bother me and I find it difficult to stay away from chocolate. There is one quote that exemplifies my relationship with it: "I'd give up chocolate, but I'm no quitter." Liquid forms of sugar, especially juices, cause instant havoc. A sugar craving escalates into never-ending radio stations, confusion and irritability amongst numerous other things.

In celebration of my recovery to date, Bonnie and I choose to host a New Year's Eve party, a reunion of sorts. We utilize the opportunity to reunite with close mutual friends. I decide on one drink, but one drink turns into two.

The opportunity to refresh our friendships serves as the highlight. A smile decorates my face the entire evening. I appreciate everyone's presence and revel in the realization my difficulties are far more noticeable to me than they are to anyone else—a blessing in disguise.

January 1: *Okay, really? I had two drinks. Two drinks.* I feel as if I went on a drunken binge and partied all night. I require several days to elevate my status. *Will alcohol always hit me this way? Does my body consider alcohol a drug much like the benzodiazepines?*

Next I try sugar and caffeine. One drink of orange juice at breakfast makes me shockingly aware of the sugar content. My brain begins to auto-search relentlessly. I make a mental note—cut the sugar.

After my trial runs, I realize management is key. Moderation will be essential. For how long? I have no idea. I also conclude that, in the scheme of things, it isn't a big deal.

To increase my nutrition, I begin drinking various kinds of green and fruit smoothies. I digest liquids much easier than solids, which makes protein hard to get in. I know best practice is to get nutrients from food itself, but I feel resigned to garner protein from protein drinks or powders. Unable to balance all vitamins and minerals, I consider drinks with minimal amounts. My twenty-pound weight gain still resides on my body in a bloated fashion. I hope more balanced eating removes a pound or two, though I sense no control over it and fear gaining more. I refuse to buy larger clothes. *Sounds like a woman, doesn't it? I will get this weight off me one way or another.*

With few daylong windows, I continually learn to manage life with symptoms in hand. I see no alternative choice to get to the other side of this. I refuse to stay stuck. To boost my feeble confidence, my next step elevates into a part-time job. Everything I do from this point gears me toward teaching the following school year. August will come up quickly.

Bonnie checks into the possibility of me working with homebound instruction within the district. It is provided to students whose medical needs (physical or emotional) prevent regular school attendance for an extended period of time. We both think it would be beneficial to instruct one or two students who possess challenging behaviors. They will be similar to those students found in the school I plan to rejoin. Homebound instruction allows me flexibility with hours, days, times and scheduling. Understaffed, the district quickly scoops me up and I offer ten to fifteen hours to kick start myself. I look to have my first student sometime in February.

By taking another step toward full-time teaching, I move far enough ahead to see the dimly-lit path in the darkened forest. I detect only one direction. The narrow dirt path filled with potholes appears to go on forever with no clearance in sight. The trail symbolizes a long walk, but I experience a sense of gratitude to have dug my way out as far as this. I am making headway.

Oh, my God. Why does this always happen? Damn it! Damn it! Damn it! Every single time I think I have moved beyond something, it comes back to bite me in the butt. The symptoms return and I realize this is far from over. I can do nothing but lie in bed or on the couch.

Confusion sets in and my mind goes blank, incapable of clear thought. I display a deer-in-the-headlights appearance. Physically, my body feels powerless. I have nothing left to fight with. The idea of surrendering never enters my mind. I feel ill, often nauseous, and want nothing more than to sleep. My hair, which had been falling out during the third and fourth month, does so again.

After a few days of desolation, I plead with benzowithdrawal.com friends for insight. They each state a similar simple response—"just be." I had been fighting hard each and every moment since day one. My body and mind demand a break. I need to surrender—to remove my boxing gloves and allow myself to rest ringside. I failed to take my own advice—the advice given to so many others on that site. I continually pushed through without recognizing the wear and tear on my mind and body. I didn't listen to my body. Surrender still comes hard for me. Sometimes, I need to be told.

For the next few days, I relish sleep. I find it difficult to allow myself the down time; my body will permit nothing further. I ease up and let things be what they will. Once capable, I make mind work plentiful. With the couch as my companion, I magnify emphasis on centering myself with frequent affirmations. Newfound attempts at meditation go successfully with little interference. My attention span improves, as well as control over my thought process.

To focus forward, I generate options for a vision board. Once more mobile, I make my selections and place them into a collaged picture frame. I hang it in clear sight so it is the first thing I see upon rising and the last thing I see before the lights go out at night. Faith, wholeness and fitness highlight the list.

My layoff lasts two weeks. Once over, I feel re-energized to jump back in and start anew. One thing refuses to pick back up. I have lost my walking endurance. I can no longer walk the two- to three-mile distances I took seven months to progress to. I fall back to square one and attempt short distances, if at all. *Shit. Is this what lack of appreciation gets me?*

As I cast a new spirit in recovery, a decision looms. My original plan had me re-integrating into life with volunteer work, moving up to part-time work, then back to my full-time position in the fall. Even though my part-time venture has yet to start and the road has been extremely rough, I vow to hold true to my plan. I don't know what the next few months hold in store for me, but I want to return next fall. The Human Resources Department informs me a decision must be made by February 1.

I verify my intent with an email to the director: "I plan on returning to my full-time teaching position for the 2010-11 school year." Full steam ahead.

36 Someday

I will prepare and someday my chance will come.
~Abraham Lincoln

February. Someone is playing games and I refuse to laugh. I stand back up on my feet, only to get bamboozled yet again. Time after time. *Will it never stop? I want off this roller coaster ride.* I find it emotionally unsettling and laborious. Up. Down. Up. Down. I already sent notification of my intent to return to teaching next fall. I can't send another notice to nullify that one. *What would they think? It's early yet. I have time. One day at a time. One day at a time.*

I start homebound instruction and am grateful most of my tutoring commences late morning to midafternoon. By midday, my body and brain gradually switch over to a calmer state.

I work with a variety of students. Some possess challenging behaviors. I don't blink an eye and find working with them effortless. *Maybe my emotional numbness has something to do with that? Maybe it's my true personality as a teacher?* Cognitively, I show little impairment. The biggest roadblock combines lack of sleep with pain in my body, headaches and flu-like symptoms. My cramping feet do not fare well in casual dress shoes. I look forward to removing those shoes each day.

Homebound instruction stretches my focus beyond my health. I have made big strides in that capacity alone. The position and hours allow me to heal and work my way back into teaching. Working with secondary-level students boosts my conviction I will be ready for the following school term no matter where I stand with recovery. All of the isolation and loneliness, self-created and otherwise, will come to an end.

Two selves exist—my true self and my lessening drug-withdrawal version. I long for extended periods with my true self, and often lose confidence, the moment the drug brain turns stations. When that happens, nothing helps my body or mind relax. I am not me. I exude high energy inside and out, often interrupting my sleep patterns at night. I find the level of energy perturbing. Everything in my body runs way too fast. I want to crawl out of my skin. My mind shifts thought patterns from one side of the spectrum to the opposite at the drop of a hat. I cannot keep up with it and the manifestation drives me crazy. My true self exhibits calmness, does not get rattled easily, and thinks rationally.

Eighteen months. Eighteen months. Eighteen months. Thinking ahead, I pray I heal more rapidly after a year's time as reported on the benzowithdrawal.com site. I read success stories and hope for the equivalent. I find it hard not to peek into the future and dream of wholeness. My main social outlet remains the drug forum, even though I know my involvement will lessen in upcoming months as I prepare for re-entry into my profession.

I still feel emotionally dependent on the site, so I make sure to be selective with my posting and the people I stay in contact with. I deem support vital to my recovery and enjoy connections with people scattered across the country and world. I consider some of them friends.

I dip farther without ever picking back up near the end of February. Barely able to speak, I experience excruciating pain—the worst yet. Beyond nerve pain, it reaches the depths of my soul. It sinks deeper than my muscle, bones, ligaments and cartilage. I lie in bed curled up like a baby with tears streaming down my face. Under any other circumstances, I would be in the emergency room petitioning for pain medication. Not this time. No way. I cannot call anyone for help.

I lie perfectly motionless in an effort to sustain myself. All of my substance holds stake in clutching to my faith and aspirations of a future life. Bonnie sits at my side, unable to comfort me and nervously unsure of what to do. I see no sense in her staying home from work to sit over me. Nothing can soothe me. I have to bite the bullet and ride it out.

I find myself hostage in bed for days, praying for strength to carry me through. My homebound student and I have our cards synchronized as she finds herself incapacitated as well. With her absence, I never need to offer an explanation for my illness.

Momentary breaches are scarce, happening mainly in the afternoon and chased by another invasion in the evening. I detest returning to the seclusion of the bedroom and try my best to access the main living area. I do not intend to remain boxed in a fourteen-by-fourteen-foot space. The A-frame living room allows sunlight to radiate throughout and affords generous views of the world outside. My vision rests upon a life outside of this house, this hell.

Someday. Someday. This thought runs endlessly through my mind. I calculate the eight months remaining until the "magic" eighteen-month recovery mark. I dream of a life far removed from this hellhole.

March arrives, with symptoms much the same. It has been eleven months since my hospital withdrawal. The convulsive activity, which had dimmed its force, returns with a vengeance.

I toss my goal of running a half marathon. *What was I thinking? What a joke.* I know why Lisa gave little response to my running ambitions now. She did not want to take away any of my aspirations. She didn't want to take away my desire to recover in an earlier time frame, even if she suspected my goals were out of scope. Lisa knew I was getting ahead of myself but did not want to dampen my spirit.

One positive development sticks out. Through self-observation the past few months, I have realized I have the ability to persevere not only over symptoms, but through the management of real life. Previously, I concentrated and exceled on the tasks at hand for hours on end. Homebound schooling is providing a suitable test for my circumstances. I realize the upcoming, full-time teaching demands far exceed those from homebound. I still have a little over four months. My faith and spirit remain high. *I can do this!*

37 First Anniversary

Your closet needs to be a place of joy and celebration of who are you now—not who you were.
~Stacy London

I close in on my first year of drug-free living—April 27, 2010. The anniversary marks two things: grace in getting me to this juncture and assurance that recovery rolls more swiftly from this point on. In many respects, my hospital stay seems like yesterday. On the other hand, what a long, horrendous uphill trek it has been. Bonnie and I celebrate with dinner out. No cake. No party. Nothing fancy. We value a quiet evening at Romano's Macaroni Grill with a favorite dish, small glass of wine and limited discussion of our paired journey. More than anything, the venture serves as a sigh of relief in the attainment of one year for both of us.

Much like me, Bonnie survived the past year on automatic pilot. She has worked full time within the school district and met my caretaking needs whenever and to whatever extent needed. She served as the sole financial provider and held down the fort for us both.

While we take respite in the distance traveled, we know the road continues to wind. Lacking a multitude of crayon colors, I fall short of displaying empathy for Bonnie's journey. My own emotional pain lies hidden. I see her at my side and know she has been present throughout. I understand our closeness to represent "best friend" status even though I cannot feel it. I see the love she showers me with but, as with all else, cannot feel the attachment. I do not realize the pain my lack of emotional tie causes, or my lack of love. Whether or not she understands my inability as part of recovery, the loss has to hurt. So does the agony of wondering whether or not my feelings will fully return.

Her favorite response is, "I am holding space for you."

Little does she know that, deep inside me, I hate the inability to reciprocate. I absolutely hate it. The more I realize my emotional ineptness with Bonnie, the more copious the degree of internalized pain.

April and May unveil smaller mirrors of the past few months, with differences only in intensity. Summer approaches and, as scheduled, my teaching contract arrives by mail. I enthusiastically sign and send it off, pushing all doubt aside. *It's do or die, baby.* I bank heavily on reported faster recovery from this point and bet on full healing by the eighteen-month mark. School begins during month sixteen and I instill a mindset that all will be well. Strong will and perseverance function as my strong suits.

I measure individual building blocks in preparation for regular life during recovery. As I march into the fourteenth month, June, a small elation sets in. My recovery process changes. The healing stages are noticeably swifter as I had prayed, even though fallbacks still exist. My cognitive ability and memory have improved dramatically, as well as my stamina. While not yet bright-eyed and bushy-tailed, my eyes no longer look empty and I possess a slight spring in my step.

Real-life opportunities begin popping up faster than anticipated. I originally planned on a quiet summer but life indicates otherwise. Bonnie and her school cohorts schedule a business trip to Colorado and invite me along.

"Great! Yes, I want to go. Oh, but wait, a plane. We will be traveling by plane."

What is the problem? This trip marks the first plane ride since this mess started in 2004. What's my concern? The altitude. The altitude can affect a healthy person—how will it affect my recovering body? I do not think of myself as healthy. Excited and nervous, I consider the vacation another stepping stone. *How can I teach if I can't do this? I have to go.*

We arrive in Kansas City for our flight. Bonnie and I will make the trip with a female cohort, then meet the others once we arrive in Breckenridge. After check-in, we have an hour before departure. I feel eager, not worried. This is real life again and I hunger for my life back. The first part of the flight is uneventful. Then we reach the mountains. I feel vibrations in my body, with electricity slowly mounting. Small jerks begin. I keep one knee faintly bouncing in an attempt to expend the energy inconspicuously. I wish to divert momentum in my body, not look like a nervous Nellie on the flight. It works. I put my earplugs in, turn my music to low volume and let the concentration begin, impatient for the captain to turn on the "fasten seatbelt" sign to announce our impending landing. It cannot come soon enough.

Once we touch down, I express a sigh of relief. I put emphasis on grounding myself and preparing for the two-hour drive from Denver International Airport to Breckenridge. I have been to Breckenridge before. I used to make annual Christmas vacation ski trips with my ex and mutual friends. It is a quaint town with unique shops and great restaurants. From what I remember, I always enjoyed the skiing and the scenery. The latter is to die for.

By evening, I have depleted my maintenance level and my body reacts. I receive little sleep as my body tosses about—brain stations turning at a high speed. My head feels like a pressure cooker and I think I may puke at any second. *Is this a mistake?* Bonnie tells me she feels the effects of the altitude as well. I experience slight relief, but know from past experience my symptoms seldom resign quickly.

Morning arrives and Bonnie heads off to her conference. Late to rise, I move slowly in an attempt to recuperate and adjust. My brain balances out for a few hours, then crashes with mind-blowing intrusive thoughts. I have not suffered this symptom in months. I want to tour Breckenridge by foot, but instead I stay tucked away in the hotel. Luckily, our room boasts awe-inspiring mountain views without ever having to leave the safety the space offers. Typical of most days, my body becomes more manageable by midday, allowing better functioning, even enjoyment.

After three conference days, the rest of the delegation heads for home as Bonnie and I extend our vacation by two days and head to Estes Park. Approaching Estes, I am consumed by the beauty of the mountains. Breckenridge is beautiful; this is amazing. I need nothing further than to relax in our condo, staring at the snow-topped Rocky Mountains and listening to the babbling brook directly behind our deck. We are here to experience the area, however, so we plan a morning hike at Rocky Mountain National Park. I walk the excursion with legs of jelly and lungs exerting enormously deep breaths. I often step aside on the trail, bending over and putting my hands on my knees. Bonnie joins me and uses the moments to enjoy the landscape. *And this is the easy trail? Really?* I'm embarrassed. I feel shocked by my lack of overall strength and stamina. On a scale of one to ten, I fall flat at a three or four.

Bonnie tries to reassure me I am doing fine. "Focus on your ability to perform the hike, not the duration of time."

By the time we reach our condo in the early afternoon, I feel spent, but do not notice any changes in my body. The bed calls my name, but I am happy. I tested myself with the altitude and the level of exercise and have come through it feeling OK. I consider the event another building block. I finished the trail.

After a nap, we both sense excitement by my accomplishment and make dinner plans in Estes. The idea is to get in as much as possible in two days. We shop. We eat. We shop some more. After a considerable amount of walking, I search for a bathroom. I spy an outside public restroom atop a small hill. Upon entering, I walk into one of two stalls—the one farthest from the door. The bathroom is unoccupied. After a couple of minutes I hear movement near the other stall—the one closest to the door and sinks.

Did the outside door open? Did someone walk in? No, it didn't open. There was no light. I didn't hear the door close. Is someone there, or am I hearing things? No one was in here when I came in. The other stall door was open.

My heart thumps forcefully. *Should I bend over to look?* No one came into the other stall. I am afraid to peek but, after several moments of repetitive self-talk, I gather the courage. Nothing. No feet. No shadows. When I sit back up, the water begins to splash from the faucet into the sink. The hand blower bellows.

I am sure no one has come in. *What is happening?* I ponder the circumstances. *Oh, my God. Is this another hallucination? It has to be.* I am spooked. I am afraid of who or what is on the other side of the door, real or imagined. Frightened and confused, I linger in the stall. I pause and hear the main door open, signifying a departure. Silence ensues. Next, I hear footsteps move toward my stall door and then back away. *How long should I wait? I can't sit here forever. Is this my brain playing tricks on me? If so, how do I make it stop? What if it isn't?*

I contemplate the distance to the door and realize my exit can be easily blocked. There is no way to prepare for this. I open the stall door, stepping forward. Out of nowhere stands a large-framed lady to which no description exists. Shock hits quickly with her emergence and I fall back into the stall as if for protection, turning my head away. She vanishes as quickly as she appeared.

Shit. Shit. Shit. Sorry, no hygiene today. Forget about washing my hands. I nearly run into the metal door, trying to get free. Scared beyond belief, I want to sprint. I walk fast paced a couple of blocks back downhill until I find myself once again bent over with my hands on my knees. After I regain partial composure, I find Bonnie and tell her of my readiness to head back to the perceived safety of the condo. I'm done. My shopping is over. I remain tucked away in the condo with Bonnie the remainder of the evening. Thankfully, the rest of the trip is uneventful, including the plane ride home. This stepping stone leaves its mark.

I spend the remainder of the summer readying myself for school. Mentally, I prepare myself for the pitfalls sure to occur. I now grasp the fact that eighteen months will fail to supply full healing. My planning must be flexible. With people unaware of my journey, I plan to meticulously return without any perceived drama. I anticipate continued healing throughout the school year with lessening degrees of daily symptoms and monthly fallbacks. I think teaching will thrust me forward on the recovery ladder. I count on it.

I spend time tanning to make my body look fit, though it remains perpetually swollen. I do anything possible to make myself look healthier on the outside to mask my inner torment. One thing I fail to recognize, though. I still carry shame from this experience. I act like my experience is akin to a bike chain slipping off the derailleur. I plan to merely reinstall the chain and continue riding full speed ahead.

38 Return to Teaching

We all wear masks, and the time comes when we cannot remove them without removing some of our own skin.
~André Berthiaume

August. I finally see it. I behold the clearance through the black forest. A long walk prevails, but the now-widened path once covered with potholes displays a declining degree of cavities. Large fissures in the tree canopy allow streams of brilliant rays of light. The black-and-white backdrop of my life turns into a colorful landscape.

Filled with numerous emotions, I turn the page, ready to begin the next chapter of my life. The start of school approaches. I have put myself through various tests over the summer through which I stumbled, yet succeeded. I prepared myself as best I could for upcoming tasks—mentally, physically and emotionally.

I seek Lisa's voice to inspire me for the return of my teaching career. She confidently motivates me. "If you can get yourself to school and make it through the morning hours, I think you will make it through the day. You have the determination." My enthusiasm overflows at the thought of merging with my old life.

First up—teacher workdays. Unable to sleep, I awaken for early arrival to the first moments of a daylong endorphin rush. I sense the feeling of irreversibly stepping into the light. I am back. I find conversations with people exhilarating and focus on something other than my health status uplifting. I cannot, however, get beyond continual self-assessment. I deem this tactic critical in keeping checks and balances on my present ability level and areas in need of flexibility and modification. No one needs to remind me I still reside in the forest, far removed from a sand-filled sunny beach.

My attention span remains short, most noticeable in lengthy meetings. What staff member does not view all-day meetings as drawn out and, at some point, boring? Teachers just want to get into their classrooms to prepare for the first day of instruction. Everyone's attention span wanes sooner or later. Through group conversations, I realize mine does more rapidly. Unlike others, my mind does not sidetrack to random topics, instead shutting off completely. I go into a fog. My brain only absorbs so much before the switch flips off.

As I assumed, people question little. Most, without knowledge, believe my status to be migraine-related, some thinking seizure. I view it similar to reading newspaper headlines or skimming a volume of work to take in bits and pieces—the process fails to yield a full-bodied knowledge of the situation. People think they are informed, yet do not know any more than they did when they started.

The simplicity of my co-workers' thought processes aggravates me, yet I offer no details into my event. It's too complicated to explain. When I do make attempts to describe the trauma, I find myself quick to the defense. Underneath the poker face, I struggle with daily symptoms and the effects of the emotional suffering. I feel judgment gets placed on me with questions such as, "Well, there must have been a reason you were prescribed the drugs in the first place?"

Before I can answer—"This began with a back injury at school"—their attention has been diverted to something else and I pursue the explanation no farther. It's a no-win situation. I do not want to deal with the judgment I feel ill-informed people will place on me. Most will not understand or take the time. Their listening skills and attention spans would be at an all-time high if this happened to them or someone close to them. Instead, I drop the topic and move on to the focus at hand—teaching.

When I return home at night, I think about the journey, how far I have come and where all of this started. I hate reminiscing. The more I try to evade retrospection, the more it plays in my mind. What is that saying? What you resist persists. I just want to move forward, but my mind prohibits me. Memories place me right back in time as if it is happening all over again. I cannot change what happened several years ago. Oh, how I wish I could.

39 Original Injury

And what seem to be a series of unfortunate events may, in fact be, the first steps in a journey.
~Lemony Snicket

It was March 2004. Picture a middle school gymnasium divided in half by a large, hanging green curtain, which separated the boys from the girls during physical education classes. That day, my class of nearly 40 girls were to work through a cooperation activity that involved navigating an obstacle course blindfolded. Before we began, I evaluated each station for chances of injury, although I had used the activity before with no problems. The girls were paired and ready to go. I illustrated the activity, then observed the sixth-grade students as they led their partners over, under and through a variety of impediments designed to build teamwork and trust.

I'd set out a lot of equipment, including several large, blue gymnastic mats. At one station, interlocking mats stood on their ends, curving various directions to form a maze. The two classes prior navigated the maze cleanly, seldom striking the structure. But this class was different. On more than one occasion, scrambling feet knocked over the mats. I found myself continually picking them up. With class time nearly over, one more set toppled to the floor. In frustration, I hurried toward the two interlocking mats that had fallen.

Without thought, I bent over to pick them up, forgetting to bend my knees for protection of my back. Grabbing hold of the end of the mats with two hands, I quickly hoisted them upward and simultaneously rotated sideways to put them back in place. I heard a popping sound that halted my motion as a slicing pain split through my lower back and buttocks.

I could not move! Voiceless and frozen in pain, I contemplated how to get through the remainder of class. There were only a handful of minutes left prior to lunch. I decided to hold my position, standing rigidly upright next to the repositioned mats, not letting on to my predicament. As I instructed the girls to line up, two reliable students were given the door key and picked to monitor the locker room. Still maintaining the same position in the gym, I anticipated my plan of action as I waited five minutes for the students to return the key. I thought about calling for assistance, but ultimately decided to make my way to the nurse's office.

I shuffled the halls slowly, paying no attention to anyone in my path. Even though the gymnasium was near the office, the pain made it feel as if I was walking a marathon. I feared becoming immobile, so I concentrated on shuffling one foot in front of the other. Each movement of unbearable agony caused me to stare with blank expression. Once I arrived in the nurse's office, I sat myself in a straight-back chair, but no relief came. Calls were made that would send me off to a workers' compensation doctor. The next order of business was to lift myself out of the chair into a standing position. The nurse noticed my wincing difficulty with the task and pondered taking me to the doctor herself. I assured her I could make it on my own.

The doctor conducted several in-office movement tests and concluded it was nothing more than a strained muscle. As an athlete, I'd lived through my share of them; it was clear to me his diagnosis missed the mark. Three months passed by. Complaining to the school district's benefits coordinator, I explained my lack of mobility and searched for more options. She explained her "hands were tied." She offered no further solutions to my problem, so I sought the aid of orthopedic doctors without permission.

I didn't care about disregarding protocol. I considered the consequences for my actions insignificant compared to the excruciating pain and lack of function. No one was helping me. The doctor seemed more focused on saving the insurance company money than on taking care of my back injury. The pain, once focalized in my back and hip, next ran down the back of my left leg. After a series of X-rays, the orthopedic doctors found a bulging disc at L5-S1.

I shared this newfound information and the benefits coordinator instructed me to return to the workers' compensation doctor. I didn't trust him much, but I was still under his care. The second week of June, he authorized a nerve-conduction study to rule out the possibility of a pinched nerve or nerve damage itself. *Oh, my God.* Nerve-conduction tests are not fun; they seem barbarous. This medical diagnostic test is designed to measure the speed and strength of electrical activity in a nerve. Basically, the patient is given an electrical shock.

The doctor administering the test sent quick electrical impulses to the nerve and recorded the time it took for the muscle to contract in response to the electrical impulse.

He informed me it would be uncomfortable, but please—uncomfortable does not even begin to describe it. I have a high pain tolerance; it's partly a personality trait and also a learned behavior from years of sports. You learn at a young age to play with pain if you want to keep your spot on a team. The test hurt to the degree I began questioning the voltage delivered. These were not minor zaps. I winced and grabbed hold of the table with each electrical current given. This was torture.

Within five or six hours of the test, my body exuded new symptoms. Tingling sensations radiated throughout my arms and legs, interspersed with periods of numbness. The left side of my face, mouth and tongue felt numb and insufferable jaw pain commenced.

Concerned about this new development lingering nine days after the nerve-conduction test, I contacted my primary-care physician, Dr. Baker. I had been under her care for thirteen years and highly regarded her opinion. She attributed the spread of symptoms to my upper body to sleep disturbance, injury-related pain and anxiety. The tongue numbness, however, could not be explained. Dr. Baker assured me nerve-conduction studies were safe and could not cause those reactions. Even though I was bothered by the timing of the new symptoms, I let it go. I believed they had arisen from months of improper diagnosis. Other body parts were chain-reacting from lack of proper care to the initial injury.

As a precaution, Dr. Baker ordered an MRI of my spine and head. The tests came back clear. She prescribed 300 milligrams of Neurontin (Gabapentin) with a gradual increase until I arrived at a daily 900-milligram dose in five days. Neurontin is an anticonvulsant used to treat epileptics and those with neuropathic pain. The pharmaceutical drug affects chemicals and nerves in the body that are involved in causing seizures and certain types of pain.

I took the drug three times a day: morning, early afternoon and evening. Because I exhibited the drug's common side effects of cognitive impairment, nausea and dizziness, the doctor instructed me to take 300 milligrams in the morning and 600 at night. The drug put me in a fog. Tremors eventually began in my lower left leg, my first experience with them.

Dr. Baker instructed me to stay in contact with the workers' compensation doctor and the district's benefits coordinator. Muscles pulling toward the left side of my physique gave the impression of my body caving. My temporomandibular joint (TMJ) pain was out of this world. With no improvement shown and symptoms escalating, I was referred to a back specialist the first week of July. X-rays once again illustrated a bulging disc. The specialist notified me that the inability of the back to fully heal could warrant a spinal fusion in the months to come. He did not view my prescription of Neurontin as beneficial, and asked if I thought it made a difference in my pain level.

"No," I said. "It hasn't helped me."

Since we were both in agreement it had no effect on my symptoms, he decided I should discontinue its use. I had been taking Neurontin for two weeks. Initially, he instructed me to cold turkey the drug, noting the short duration of time.

On second thought—and without discussion—he did an about-face and told me, "Just to be safe, let's change that to a two-day taper to make sure there is no rebound effect." He instructed me to drop my drug intake from 900 to 600 milligrams that day. The following day, I was to take 300 milligrams and none the next day. The side effects from the drug caused an ill-at-ease feeling with the thought of tapering so quickly. He acted confident with the decision.

On my first Neurontin-free day, Bonnie and I were flying from St. Louis to Florida, meeting her family for a Caribbean cruise. Upon rising, I felt apprehensive about the quick taper due to the side effects while I was on the drug. I noticed no ill effects. By the time we arrived at the airport and prepared to board the plane, the story quickly changed. As we stood in line at the gate, I broke into a sweat and felt so nauseous and weak I wanted to sit down.

Once in my middle-row plane seat, I considered options, hopeful the feeling would pass. I was in a tight spot. *Something's not right. Something's not right. I need to get off the plane. I can't. We're moving. I don't know what to do.* I turned the overhead air nozzle on high and directly onto my face in an attempt to cool down. As the plane taxied to the runway, my leg muscles began contracting so fiercely my veins looked as though they might pop out of my skin. I watched in disbelief as my veins felt as if they exploded like popcorn and my skin stretched to what seemed like its bursting point.

My legs quaked so violently they shook my entire body, but, luckily, the fastened seatbelt held me in. I turned toward a young male teenager sitting to my left doing his best to gaze straight ahead as if nothing was happening. Who knew what he was thinking? He appeared nervous. I felt bad for him.

If this isn't a partial seizure, I don't know what is. Later, I learned seizures are noted on several Neurontin-withdrawal web pages, including the Epilepsy Home Page, which notes they are the most dangerous adverse effect from a quick taper off Neurontin. This is across the board for epileptic sufferers, as well as those never experiencing one before. Sitting positioned for take-off, Bonnie debated flagging down a flight attendant to stop the plane. I shook my head and waved her off.

"No, you can't do that," I sputtered, so as not to cause a scene. Back to my wallflower mentality. I didn't want a plane full of people on hold for departure due to my health issue.

Luckily, I'd had a premonition and something told me to hang on to the unused Neurontin pills instead of trashing them. They were safely stowed in my carry-on bag located in the overhead compartment. Once the plane was in flight and the seatbelt sign off, Bonnie pulled my bag down and I ingested one 300-milligram pill of Neurontin. Within minutes, the shaking ceased and within a half hour, the nausea faded. *It stopped. Good. Oh, but wait.*

I turned to Bonnie, concerned about the vacation. "I don't have many pills left."

Bonnie assuredly recommended taking one step at a time. "Let's just get to Florida first and off this plane."

The teen never once looked in my direction the rest of the flight. Poor kid. Later, she and I jested of the occurrence and of the boy's reaction in the seat next to me. "He probably thought, 'Great! I have some druggie sitting next to me,'" I laughed. It was our way of making light of the situation—another family trait.

Bonnie shook her head in disbelief. "Your body looked like it was turning into an alien."

Once on the cruise ship, I formulated a plan. I had only a few surplus pills for our weeklong vacation, so I resolved to cut them into small chunks and dole out a hit each time the shaking resumed. It was not of the seizure-type as experienced on the plane, but extreme full-body shaking, nonetheless.

After we returned home, I concluded Neurontin withdrawal was to blame. Several medical websites listed tremors and shaking as common side effects: Drugs.com, RxList and Health Central, to name a few. Never in my life had I experienced seizure-like symptoms or tremors prior to taking and getting off this drug. More research under the Road Back, which I discovered through my website searches at the time, revealed tremors were also associated as a symptom of withdrawal. Emedexpert.com states that abrupt discontinuation of Neurontin is associated with the development of a syndrome resembling alcohol and benzodiazepine withdrawal.

Surely Dr. Baker was aware of these side effects. I scheduled an appointment with her and felt confident my health would improve once she reinstated Neurontin at the uppermost prescribed dose and tapered me off appropriately. That would not be the case. Neurontin was not deemed the culprit. Attempts to discuss the possible connection with Dr. Baker were futile. I got to the point of handing a copy of my Neurontin side effects and withdrawal research to her secretary. At the time, the drug manufacturer, Pfizer, was locked in a series of lawsuits related to complications of the drug and promoting the drug for unapproved uses. I received no response back from Dr. Baker.

Four months into my ordeal and, on top of the newly developed tremors and body shaking, I still bore the pain from my back and hip. Searching for help and hoping to find someone who would listen, I turned to Steve, a highly recommended chiropractor. He diagnosed a sacroiliac joint subluxation, commonly caused by jarring-type accidents and lifting heavy objects.

Steve explained the sacroiliac joint (SI) is formed by the union of the sacrum—the triangular bone at the base of the spine—and the ilium, which is the main bone of the pelvis. Subluxation means partial dislocation of the joint. He said that, when a movement of the joint goes beyond its maximum passive range, the alignment between the joint surfaces becomes distorted. Subluxations cannot be detected by X-ray; however, motion palpation revealing joint dysfunction and visual examination can reveal an unleveled pelvis. Left untreated, subluxations can throw off the alignment of the entire spine. That was why I felt my body was buckling to one side.

Steve used standard procedures in an effort to restore the joint. My lower back and hip region received twenty minutes of mild electrical stimulation and hot-cold contrast therapy. He massaged the soft tissue of the lumbar paraspinal muscles.

He then began diversified manipulation in the SI joint using a side posture. I lay on my side with my top leg and hip fully flexed while keeping the opposite leg straight. He put one hand on my shoulder and the other on what he referred to as the posterior superior iliac spine. He explained the SI joint would be stressed to the end range of motion to lock out joint play. Next thing I knew, he applied a high-velocity thrust to the joint. I heard a small popping sound. Shock and relief hit simultaneously.

I turned over for manipulation of the other side and expressed a sigh of relief. Although the manipulation was quick and easy, I found it difficult to fully relax during treatment. It was similar to someone telling you to take a few deep breaths, and on the count of three they were going to pop your neck with a quick twist.

I then switched rooms, moving to the pelvic drop table. My homework thereafter was a daily regimen of stretches. Treatments started once a week and gradually spread out over time. Within two to three treatments, I noticed a big difference. I could walk with less pain. After five or six sessions, I felt I was back on track even though my joint slipped occasionally. Steve became a common face as it took a year before my SI joint was stable.

I waited four months from my initial injury for an answer to the chronic pain. If only I had gone to the chiropractor earlier! I decided against it, though, in view of the workers' compensation policy. Various doctors, tests and certainly no drugs would have been involved. With my back pain easing, my immediate focus returned to diagnosing the cause of my tremors and shaking, and putting an end to them once and for all.

Once focused in my torso, they were now stretching into my extremities on more severe days.

Full-body shaking sent me to the ER twice. Visit one—the doctor injected me with a hypodermic needle filled with who knows what. When the drug did not work, I received a second. Three hours after my arrival, the second hypo finally stopped my body shaking; it also turned me into a noodle. Sent home, I slept for twelve hours. Knocking me out seemed to be the ER doc's solution. Visit two—Bonnie escorted me to the hospital after an early-morning gym workout. My body began ceaseless shaking upon cool-down stretching.

Dr. Baker was called by hospital medical staff. Unable to determine a cause, she scheduled an appointment with a neurologist. Dr. Baker informed me that, whenever a diagnosis was unknown, the doctor randomly coded three possibilities. Can you guess what one of mine was and which random position it was listed in? Anxiety—number one. I questioned her about the influence these codes might have on a doctor, especially one not familiar with me or my history. Isn't the next doctor influenced by these three codes? I didn't like anxiety sitting in the number one position. Dr. Baker found it irrelevant. I still beg to differ. Why can't they type "presently unknown?" Why the need to fill in a code at all?

Initially, the referral to a neurologist, Dr. Murry, came as music to my ears. He was a slender, slightly tanned man with brown hair parted to one side. His demeanor seemed lackadaisical, though, as he made no attempt to observe my disorder after multiple visits. Bonnie attended the appointments as a witness, but he did not value her input. She and I decided to take matters into our own hands. We borrowed video equipment and recorded my shaking. We delivered the videotape to him directly and awaited his opinion. We waited and waited and waited.

During the next appointment, he joked how his wife frequently reminded him to watch it. The video had been sitting on top of his television this entire time. He laughed. I found no humor in it. After a series of neurological exams and blood tests, no answers were found. I did not expect any of the exams to turn up a neurological problem, virus or infection. I was convinced the problem stemmed from my fast taper off Neurontin. The doctor, however, discounted Neurontin withdrawal and rejected discussion. He thought the shaking in my video appeared anxiety-ridden.

After leaving Dr. Murry's office, I turned to Bonnie. "Does he know what it's like to have your body shaking uncontrollably? Any anxiety I have is caused by what my body is doing. Jerk! I would like to wipe that smart-ass smirk off his face." I thought myself quite calm under the circumstances—definitely calmer than most people would be. In time, body shaking occurring primarily in a restful state began to cause dysfunction in an active state.

Dr. Murry had already prescribed a benzodiazepine called Xanax before observing the video of my body shakes. Clearly, his mind was made up beforehand. I took the pills without fully understanding their use to manage anxiety disorder, relief of temporary anxiety and/or panic disorder. With the Xanax not working to stop the shakes, he ran out of ideas and referred me to another local neurologist, Dr. McDonald. Bonnie escorted me to the appointment.

Our first impression was positive. He came across as experienced, denoted by his thinning white hair—typical of an upper middle-age man. Most important, he appeared attentive. During the appointment, both Bonnie and I carefully laid out the timeline for the Neurontin removal and the symptoms that appeared thereafter. No matter.

As Dr. McDonald put it, "Neurontin is nothing more than colored water with a little something in it."

He concluded Neurontin was not potent enough to cause tremors as a withdrawal symptom, certainly not after two weeks of use. Bonnie—serving as a testament to my partial seizure on the plane and the now-more-frequent episodes of tremors and shaking—was of no interest to Dr. McDonald, nor was my emotional stability. Maybe I shouldn't have taken a pill on the plane when I started shaking. Maybe if I had let the flight attendants take care of me, doctors would have realized right then and there what the cause was. This would all be gone. Then again, maybe I would have been prescribed another drug. That didn't matter now. Here I was.

40 Next Prescription

When things aren't adding up in your life, start subtracting.
~Anon

Dr. McDonald altered my prescription from Xanax to three milligrams of Clonazepam (Klonopin), another benzodiazepine, used to treat panic and seizure disorders. Taking a pill every four hours, I needed to set my alarm in the middle of each night to keep a balanced dose. Depakote was listed as the next drug on deck should Clonazepam falter. I already declined it when it was mentioned as the first option. It held the potential for too many horrid side effects. When I looked over Clonazepam, I felt confused as to the greater evil. I fell deeper and deeper into a hole with no safety net, unsure how to climb out.

The two neurologists put me through test after test after test—and zilch, I got no answers. Neither neurologist considered simply observing me to analyze the symptoms. With tests offering no answers, my diagnosis staggered back and forth between questions of further back injury, myoclonus or anxiety.

It took me several doctors to realize that, any time a doctor had no knowledgeable diagnosis for my neurological symptoms, a verdict of anxiety quickly topped the chart. I later wondered if this diagnosis was due to the insurance company needing a proper code in order for monies to be distributed, or plain and simple medical arrogance. I also realized the drug companies themselves fit into the equation in the fact they often had their own doctors educating the physicians who prescribed the medications we patients received. To this point, I had not found one doctor willing to probe the possibility that Neurontin withdrawal was responsible for my symptoms.

Neither Xanax nor Clonazepam proved beneficial. I wanted no other drug. I was not a guinea pig. Shaking had increased in intensity, frequency and duration. Body shaking was more violent, primarily at rest. I noticed that extended aerobic activity set my body off. My heart rate abnormally increased as did my respiration. Neither achieved a state of normalcy between cardio intervals or after any kind of workout. My body also found it difficult to regulate its temperature.

I requested a referral to a larger, more prestigious medical center. I didn't know why I thought one well-known Midwest hospital would differ from any other. Here I was, convinced from day one we needed look no farther than the Neurontin itself. I struggled, however, to find one doctor with an ounce of common sense who could see what I clearly saw to be true. I had always been in great health with no medical or family history of any problems. Surely the timing of the tremors and shaking would be enough to compel one to indicate the drug as the villain?

December marked an appointment with a third neurologist, Dr. Tucker, who was affiliated with the prestigious institution from which I desired treatment. My hopes were that this larger institution connected with research would have a prompt fix. I wanted someone to listen. Was that too much to ask? The neurologist conducted some in-office memory and physical tests, which seemed like old hat after performing them for each of the prior two neurologists.

The memory test consisted of reciting three words I would be asked to recall later in the appointment. I focused on remembering the three words, not listening attentively to him. Once I was asked to repeat the three words, I shifted my mind back to listening to his every word. I focused on the test I wanted and cared about. I was looking forward to the opportunity to lay on the bed to let my body show its song-and-dance routine. I wouldn't need to chime in. My body would say it all.

To check my coordination, the neurologist asked me to place my finger on my nose. He then held his finger out directly in front of his face, nose high, and asked me to move my finger back and forth from my nose to his finger, touching the tip of each. I was also asked to tap my forefinger and thumb together as quickly as possible. None of these tests were difficult, but I was not sure how they could rule out tremors. *Just let me lie down. I'll show you what my body does.*

I repeatedly told Dr. Tucker the tremors and body shaking occurred primarily in a restful state. Symptoms were not 24/7, but had definitely increased. As with my previous neurologists, Dr. Tucker did not allow me to lie down to illustrate the symptom. He ignored my reference to resting tremors and shaking. Over the months, I had learned that pressure on my spine upon lying instantaneously sparked body shaking. Surprised by his refusal to observe, I quietly contemplated the issue. Why wouldn't he want to see that? The bed was right there. Lying down would alleviate all doubt. Once again, I struck out. I found myself questioning him and all previous doctors. What were they afraid of? It wouldn't have taken but a minute to show him.

Astonishingly, he quickened the pace of the appointment and, before I knew it, it was over. Nearly laughing with his assistant, he stated, "It's a no-brainer." Without saying the quick taper of Neurontin was at fault for the withdrawal symptoms, he prescribed it again.

"This will take care of everything," he said.

The doctor's attitude suggested nothing was really wrong and, again, it was all in my head. I was being ridiculed. I was once more perceived as an anxious crazy lady. I was wasting his time and he wanted me out of there to deal with what he considered more pertinent health issues.

Dr. Tucker prescribed 900 milligrams of Neurontin daily with a sequential monthly taper plan. I was instructed to reinstate its use immediately. Simultaneously, he wanted me off Clonazepam. I had been on it a little over two months. At that time, I ingested three milligrams daily. He wanted me to taper off one pill a day, 0.5 milligrams, beginning immediately. I asked questions, concerned about another quick taper, but he assured me the Neurontin would balance out the symptoms associated with the taper of Clonazepam.

Bonnie and I decided to eat at Boathouse Forest Park, a nice lakeside restaurant, as a treat for getting through another demeaning appointment. Directly after eating, I pulled out the newly prescribed container of Neurontin, looking over the prescription once more. I removed the lid, turning the bottle to its side. I pulled out one pill and looked it over with a sickened heart and mind. I bittersweetly washed down 300 milligrams of Neurontin as instructed. While believing I needed to reinstate the drug to taper properly for the removal of the shaking, I found it hard to put it back into my body. Instinctually, I knew the tremors and shaking came from it. I had absolutely no doubt whatsoever.

Within 30 minutes, full-body shaking occupied the helm. The severity of the shaking hit a new level. It was a two-hour drive home. My upper body stayed contained, held in by the passenger seat and shoulder strap of the seat belt. My legs, however, repeatedly ricocheted off the console. I grimaced with each contact made, voicing the agony felt. I was unable to stop the leg action. I lowered the back of my seat to a more level position. Attempts to slide farther back in it to protect my legs failed.

Bonnie nervously eyed the interstate and mulled over her response. She could not locate anything in the vehicle to guard my body from impact. It would be a long ride home for both of us. My body did not stop shaking. Once we arrived home, Bonnie assisted me in. I feared not taking the other 0.5 dose of Clonazepam to begin my quick taper. How would my body react to a Clonazepam taper when it was already shaking from Neurontin? In the end, I did as the doctor directed. I didn't know what else to do. I left off one 0.5 dose and began my taper off Clonazepam.

Bonnie called the hospital the following day to inform the doctor of my deteriorating condition. Office staff conveyed to her I should continue what I was doing. "The Neurontin will balance out the Clonazepam taper. Give it another day or so." Bonnie informed them the shaking started with the ingestion of Neurontin, but it was as if they didn't listen. I continued with the plan in hopes the doctor was right.

With each 0.5 daily taper, my body reacted more furiously, moving from tremors and body shaking into major "coherent" seizure activity.

Two weeks after the last dose of Clonazepam following the slow taper, symptoms continued to mount. The world spun about me, and it was evident that something had gone madly wrong. Tapering Clonazepam by 0.5 milligrams a day from three milligrams daily was too fast. Dr. Tucker assured me the installment of Neurontin would balance out the taper off Clonazepam. He was wrong, dead wrong.

Bonnie and I left countless messages, but received no response from him to our desperation. After constantly harassing his office staff for help, we were told he was out of the country. Like many doctors at this hospital, he normally saw a patient only once a year.

Anger and fear hit at once. *What? Once a year. Who does that? What am I supposed to do?*

I finally conversed with a nurse from his office, who told me I could have an appointment with another doctor at the hospital—a psychiatrist. She informed me there was nothing more Dr. Tucker's office could or would do. I crumbled and lost control. Far from polite, I took no mercy on the messenger. It was like a customer taking a poorly cooked steak out on the server. I impugned the suggestions made by the doctor.

My voice was loud and sharp as I launched into a breathless rant. I filled her ears full of the number of days I tried contacting the office. I admonished the doctor for the gross neglect of symptoms encompassing my body and for not taking time to observe my tremors and shaking during the original appointment and for insinuating this was all a fantasy as if I were crazy. Once I'd finished spewing out my frustrations, I heard nothing but silence on the other end of the phone, so I hung up. Black thunderous clouds of thought ruled my mind. A long-lasting storm, I grumbled for not only hours but days.

The reinstatement of Neurontin and quick taper off Clonazepam forced me to take a leave of absence from school. Crestfallen by December 27, Bonnie wheeled me into that same prestigious hospital after witnessing five hours of tremors, shaking and "coherent" seizures. After we reached the hospital, the seizures and full-body shaking de-escalated to tremors and trembling. I spent an hour shaking in the waiting room, anticipating a doctor's availability. I could not believe they were letting me sit here in that condition. But after that hour, my symptoms diminished to nothing. My body was spent.

It was like when you take your car into the shop, only to have the mechanic look at you like there is nothing there. That ping will be in the engine all day long, but the moment you take it in, it's a well-oiled machine. The doctors were supposedly busy so they appointed me an intern, who came to the same conclusion as my other doctors—anxiety.

The intern asked a series of questions regarding side effects. Though I could usually offer an extensive and detailed account, my analytical mind could not remember much that day. My body was exhausted; my mind was foggy. It was typical of what happened to me after such harsh "coherent" seizures. I could barely speak. Memory issues had also been apparent since my Clonazepam taper three weeks earlier. The intern instructed me to perform arm and leg movements; functioning was limited. She noticed elevated breathing upon simple movements, which she attributed to anxiety. *Here we go—again.*

The intern suggested I search out a psychologist or psychiatrist to uncover hidden emotional issues. Dumbfounded, I remained silent. Trying to talk common sense to those people seemed not to work. It was all I could do not to laugh in her face. After just a few moments of observation, she concluded I would not be able to teach again for at least two to three months—maybe more—until I resolved my distress. All I could do was stare at her in disbelief, thinking the entire time how ridiculously overambitious and obtuse she must be. How did these people become doctors? I didn't care what she said and just wanted out the door. She had proven her ignorance and was squandering my time.

During the course of our conversation, I repeatedly asked to lie down to let her observe my tremors/shaking, knowing "coherent" seizures would resume once my back touched the table.

"What you are exhibiting are not Neurontin tremors," she told me. She was going on nothing more than my increased respiration and noted shaking during the movements she asked me to perform earlier.

In agreement, I stated, "I know. They are from tapering Clonazepam too fast and the installment of Neurontin."

I tried to explain, but could not remember the full timeline or effects. I was dazed. She refused to listen. My inability to recall events and organize thoughts elevated her belief in her earlier diagnosis of anxiety. Her mind was made up. *Good grief.*

"I've seen a thousand tremors," she replied. "I know what one looks like."

I am sure my eyes turned black with malice. *You have not seen my tremors! You have not seen my "coherent" seizures! You are an intern! How can you possibly know it all?*

My medical terminology might have been incorrect for my body shaking, but it would shock her to see what my body did. I wondered if that would turn off her arrogance. I questioned the idea of getting onto the bed without her permission. I did not. *What if she increases the dose once she sees how neurologically crazy my body gets? What if she puts me on another drug? I don't trust her. Get me out of here.*

Per her suggestion, I went down to 600 milligrams daily of Neurontin. She wanted me off the remaining Neurontin within three to six weeks, feeling it was serving no purpose. "No pill is going to fix this," she said. She was stuck on the anxiety diagnosis.

Bonnie and I left the appointment knowing we would never call upon these people again. We both found their arrogance suffocating. In that moment it hit me. She and I would have to figure this out on our own. I was grateful I knew who I was and had the ability to hold true to that. I felt an overwhelming sorrow for other patients who would be misled down an erroneous path, believing the total absurdity of these seemingly intelligent, but yet uneducated, people in the field of drugs. I wrangled with a symptom of drug withdrawal and the medical field at the same time.

The instructed drop in dose lowered the frequency, duration and intensity of my body shaking. Within days my mind was not as foggy. I was finally on my feet and more active. The improvement was significant.

I sent a letter to Dr. Tucker informing him of my visit with the intern and my present status. I informed him of the drop the intern insisted upon. At 600 milligrams daily, I notified him I intended to hold at that intake until I heard instructions otherwise. It was a last-ditch effort to contact him and get feedback. I never heard from him other than to receive his signature on a medical release form for school.

I resolved one thing. I sure as hell was not going to taper off this drug quickly. I counted the number of pills remaining out of the 270, and planned the safest and slowest taper possible. These damn doctors didn't know what they were doing. I had seen two doctors in a month who told me two diverse things and prescribed two different tapers. Whom should I believe? I chose neither one. So much for well-known hospitals.

Bonnie and I began our united walk through Hades. We needed support from knowledgeable people. Doctorless, I contacted Lisa, a licensed psychologist. I saw no choice but to continue my taper off Neurontin and hope for the best. I contacted my primary, Dr. Baker, in case any complications arose along the way.

I started up school on time in January 2005, despite the intern's prognosis otherwise. Thankfully, school administrators affluent with my character and status supported me without question. Needing only one day off a week for the first month, I made continual progress with fewer and fewer setbacks. Tremors and body shaking hit every two to three days or upon exhaustion. All other symptoms were still present, but I showed gradual improvement.

I read a Johns Hopkins Health Alert, which stated that more than one third of people using Clonazepam become dependent after one month of use. Dependence is a physiological response, not behavioral or psychological. Physical dependence means withdrawal effects will occur if a substance drug is abruptly stopped or dramatically decreased. The side effects that each drug is prescribed to alleviate can thereafter become the dreadful withdrawal symptom in too fast a taper. I would just have to ride it out. Neurontin was my first withdrawal, and now the addictive benzodiazepine Clonazepam would be my second.

41 Rear-View Mirror

What lies behind us and what lies before us are tiny matters compared to what lies within us.
~Ralph Waldo Emerson

Stop. Stop. Stop. What good does reliving the nightmare from five years ago do? I don't want to think about it anymore. What's the point? It doesn't change anything. It won't change where I am in recovery. Just stop! Change your focus. Live in the present.

It is 2010 and I decide to put everything behind me and focus on my teaching position. I am willing to share only limited details of my experience. Part of it is due to the vast harshness of the trauma, as well as the lack of support I felt. *If people weren't concerned in my absence, why would they be in my presence?*

I carry a great degree of anger and hostility with the medical community over what has transpired. That bitterness displays itself any time I perceive a negative reaction to my circumstances. Life has been hell. I have fought to get myself to this point and the undertow of emotional pain weighs heavy. Screw people's judgment.

I do not want to live in the past. I wish to break free from this storyline. School offers the opportunity to take a big stride forward and move beyond all of my health issues. My identity and life await me.

The school mode begins; everything shifts to conversations on related educational and behavioral topics. I enjoy the company of school staff again, but keep my primary focus on the task at hand—teaching. I am well aware of my stamina level and know that planning and instruction alone will suck it dry.

Lisa told me she believed that, if I could get myself through mornings, I would make it through the rest of the day. She based this on my fight and perseverance alone. She also instructed me and Bonnie to free up every weekend for the first two months for down time. She depicted social interactions as the most stressful as a person has to be constantly listening, thinking and interacting. The brain stays alert the entire time. Teaching adds a higher echelon and the behaviors I encounter at this middle school are far from the norm. Lisa felt quiet time, even periods alone, would be beneficial to allow my brain to unwind and restore itself.

Preparation for teaching classes of 30 to 40 middle school students must be thorough. I plan my curriculum in the most detailed, step-by-step manner in case of an infrequent maladaptive brain, strategizing weeks in advance when my mind is cooperative, which allows adrift moments to occur without concern.

I experiment with and gauge my physical movements for each skill to be taught. I resign to use my cohort or a student for skill demonstrations when needed instead of illustrating myself, but do so myself without hesitation when working with individual students. My body parts and brain lack synchronicity; my brain itself slow to transfer thought to action. My balance gets thrown easily and too much movement makes me feel as if I'm a passenger on a Tilt-A-Whirl.

Athletically inclined, I catch myself throwing off of the wrong foot in activities, my depth perception misgauging in all kicking and striking skills. Are my mind and body relearning? Movement with my left arm remains non-existent, my right arm limited. I cannot raise my arms above my shoulders or electrical shocks shoot through my body. No body shaking or jerking, please!

My cognitive ability seemingly intact, I plan activities and break down proficiencies to the nth degree. I teach individual students concepts in the most diminutive form to substitute for any physical meagerness.

I intend for all of my physical education curriculum development and instruction to be on par or above, using whatever adaptations are necessary to make that possible. *Sure. Why not put more pressure on myself?* I exhibit the perfectionist I work to free myself of. I never want my professionalism questioned. While my job lacks flexibility, I personally need to be more than ever. My planning going into this entire year is indisputable.

Despite this, I lack control of what my brain and body bring to the table each day. Sometimes, they bring moments of embarrassment. On occasion, I have ducked at the last moment after barely catching sight of an illusionary flying object—usually a ball of some kind—coming toward me. Luckily, that's not so out of the ordinary given I teach PE. I learn to laugh at myself after the first time. Since the ball isn't really there, I joke with students that seeing things must have to do with aging. The kids laugh and we carry on. No big deal. I am the only one who truly knows what is happening and learn to make light of it as best I can.

At this point, my stamina fails to increase and remains at a standstill due to an already over-fatigued body. Biking, lifting weights and all other activities outside the school day are out of the question. They deplete me farther, fostering more difficulties. School in itself overflows my cup. I aspire to maintain my present physical level with the increased load of teaching. Rest is crucial. My focus sticks to getting myself successfully through the school year.

August into October passes like a breeze. I feel pleased with how my body has responded and with school itself. Can it be a dream? Mornings remain typically tougher. Lisa was right. I need the weekends to regroup. Even though my classes are some of the toughest in my tenure, I am confident the positive trend will continue. I feel good about my ability to adapt and securely believe in my gradual healing as the year goes on. I enjoy this honeymoon period.

You know what happens with a honeymoon? It never lasts. The combination of classroom management and long hours begins to take a toll. The fatigue and stress cause dramatic monthly flare-ups. In my original plan, I perceptively plotted to take one of my designated sick days per month to attend to them. The addition of school aids recovery on some levels; hinders it on others. I have no idea whether I will be able to cope with whatever may lie ahead.

42 On the Shelf

If you don't sacrifice for what you want, what you want will be the sacrifice.
~Unknown

I leave a productive day at school in October 2010 with the positive belief I can manage the year successfully amidst the struggles. One voicemail from my sister as I climb into my Honda Pilot to head home changes the scenario. A beaming smile turns to a frown. Mom has been taken by ambulance to the hospital. Frantically, I call in search of answers. My sister relieves my concerns momentarily, though I quickly realize Mom's congestive heart failure has reached critical stages.

Except for general aging and a serious bout with pneumonia two and a half years ago, no one noticed dramatic changes in her health. At least, I didn't. Besides showing some frailty, she never let on to any ailments. I am blown away to learn her heart now functions at 30 percent. *How does anyone live with so little functioning? I thought anyone below 50 percent was a goner. Thirty feels so close to lifeless. How low can it go before she ceases to exist? How long before other body systems and functions give out?*

I deem a road trip imminent and make arrangements for a northbound journey to Mercy Hospital and Trauma Center in Janesville, Wisconsin. A bit of a lead foot, the road trip goes quickly. Arriving to see Mom in the hospital bed puts a lump in my throat. I question the possibility of a pacemaker, but my thought is short-lived. The doctor explains her condition; her heart contains holes. Options for her age and heart condition appear limited. Her doctor informs us of a surgery performed at another hospital in another state—but only for a highly selective group of candidates.

Is her age against her? Is her heart strong enough to get her through surgery? How would she get there? Wouldn't travel be too stressful at this point? What is the cost? How long does she have? Is this just a means of providing hope when none exists?

Probabilities produce anger. I am just starting to find myself and the relationship I yearn to revitalize with her. I am returning; she is departing. *How much time do I have with her? How can this be happening right now? It sucks!*

I return from the hospital each night to stay in her home alone. My older sister asks me to stay at her house, but I consider Mom's place my childhood home. With Mom's ailing health, I realize the possible loss of this cherished dwelling and, most important, her. I sit and contemplate life in the quiet surroundings of the house. I feel emotionally fatigued by travel and the situation itself. The more I relax, the more memories of my own health challenge force themselves upon me. Attempts to starve them prove ineffective. I sit back in Mom's favorite recliner and allow them to wash through. My mind swiftly falls back to May of 2005.

I had just completed the Neurontin taper. The best news—all body shaking disappeared and most of the Clonazepam withdrawal symptoms ceased their grip. Withdrawal-induced anxiety and menstrual irregularity, however, ruled my life. The anxiety was caused by chemical imbalances, not thought processes. Notable difference. Dysmenorrhea had been an issue since puberty. At that point, unbearable cramping had escalated to the point where I needed to sit on a balance disc to relieve discomfort. Six months into my Clonazepam withdrawal, Dr. Baker referred me to a gynecologist, Dr. Lind. Her concern highlighted fibroids and the beginning of endometriosis.

Clonazepam withdrawal can cause complications with a menstrual cycle, including severe cramping, according to Psych Drug Truth. Withdrawal-induced anxiety meant I still suffered withdrawal. Major surgery would not be a good idea. Proper planning on my part would have put the surgery on hold for a minimum of a year. Without hesitation, I scheduled a total abdominal hysterectomy for July. Bonnie insisted I wait, but I moved ahead. Quality of life meant ridding myself of the nuisance of a menstrual cycle that caused monthly pain and discomfort, as well as lack of function. Ill-informed, I was not aware surgery could not only knock me back, but send me into a downward spiral.

I lay calmly in the waiting area for my turn to be wheeled to the operating room. I looked forward to the conclusion of the surgery. Dr. Lind met with me beforehand to discuss the operation and go over any last-minute questions or concerns. I was ready to go. My demeanor changed within minutes of being administered Versed (Midazolam), a drug meant to relax my body. I suffered a paradoxical reaction. Instead of a relaxed state, I felt a heightened sense of anxiety. *Code red. Code red. Code red.* Panic hijacked my brain, allowing no rational thinking as the hospital bed traversed the hallways into surgery. My frenzied thoughts were rapid and fear-filled. Finally, I was lifted onto the operating table. The next injection released me from all apprehensions as I drifted off to sleep.

Lying in my hospital room later that evening, I felt no pain. Once the medication wore off, however, my muscles began to tremble as if I were chilled. My entire body was affected. I pulled Bonnie aside to take notice, knowing something was out of the ordinary. I had never experienced this. I requested a painkiller to mask the manifestation. The presence of painkillers in my body kept symptoms at bay for two weeks.

As I moved into August, I began to taper the amount of pain medication until none was taken. Depression hit callously. I could not sleep. I could not think clearly. Suicidal thoughts were present throughout the day and evening; nothing worked to cure them. Thoughts were not graphic, just fluid. No notion of method existed. The idea of killing myself raced through. I tried stopping my thoughts. I tried meditation. I kept busy with friends and activities. I listened to relaxation music; nothing helped. Thoughts seemed worse in the middle of the night and early morning. I was hopeful that, as the days passed, the destructive ideas would diminish, but the lack of sleep fatigued my entire body.

During my follow-up visit with the gynecologist a month after surgery, I inquired about the normalcy of depression after a hysterectomy. Without hesitation, Dr. Lind responded, "Only to those who had been predisposed to it prior."

I am confused. *What? How can this be?* My mind scrambled for an answer. The two transgressors must have been the combined effects of major surgery along with the introduction of the anxiety-reducing drug Versed. Another benzodiazepine, it is used for preoperative sedation. Side effects include drowsiness, relaxation and some memory loss. Due to my difficulty coming off Clonazepam, I should never have been given another benzodiazepine. I never made mention to Dr. Lind beforehand. I didn't understand the relevance. Now seven months into Clonazepam withdrawal and two months clear of Neurontin, I thought myself clear of complications. Not only was I falling backward with withdrawal recovery, but spiraling way off-course in the opposite direction. Scared, I didn't know what to do.

When one domino falls, they all follow suit. The series of doctors continued. Depression meant seeing a psychiatrist. I got a referral to Dr. Reynolds and headed off to my appointment. Bonnie and I gave my full medical history; his interest lay with the recent hysterectomy. I made him aware of my concern over the prescription of more drugs. I carried a noticeable chip on my shoulder from previous experiences with physicians. After several self-talks, I persuaded myself to optimism. *Everything that happened is in my past, and this is a new doctor. Give Dr. Reynolds a chance!*

He prescribed a new daily regimen—three milligrams of Ativan (Lorazepam), 75 milligrams of Lamictal (Lamotrigine) and 50 milligrams of Zoloft (Sertraline) to start with, increasing to 200 milligrams a day. The Lamictal prescription was from free samples in his office. *Why so many drugs?* I did not know, nor did I ask. I was in a bad state and trusted him to get me out of it. Dr. Reynolds appeared very confident in his decisions.

Naturally, we discussed how my depression transpired. "The majority of women undergoing a hysterectomy experience depression," he said. "Up to 75 percent." I still had my ovaries, but he insisted it did not matter. This information was quite contrary to the words of my gynecologist. Dr. Reynolds suggested a two-year stint on Zoloft would resolve my depression. My inner talk ignited. *Wow! Two years! How do you know exactly two years? How can everyone be the same?* Though I felt uneasy, I held myself back. *Oh, yeah. No questions. Trust him.*

I will never forget his words: "You can stay on it a lifetime if you want to. There are no side effects!"

43 The Perfect Storm

She is tossed by the waves but does not sink.
~Unknown

By the summer of 2006, I felt balanced psychologically and wanted to reduce the medication in my system. Surely I was beyond any temporary necessity? Dr. Reynolds instructed me to cold turkey the Lamictal. My third drug withdrawal in two years, though minor. Noticeable symptoms lasted a month. While lethargy, exhaustion, dizziness, habitual headaches, nausea and lack of focus were no picnic, my eagerness to be free of the pills stopped me from complaining. Compared to Clonazepam withdrawal, it was a walk in the park.

The fall of 2007 marked the two-year anniversary since I began care under Dr. Reynolds and his regimented drug therapy. I requested tapering off the remaining two drugs—Zoloft and Lorazepam. In agreement with my wishes, he instructed me to take Lorazepam as needed.

I looked at him. "As needed?"

"Yes," he said. "Take whatever amount you feel is needed in a day but don't exceed the original prescription of three milligrams."

"Okay," I replied, thoroughly confused.

To me, "as needed" meant none, but I decided to take an infrequent 0.5 as I thought I should. Simultaneously, he directed me to taper down 100 milligrams of Zoloft in a two-week period, half of what I had been taking. I was to drop 50 milligrams the first week and 50 on day eight. The concept of removing the drugs from my system filled me with excitement and relief; however, the second taper made my body rebel.

So much pain! So many symptoms! Body tremors, jerking and shaking occurred frequently in the evenings and mornings upon waking. A build-up of energy stored in my lower back prior to unleashed "coherent" seizures. I thought I had gotten rid of those. These episodes occurred minimally once a week, lasting up to an hour. Vision blurred, I often felt dizzy and faint. Bed spins were typical. My balance was off and my legs got stuck in place. I stared at them, trying to force my will upon them. They didn't budge.

Bonnie came to the rescue, escorting me to my destination. Severe abdominal cramps combined with nausea depleted my appetite. Even so, I gained weight. I belched upon drinking or eating anything. Insomnia presented itself daily; I felt overwhelmed on every level. Electrical shocks zapped my body, primarily my back region. Generalized pain occurred primarily in my back, legs and the bottoms of my feet. Tingly sensations soared through my body and head. Limbs fell asleep like tree stumps.

I was unable to concentrate and had difficulty putting thoughts and words together. I was easily agitated with hostile thoughts. With Bonnie in close perimeter, many were aimed at her. My memory often vacated me. My thermometer gauge stuck on freezing temperatures. Anxiety became an up-and-down cycle with bouts of short-lasting depression. Imaginary people showed up in my peripheral vision. My head ached; my ears rang. I could never seem to take in enough fluids. I was always thirsty and diarrhea, well, it was such a pleasantry.

With such drastic changes in my body, I rushed back to Dr. Reynolds' office. His undaunted rebuttal was to maintain the dose of Zoloft for two more weeks, waiting for my body to adjust. My body did not. His next decision elevated my Zoloft dosage back to 150 milligrams a day. My body refused to harmonize during another month-long waiting game. Symptoms had calmed but were still apparent. Tremors/shaking, blurred vision and dizziness maintained their strength. His next step led to a continued taper off Zoloft at 25 milligrams a month. I started it immediately.

Once I hit the 100-milligram dosage of Zoloft in January of 2008, severe tremors and body shaking collapsed me to the school hallway floor. I was stuck in a sitting position just outside the main office. Filled with pain from muscular contractions in my legs and unable to move, I was lifted off the floor and assisted to the nurse's office with one person on each side of me. Legs practically immobile, one of the guys aiding me wanted to carry me into the office. I shook my head and half-jokingly told him, "Hey, Bud. My arms still work. Do you want to get slapped?" Wallflower mentality again. Maybe a little sass, too. I didn't want to be carried. I was heavier than I looked. The thought of someone carrying me also made me feel completely debilitated. I waited on a bed in a closed-off room in the nurse's office as Bonnie was called to drive me home.

March. I tapered from 100 milligrams of Zoloft daily to 85. Chaos ensued with a higher frequency and severity of symptoms. My body and mind appeared angry from the taper. Moody was an understatement. I waited one month for my body to adjust. It did not. I was frustrated my body would not tolerate any attempt to lower the 100-milligram dose. *I want off the stupid drugs! Why won't my body let me?*

April: I should have realized Lorazepam is a benzodiazepine, the same as Clonazepam! Instead of educating myself on the doctor's method of treating depression, I gullibly trusted his presumed expertise and conclusion. You know what they say when you assume something? I always did some research, but I never did enough and too often after the fact. I learned how morally monstrous it was not to taper a highly addictive drug such as Lorazepam. It was insane for the doctor to instruct me to take it as needed, especially after two years of intake.

Without discussion, I unintelligently hiked my intake of Lorazepam from "as needed" to 1.5 milligrams daily—half of the original dosage. I felt Dr. Reynolds was inept and would be of no help. He was the one who told me to "take as needed," which started this mess. Having no reference point, I hoped it would be enough to diminish the symptoms. By the end of April, Dr. Reynolds upped my Zoloft intake back to 100 milligrams.

May: Tremors and long bouts of "coherent" seizures hounded me 24/7. On May 5, the school year ended for me. I was driven home weak, nauseous, dizzy and straining to see through blurred vision. There was no way I could finish out the year. Medical leave was inevitable as the barrage of symptoms showed no signs of ceasing. With numerous emotions running through me, Bonnie and I returned to Dr. Reynolds' office.

His response was pretty direct. "You did okay on higher levels of Zoloft. Maybe you can't get off because you need it. Maybe you should move up to 150 milligrams."

"I *need* it? What?" I reminded him of his bold statement. "You told me the drug has no side effects—that I could take it for a lifetime if I wanted to. You told me I would only need it for two years."

Dr. Reynolds sat expressionless in his chair. Biting my tongue, my mind was silently attacking. *No comment! I didn't think so! What the hell did you do to me? Why did I trust him? Oh, my God! Why did I trust him? What have I done?* The ignored chip on my shoulder surged. I wanted out of his incompetent sight as quickly as possible. Once more, I had shrugged off my instinct, putting myself at the mercy of unqualified hands. With anger burning inside, I nudged Bonnie. There was nothing more to say. His sight sickened me. I needed a new doctor.

Not only did Dr. Reynolds falter with Lorazepam, he concurrently tapered the Zoloft too quickly. Tapering down 50 per cent in eight days was absurd. Protocol suggests slowly tapering one drug at a time too. Once the body is allowed time to adjust, the second drug can be slowly tapered.

Side effects were still present, with a gridlock distinguishing which drug caused which symptoms. Withdrawal symptoms for Zoloft and Lorazepam are similar. I was in trouble. Big trouble!

I searched the Internet continually for prospective doctors. I called one office after another. It would take months before admission as a new patient was possible with a new doctor, no matter what expertise area. I could not spare it. Appointments with my primary doctor, Dr. Baker, became habitual. Under her direction, I moved Zoloft to 125 milligrams in an attempt to alleviate the symptoms. As usual, my body reacted.

Within a couple of days, anxiety increased; anger filled me. A change occurred. Within minutes of ingesting each Lorazepam pill, I now experienced short-lived panic attacks, extreme nausea, blurred vision, tremor and muscle twitching. My body revolted to any change in Zoloft, up or down.

With Dr. Baker's recommendation, an appointment with another psychiatrist, Dr. Clifford, became available. According to Dr. Baker, psychiatrists were the ones who prescribe these drugs and knew best how to remove them. I was not fond of psychiatrists. This was my second. I believed myself to be an emotionally well-balanced person, but the social taboo suggested a mental-illness diagnosis. I also felt like my time with Dr. Reynolds revolved more around drug management than counseling. Now, here was another one.

Thankfully, Dr. Baker's insight with my history pre-empted my appointment with Dr. Clifford. After the disillusionment caused by previous doctors, I planned to evaluate this prospective doctor, more so than him me. There was no need to see any given doctor if I did not trust or believe in that person's capabilities. Bonnie and I headed to the appointment.

"Who prescribed Lorazepam and Zoloft and told you there are no side effects?"

"Dr. Reynolds, another psychiatrist."

Dr. Clifford smiled. "He is well-known for loading up on patients. He likes to live well."

I did not give any thought to his statement or consider how ludicrous it was for a doctor to do such a thing if it were true. It was not really very professional on Dr. Clifford's part to tell me in the first place. All I wanted was immediate assistance.

After a discussion on my state of affairs, I asked him what he thought. His first words—"I think you're crazy!"

Though he was laughing, his demeanor told me he was only joking. Noticing his humor, I began a rare laugh myself and replied, "Good, what should we do then?" He said he would contact the physicians connected with Pfizer, the drug manufacturer, to find the relevance of the symptoms illustrated in me, as compared to those claimed as possible side effects and withdrawal symptoms.

During my next appointment, Dr. Clifford informed me contact had been made. Sure enough, it was a match—my symptoms matched side effects noted by drug company doctors. He, however, made no more comment other than to set a plan of action in place. The remaining Zoloft taper would be as slow as needed. Appointments with him would be for no other reason than medication management.

His first priority was tapering off the Zoloft. He and I initially disagreed on which drug to taper first. From website readings, I learned the shorter-acting benzodiazepine should go first. He stayed unbending with Zoloft, so that was what we decided to do. I asked if Lorazepam would then follow, to which he nodded and said, "Yes." I wanted to be drug-free. It was all I cared about.

I endured a bumpy ride for several months to come. The depression Zoloft was originally prescribed to abate was now a mainstay. As if things weren't bad enough, a new symptom prepared to introduce itself.

Vivid hallucinations became prevalent. Dr. Clifford lacked shock or concern at my next appointment. Anxiolytic properties found in both Zoloft and Lorazepam are known to cause hallucinations. An anxiolytic is a drug that inhibits anxiety and/or panic. He told me the brain is nothing more than a computer chip, and what we see often gets played back to us. He brought up the use of another drug to curb the hallucinations, but neither he nor I intended to add another medication to the mix. There would be no more drugs, no matter what.

Throughout the summer, my computer chip displayed various scenarios. A few visualizations dilated my eyes and shocked my heart. All appeared when I was at ease, not stressed.

In August 2008, school started back up; I was present, hopeful that the final taper off Zoloft would nullify all symptoms in a timely manner. I was accustomed to pushing myself through adversity after all I had endured through these drugs. I remained focused on the day at hand, not allowing myself to look too far in advance.

My hands were full with teaching, coaching basketball and dealing with the complications of tapering off my prescription drugs. I was determined! Being a fighter by nature had its strong suits. Bottom line, I wanted to be Zoloft-free and, eventually, drug-free.

44 Grace

Grace has been defined as the outward expression of the inward harmony of the soul.
~William Hazlitt

The sound of a ringing phone jolts me back to the present moment, October 2010. *What? What the heck?* I realize the voice on the other end of the phone is my sister. She has called to check up on me at my mother's home in Wisconsin and make plans for the following day.

Even a few short days with Mom at the hospital are long, tiring and stressful. There are no solutions for this type of predicament. Upon her release, family concerns emerge for home care. Aside from Meals on Wheels and a Lifeline medical alert subscription, Mom nixes other options. She needs time to process her feebleness and the idea of other people occupying her house. I head back to Columbia with one thought—my return visit.

I exchange the sick days I planned for the benefit of my own healing and use them to travel home for Mom. Internal conflict ensues. *How often can I handle driving home by myself? What will the stress and fatigue do to me?* I desire to be at her side as often as imaginable. I decide to tackle trips once a month unless an emergency arises. Each phone call I receive generates fear of bad news on the ring alone.

In November, I discuss the new set of circumstances with Lisa. She addresses the remaining phase with Mom as a grace period and considers the timetable of events a blessing. Mom's heart did not fail earlier in my health crisis, which allows me time, no matter how small, to spend with her. I need to make the most of it. Lisa points out my individual healing may suffer as I focus on my mother. Mom, too, makes a point to frequently discuss the possible effects on me, not wanting to diminish my health further for hers. No matter. I vow to shelve my healing to spend as much quality time as I can with her. This is my mom we are talking about. Time is precious and I have no idea how much remains.

Christmastime provides a focal point for having the entire immediate family present, constituting one of the best holidays ever for Mom. We all know it will be her last. She does, too. Her main joy lies with the family itself and making sure everyone has a gift to open. An extra twinkle shines in her eyes. It is unlike any other Christmas.

After the holidays, I continue my monthly trips to Wisconsin. I notice an advancing decline in Mom's status with each visit. Quality time soon lies in the realm of caretaking. She fights to be as autonomous as possible under her conditions. As her body weakens and systems begin to fail, she rapidly loses independence.

Mom's health takes precedence over everything. Death serves as no stranger to our family. I don't know if a person ever really heals from the death of a loved one; maybe, instead, we just do the best we can to adjust to life without the person. As part of my ingrained upbringing, I attempt to continue my first-rate teaching at school and simultaneously try my best to be a support to her. The difficulty lies in the distance. School, my health and, now, Mom. My candle burns at both ends.

My fallbacks become more frequent and obvious, a definite sign of physical and mental exhaustion. In January of 2011, I decide to suspend my participation in after-school activities which I normally coordinate. I release any tasks I deem non-essential to my primary teaching position. I need to protect my shrinking energy reserves.

In February, Mom decides she wants one last weeklong stay with Bonnie and me. The phone rings frequently as siblings discuss the prospect of her traveling this distance. I nervously anticipate the consequences of the long haul down. When all is said and done, Mom wins out. My sister and brother-in-law bring her. Mom makes no mention of a fall she sustains the day before leaving, knowing full well they would cancel the trip. After she settles into our home she shows me the bruises. The red, deep blue and purple colors cover her entire right shoulder region down into her arm. *Good God.* I shake my head in amazement of the magnitude.

Her ankles show bruising as well, the left more than the right. Mom caught her foot in the blankets as she rose out of bed and twisted an ankle. She fell not knowing, or at least not stating, what she hit on the way down. She admits she had fallen another time within the same week, possibly from fainting. I shake my head, yet admire her determination. I do not fall far from the same tree.

Each night we sit in front of the fireplace. Bonnie and I soak Mom's injured feet in a warm Epsom saltwater solution and apply ice to her upper back, shoulder and arm. We garb her in a heavy white robe, similar to the ones found at swanky hotels.

"I feel like I'm at a spa," she comments one night.

Normally short with words, she fills the evenings with storytelling. Bonnie and I enjoy listening to her reminisce about her life, especially memories of childhood. Mom appears at ease, which instills peace in me as well.

She becomes more and more fragile with passing months, accompanied by a couple of trips to the emergency room. I travel home as often as I can; I feel conflict as a daughter not being there more. My two sisters shoulder much of the caretaking role, which begins to take a toll on them. My body seems to hold up throughout the week and allow me to travel home for long weekends; however, my body revolts on alternate weekends.

My second year of recovery anniversary in April of 2011 comes and goes with little appreciation. As the end of the school year approaches, I miss more days to participate in Mom's care. I know her days are numbered. She looks like she weighs all of 70 or 80 pounds soaking wet, if that. Some days she shuffles behind a walker; other days she requires assistance.

Balancing work, Mom, stress and rest is nearly impossible for me. I discuss with my sisters the option of leaving school with two weeks left. This is my first year back from medical leave; otherwise, I would already be home with her. My sisters are stressed as caretakers; Mom continues to decline. I have every intention of being with her when she passes. That is the most important thing right now.

The heavy, stressful load becomes unbearable and, with a week left of school and all in order, I eliminate the internal conflict. I prioritize and head to Wisconsin to be with one of the most important people of my life.

45 Role Reversal

My daughter,
The day you see I am getting old, I ask you to please be patient, but most of all, try to understand what I am going through. If I occasionally lose track of what you are talking about, give me the time to remember, don't be nervous, impatient or arrogant. Just know in your heart that the most important thing for me is to be with you.
~Guillermo Peña. Translated into English by Sergio Cadena

The prior concern I entertained about retrieving my teaching title and role after recovery seems all too trivial compared to what lies at hand. Everything is once again put into perspective. I relieve some weight from my shoulders as I leave school and head to concentrate on my mom's waning health. That in itself brings its own Herculean task.

Mom's doctor finally persuades her to use hospice care. Hospice managers frequently note most people wait too long to use their services. We knew that to be true in our case. The hard part was waiting for Mom to come into alignment with that thought process. She didn't like having "strangers" in her house or someone other than family caring for her; however, once she meets each care person individually, her mindset changes. Nurses and aides attend to her one to two days a week with primary care still coming from my two female siblings, and me when I am able.

I stay with Mom for caregiving two to three weeks at a time, as summer affords me this luxury. I often take Buster with me as a source of comfort and distraction for us both. She has never been much of an animal person, yet she loves Buster. Love might be a strong word. He has always risen quickly in the morning when she is around, knowing full well he would be greeted with a treat each time. She gives an extra for retrieving the rolled newspaper in the driveway as well. Instinctually, he knows these trips differ and often lounges around, waiting for each day to start.

I am unable to catch any long periods of sleep. Roles reversed, I listen for every sound as she sleeps, as a mother with her newborn child. I continually check her breathing during the night to make sure she is still with us and assess her pain level. Knowing Mom has a mind of her own, I need to be available for assistance at the drop of a hat so she does not take matters into her own hands. She lacks patience, always has. A fall would turn the tables quickly for sure. The more I observe her body wasting and her mind gradually preparing for transition, the more grim things become.

My mind wanders often, especially at night. I lie in bed and allow memories of both parents to flood my thoughts. The one thing I always desired from Mom was to hear the words, "I love you." I remember hearing it only once. Her lack of shown affection has nothing to do with my lifestyle. While Mom may not understand, she has been fully supportive and accepting, never once questioning me or Bonnie.

Mom has always kept an updated 8x10 of us on the family wall alongside pictures of my siblings and their families. She is always quick to remind us when she needs a new one. She treated Bonnie like another daughter from the moment they met and instantaneously welcomed her into our family. People who speak in a derogatory fashion about us place themselves on the battlefield with her. Believe me, that is not a good place to be.

So what holds her back from expressing her emotions? I don't know. I used to take pity on myself and, at a younger age, felt as if she did not love me at all. Over time I began to understand her better, withheld judgment and felt bad for her. I doubt affection was shown to her as a child. What happened to close her off? I do not doubt her love and appreciate she would do anything for me. I have crossed paths with parents who speak of unconditional love, yet often try to feverishly manipulate their child to meet their expectations. Their ego takes priority over the individuality and well-being of their child. In that matter, as an adult, I am lucky. Mom told me her only wish is for me to be happy. What more could I ask for? Subconsciously, though, I want to hear the words.

One of my older brothers and I joke with Mom about her inability to say them. One of us says, "I love you, Mom," and, when there is no response, except for maybe a hug, we turn the conversation over to each other.

"I love you, Tarry."

Tarry responds with a big smile, saying, "Ditto!" or "Back at yah." Then we often reverse roles. Mom just smiles and shakes her head. We only throw out a few words here and there in an attempt to make jest of the situation and ease her discomfort. You will not meet a Laube who does not joke.

Through it all, my body somehow maintains, but my strength dwindles. I relieve stress by taking daily walks or napping when Mom lays down to sleep. I am caught in a vacuum.

The doctor has given Mom a Lorazepam prescription as an anxiety-reducer. I have observed it in the upper shelf of the corner cabinet many times as I prepare her cocktail of daily medications. I know numerous side effects could arise within days or weeks if she takes any. Why take a chance? I discuss with my sisters my unwillingness to give Mom the drug. We need to weigh the pros versus the cons. Unless I notice discernable anxiety or realize Mom is close to death's door, that drug is staying in the cabinet. She knows the pain the drug has caused me and I do not believe she would want it given to her unless absolutely necessary. I feel somehow like I would betray her.

As I wake one morning, I lie in bed contemplating rising to prepare her daily regimen of medications. One single thought of that drug in the cabinet overturns the radio station in my brain and sends me into a frenzy. What I'm sure reigns no longer than a few minutes, but seems like hours, becomes a drug craving I have not experienced in more than one and a half years. To say it overtakes me is an understatement. Scared, fighting, holding on, I cling to the covers of the bed.

My mind takes a hard-right detour. I fearfully cling to hope and faith but can't shake the thought of that drug just sitting there. Waiting. I crave not just one pill, but the entire bottle. I personally do not want the drug any more than I previously wanted to injure myself or anyone else. Unfortunately, a part of my brain has its own entity; it is the remainder of my drug brain. That part does not think like the real me. Once it finally terminates, a huge sense of relief fills me. Uniformly, I now realize my life will never be the same. I am not the same. There will forever be a part of me that, no matter how hard I try, I cannot rid myself of. *How do I make peace with that concept?* Shaken from the event, I pause to pray for strength to overcome any obstacles should it appear again.

Mom composes a strong, inexplicable comeback in July. She could barely walk, looking like death warmed over, and now she is mobile with use of the walker. I had her on death's doorstep; now she claims the appearance of someone who has walked through a different door. A smile and sparkle return to her hazel-green eyes. It is remarkable! Then one morning, I hear Mom rise and I yell to ask if she needs assistance to the bathroom. I am packing in my bedroom in preparation for my return trip to Columbia. Whether she states "yes" or "no," I always head in her direction to support her. I pace behind her for safety. On this morning, I do not hear her response to my question. She already made her move without waiting for my assistance. I hear a loud thud and a moan. In shock, I stand up straight and pause to listen. I hear more groaning. *Shit.*

As I turn the corner into the bathroom, I see a pale, naked and frail 87-year-old lady slumped over on the linoleum floor, lamenting in pain. Her skeletal bones protrude through her wrinkled skin. She lost her balance when she bent over to see her numbers as she weighed herself. Hospice nurses had previously asked her to get weighed whenever possible, but with no hurry. When someone asks Mom to do something it means sooner rather than later. She didn't ask for my assistance, instead feeling well enough to do it on her own.

Now, the life-changing fall I had been concerned with has happened. I crouch over her and contemplate how to pick her up, if I should at all. I can't leave her here. She bemoans her hip. The appearance of her emaciated body takes me aback. I bend down as low as I can and lift her to a standing position to cloak her. With my arms around her, I cautiously walk her to the living room recliner and position her with the least amount of pressure on the injured areas. She moans with each and every movement.

Flabbergasted, I put her oxygen mask in place and call a sister who swiftly arrives. There will be no 911 call. That had been decided much earlier in the summer. Mom loathed the thought of dying in a hospital. She had recently watched her sister wither away in one over a period of months until her subsequent death. My sister and I do our best to make Mom as comfortable as possible. Ice seems so paltry. We call hospice. A nurse is dispatched, but will not arrive promptly due to the distance of travel.

I mull over a big decision. Today, I planned to head home for a reprieve and to switch sibling caretakers. I am holding on with the smallest stitch of thread having reached an emotional stymie. My symptoms have been appearing more and more. I feel completely worn down on all levels, and now this. Guilt fills me. I gaze at her in the recliner, suffering pain from the fall, and I feel overwhelmed. As I talk with my sister and coordinated plans are made with hospice, I decide I need to keep with my plans to return to Columbia, even if only for a few days. I talk with Mom, who supports my decision. I feel ill. When the fall occurred I knew the outcome. Mom did as well.

Will I have time to go home for some much-needed rest before Mom regresses farther? I sense I must leave now if I plan to receive any respite. I load up Buster and the suitcases in the vehicle and head for Columbia, guilt-ridden. I periodically check in with my sister for updates on Mom's status. Hospice arrives and determines with a physical exam she has no broken bones.

Hospice and my sisters make the decision to keep her at home instead of transferring her to a hospice nursing facility to recuperate. I think a common thought prevails in all our minds that, if she leaves, a high probability exists she will not return. Pain management becomes the focus.

Once Buster and I arrive home to Columbia, I endure one full day of symptom onset. I can do nothing but let my body have its way with me. I am sicker than a dog and, in a fog, unable to think clearly about anything. Days pass before I sense a functioning level return. I realize how unattainable it is to moderately decompress as my heart and mind are always in Wisconsin. Emotionally numb and downright exhausted, I spend the majority of time sitting in nature, doing mindless small indoor or outdoor projects and finalizing tasks after being gone most of the summer. To add another element, teacher workdays start in a few weeks for the upcoming school year. I need to prepare for various scenarios. My current aspiration, however, entails regaining strength and energy for more intense caretaking upon returning to Mom's side.

The injury knocks Mom off the fence and throws her into an unwavering downward spiral. Kidneys failing and running out of systems to compensate for each other, she has nothing left to fight with. She becomes fully bedridden with overwhelming pain. The tables have turned—drastically. As hospice works to find a level of medication to curb Mom's pain, my sisters' stress levels reach a new high. They order a hospital bed and move Mom from her bedroom into the living room to remove her isolation. *Why didn't one of us think of that sooner?* My sisters speak of how far and rapidly Mom is plummeting.

After staying home for two weeks, Bonnie and I prepare to head north. I plan to stay as long as needed. As we head out, I receive a message from my sister questioning our arrival time. *Oh, my God. No!* I can easily read into the inquiry. When I call to inform her of our travel plans, she states the head nurse is concerned about my arrival time. I tell my sister 10:30 p.m., to which the hospice nurse responds, "Good, she will make it in time."

46 No Words

A mother is she who can take the place of all others but whose place no one can take.
~Cardinal Mermillod

Make it in time? What? I knew Mom had worsened, but I am alarmed to learn time is of the essence. The ride home is a blur. Fast and safe become conflicting terms. I call or text frequently to check her status, let them know where we are and how much longer we have. Instinctually, I have always believed I would be at Mom's side when she died, just like I was with my younger sister. Fear, however, can shake faith.

Upon arrival, I rush into the house without grabbing anything we brought along for the stay. I nervously yearn to get to Mom's bedside. I am momentarily relieved as I enter the living room and find her awake. She sits up with assistance and gives me a hug.

"Thank you for coming."

I still see life in her eyes, though few words are spoken. No anxiousness, only peace. There may have been times Mom felt anxious about her circumstances and the inevitable outcome, but she didn't show much of it. Not to me anyway. Maybe it is her playing the role of a strong parent no matter what the circumstances. She has always been one strong, resilient lady at the hub of our family. Without complaint, she lived each day to her fullest, stating in June, "I'm not going to just give up!"

Mom falls back asleep and I assume the caretaking. A defining event happens the next morning, a Saturday as pain once again takes hold. Discussion with hospice leads to increased morphine. The head nurse acts surprised Mom is still here and questions our need for care workers or someone to physically check in on us daily.

"I'm glad you made it home in time," she tells me. "I know you and your family have taken care of her all along. It's a hard task and I commend all of you for how well you have done. This next part is beyond difficult."

"I know," I tell her. "It will be okay. Family will be here often, and I'll let you know otherwise. I'll call if we have any questions or concerns or need assistance."

"Are you sure?"

"Yes. We're okay."

We serve as Mom's primary caretakers and will be in charge of everything: hygiene, medication, pain management and the dreaded check of the pulse and call in after death. None of it will be pleasant, except the fact we are doing it for Mom.

Her house is steady with people from morning until evening. Sons, daughters, sisters, in-laws and friends alike attend a daily vigil. Let's not forget the 25 grandchildren and 28 great-grandchildren. Her two-car garage turns into a communal area for everyone to socialize, ruminate and support one another.

Within a couple of days, Mom no longer fully wakes, but knows our presence. A rattling sound occurs in the back of her throat from the accumulation of saliva. A "death rattle" develops and she lacks the ability to swallow. Nurses guarantee us her breathing is not hampered and the sound distresses us more than it affects her. The hospice nurse instructs me to administer another medication to dissolve it.

Mom fades farther and farther away. Each evening since our arrival, Bonnie and I have been the lone overnight caretakers. I lie up against the couch arm closest to Mom's bed to hear the slightest change in her breath, or to hear the faintest sound from her mouth. I don't think of sleep. Bonnie sleeps in the bedroom and sets an alarm for us to switch midway through each night, but I can't leave Mom's sight. *This is it. It can be any moment.* The only thing differentiating day and nighttime is the number of people in the house and darkness of the night.

By Tuesday evening, it appears obvious Mom will not reach dawn. Bonnie and I are joined by family members in the living room as we contemplate the next 24 hours. Out of nowhere, Mom sits up and starts to get out of bed. We are shocked. Each of us takes a running step to grab hold of her and lay her back down. We try to talk with her; she doesn't act coherent. We put the rails up and anxiously watch bedside in wonderment of what just happened and how it happened.

As quickly as she got up, she sacks out cold again. Everyone eventually leaves the house and some talk of an early arrival tomorrow morning to visit her again. I know better. I think they do, too. Tomorrow will not exist for her here. I securely close the vertical blinds that cover the large picture window. Bonnie and I sit and talk on the floor, often glancing at Mom in the silence—a tranquil silence.

I remember how Mom enjoys listening to music. Her childhood home was filled with song and dance. Several of her siblings played musical instruments. She herself occasionally sang as she performed daily chores around the house. During these past few months of caretaking, I often played light jazz. I think Mom would like to listen to some relaxing music on her way out. I search my iPod for what I deem appropriate serene music. There it is. Soft, peaceful and somewhat angelic. Ambient radio. Perfect.

In the early morning of July 27, the heart-wrenching job of checking for her pulse, then robotically calling hospice, and the beginning of the family tree, soon ensues. I anxiously tried to check Mom's pulse two or three times during the night. I wanted to make sure I had the right spot when the time came. With each attempt, her body twitched as if to push me away. I took it to mean it wasn't time yet—she was letting me know it. Later, after one large, loud, startling and seemingly forced respiration, there would be no movement.

Once Bonnie and I hear the sound, we know she is gone. I have heard of this type of occurrence referenced before, and now I will never forget it after experiencing it. It is no ordinary breath… more like someone who is suffocating and straining to get as big a breath as possible.

Bonnie and I are at a loss after her last breath. We stand over her, rechecking her pulse for error. There is none. I gently run my fingers over her eyes in an attempt to close them. The eyelids don't shut. *All of those movies where they show someone closing another person's eyes after death are just that—movies. Weird, the stuff that comes to your mind.* I pull the covers up slightly, as if to tuck her in, and tell her time and time again, "I love you." Buster instinctually climbs directly underneath the hospital bed where he curls up to sleep.

A chain of calls goes into effect. An hour passes before anyone arrives. *Now what?* We survey the living room and once again make sure the blinds covering the large picture window are securely closed. We often closed them each evening over the summer to protect her dignity from passersby. I sit by her. I stand over her. I move to peek out the covered windows. I leave the room to return shortly thereafter.

I feel empty and lost. I want to take her in as much as I can with knowledge I will not see her again until my turn comes. I know the reality is that she is already gone. However, her body remains, and that is all I have to hold onto right now. I gaze at her, move away for a period of time to catch my breath, then come back to view more. I am grateful to be here. I find no greater gift than to be with loved ones when they die, hard as it may be.

We hear rumblings of thunder in the distance as a storm brews. I turn the front porch light on for arriving family members. Our hospice nurse follows and immediately checks Mom's pulse. A family pastor and the funeral director are not far behind. The wait seems long as they get all of the necessities out of the way. Then the time comes. The funeral director makes his way into the living room and asks for assistance to move Mom's body onto his mobile cart.

First, we move Buster from underneath her bed to prevent him from acting overprotective. I attempt to shut off whatever emotion remains as we ready ourselves to lift her. A person stands at each corner of the bed. Using the sheet underneath, we transfer her lifeless body to the cart where a black body bag lies. In an automatic and routine mode, the mortician zips the bag up and over her head. My heart stops. I stand frozen. We all do. The hospice nurse immediately directs him to lower the zipper to chest level. He apologizes and carries on.

I'm traumatized. I have only seen occupied body bags on television via news reports, war stories or drama series. During those, I had the ability to turn my head away if the scene disturbed me. When I watch Mom's body bag close, the realization of her lost life hits me in the face. The black bag turns into a lifeless cocoon and reminds me of something to be thrown out in the trash. It makes me sick.

We help guide the rolling cart out the front doorway. In the cover of the closed living room shades, I failed to realize the change in Mom's color. White—pasty white. I stare from the front porch as the mortician positions her directly behind the hearse. The cart legs break down and he slowly slides her in. The black body bag carrying my mom slowly disappears into the vehicle. I watch until her face is no longer visible, the door closes and the vehicle disappears. A chorus of thunder bellows loudly overhead and lightning streaks across the horizon. *How poetic!*

As we sit amongst family members and wait for the remainder to arrive, little conversation exists. Lacking sleep and emotionally spent, I am at a loss for words or conversation. You never know what response siblings will give when the last parent goes, or the reaction each will have with such a loss. In a family with many children there will be different coping methods, priorities and opinions. A solemn day quickly turns complicated.

I perceive some family members prioritize business matters over grief. Maybe that in itself is a means of coping. I see nothing crucial beyond sharing memories, spending time with family and friends and supporting one another. For those of us actual caretakers, downtime and sleep are also vital. The obituary, visitation and funeral arrangements are necessary; all else can surely wait until after the funeral. From my viewpoint, I just took my mother's pulse—she is gone. I hurt deeply.

I believed a respite would occur after her death. Nope. Mom's house continues to be a collective meeting place each day. I yearn for serenity as I bask in memories but instead find staying here distressing. Worn down physically and emotionally, I fear a major fallback and pray I make it through the funeral without occurrence. *How did I make it to this point?*

As a family, we schedule a Saturday morning visitation followed by the funeral. Mom looks great. *Isn't it crazy how much emphasis we put on how someone looks in the casket?* I have heard people say she would be happy with how she looks. *Really? In the scheme of things, why would she care?* The looks of someone in a casket are for the benefit of those attending. A vivid flashback of the person will remain for several months to years. It is our last mental picture and we want it to be a good one for our own psyche.

I hate the challenges of a visitation. My goal is to get to the funeral without breaking down. Once I begin to cry, I will struggle to compose myself from then on out. The visitation presents a test. People attend to pay respect to the deceased and family members. I address people I have not seen in a long time and appreciate their attendance; I find it difficult to talk. People discuss Mom, her illness and its longevity, family and, for some, how long it has been since we have seen each other. It is all good. It is just so damned hard. In my mind it is the first step in laying her in the ground. I already miss her terribly.

People fill the chapel, standing in the back and flowing out the doorway. The pastor makes note of the number and reflects on how her life has affected so many people. Sitting in the front row, I cannot restrain my tears. I don't try. Tears flow freely like a broken faucet for most of the service. During a pause before a hymn, I lean over to Bonnie. "It must be hard for a pastor to deliver a eulogy with people so visibly upset."

She has a quick response. "Maybe they find comfort viewing how loved the person is."

I nod. "Good point."

I fully appreciate having Mom's casket open the entire service. I never want the funeral to end, just to keep her in my presence. I relish the playing of the instrumental version of "Take Me Out to the Ball Game" in respect for Mom's love of sports, especially the Chicago Cubs. Many of the grandchildren garbed themselves in sports jerseys to honor her.

Once the service ends, I find it tough to leave. Family members depart first. I want to remain last as the casket remains open until the final attendee departs, but leave with family members to line up for the procession. The procession to the cemetery and the proclamation of the final rites transpire quickly. Afterward, I hurry myself through the luncheon and return to Mom's house in an attempt to acquire some quiet moments. Other family members decide the same. Before I know it, discussion turns to business matters surrounding Mom's will and estate. For me it is too soon. After discussion, we agree to suspend all matters until Labor Day. Bonnie and I plan a Sunday morning departure. I need to convalesce.

Losing Mom hurts. I held my bond with her in the midst of all my withdrawal symptoms. Lacking attachment to most people and things, I now feel alone and emotionally tapped out. All facets of the event and my own health overwhelm me. Hurt by family discord, I perceive my only resolution to grieve on my own.

Grace not only allowed me quality time with Mom, it gave the opportunity to take care of her. My health, while greatly saddled, has weakened, but held out. My gratitude flows. Here and now, I look to prioritize my well-being to the number one spot.

47 Watershed

No matter how you feel, get up, dress up, and show up.
~Regina Brett

It is August 2011—one and a half weeks have passed since Mom's funeral and school prepares to start. I have no reservoir of sick days, only what the new school year affords me. Though psychologically spent, I decide not to use any of those sick days and start the school year on schedule. Autopilot engaged, I turn my energy and mental focus toward preparation. My grieving process and health recovery combine with regular instruction for a trifecta of mental stress.

Both of my parents are gone. At mid-life, I suddenly feel like a child all over again. As John F. Kennedy, Jr., once said, "You are not a true adult until both of your parents have passed on. You are then an orphan."

I didn't understand the impact of Mom's death until now. While there may be people to lean on, discuss matters with and support you—it's not the same. Love for a parent is like no other, much like it would be for a significant other or child. I lost the sanctuary of her presence. I talked with Mom frequently, through my health crisis and hers. An impulse frequently crosses my thoughts each day to call her and check in.

While grateful to have been with her at the end, I experience vivid flashbacks that disturb me as events replay in my mind. Memories of other family members passing surface as well. Grieving is lengthy and difficult, tugging at the core of my being. I agonize over dueling emotional roller coasters: one of grief, the second from recovery.

As a family, we decide to congregate in Wisconsin over the Labor Day weekend to deliberate over affairs. Sibling differences of personality and opinion appear instantaneously. By the end of the weekend, we clear out Mom's house of all items except that which will be sold. I asked Bonnie to take pictures of each untouched room beforehand. My siblings agree to list her house on the market as soon as possible. Mom's house, one of two I consider a childhood home, will serve as a sentimental loss.

I stand on my own as no other sibling owns this connection. My brothers and sisters experienced all of their nurturing on the farm. The term "home" takes on a whole new meaning for me. I inhabited Mom and Dad's house whenever I visited, no matter where I lived. Soon, a "for sale" sign will be positioned in the front yard of their corner lot. *Why is everything moving so fast?* Emotionally crushed, I prepare to head back to Columbia and jump into the school year.

The typical honeymoon period, which exists at the beginning of the semester virtually every year, never occurs. I hit the ground running without catching my breath and devote my attention to teaching. With student behavior more intense, I notice subtle changes starting to mount.

The first red flag occurs during morning cafeteria duty. A crowded table of seventh-grade boys instigates a small food fight. I shift to their table, without making it a big deal, and simply direct two students to move to another area. The first moves quietly; the second stands in opposition. I patiently wait for him to finish his rant. When I do not give in, name-calling ensues.

"You motherfucking bitch!"

The boys at the table start laughing. "Oh, you're going to get suspended," they chide and continue to tease him as they anticipate my response.

I stand calmly gazing at him. "Really? That's your response because you didn't want to move? All right. Come on."

He lowers his head and willingly follows me to the main office a few short steps away and sits to await his fate.

Midday, we cross paths in the main hallway. I plan to walk past without discussion. He walks over to me. "I'm sorry for what I said to you earlier. I didn't mean it."

I make direct eye contact. "If you didn't mean it, then why would you say such a thing?"

He shrugs his shoulders and gives no response.

"Do you talk like this at home?"

"No. Not ever."

"What would your mom do if you said such a thing to her?"

"Slap me across the face."

"What would happen if she knew you said such a thing to me?"

"The same."

"Interesting. Yet you said it anyway." I pause momentarily as he loses eye contact. "Thank you for your apology. I know saying you're sorry is difficult. Realize, though, that sometimes saying you're sorry doesn't take away the damage it has caused." After another brief pause I ask, "Where are you off to?"

"I'm going home. I've been suspended today and tomorrow."

"Okay. Well, I'll see you when you get back then."

He nods and we both continue on our paths.

I have been called such names before—usually indirect and under the breath. The words never once soaked into my skin. Today was different.

Maybe I had been too numb from the drugs before. Maybe I tire from the foul language I incessantly hear on a daily basis. It could be the total lack of respect an increasing number of students show their teachers.

I realize this school year will test me on a number of levels. During the first semester, I believe much of my struggle with teaching stems from my overflowing cup of grief and my own health. While I carry a great deal of weight, my cognitive ability and memory vastly improve. Multi-tasking is a cinch. I eliminate the need for reminders or index cards, instead relying totally on recall. I plan curriculum in detail, yet I have regained the capability of spontaneity without over-the-top organization. I can think on the move and change directions for lesson plan flexibility in a heartbeat.

My physical ability picks up slightly as well. I fully illustrate and instruct without supplementation or thought of malfunction. I limit my physical performance to skill demonstration only. On occasion, I experiment with my ability, but I don't get carried away for fear of retaliation. A neurological beating lingers a short reprimand away.

I still feel compromised in the mornings and gradually improve as the day wears on. I wear cheaters for reading. I question the need for contacts or regular glasses. My distance vision remains blurred. I cannot distinguish the cause of the imperfection—is it a withdrawal symptom or declining vision? I decide to wait until farther down the road to re-evaluate.

My left side remains at a deficit. My brain forgets a left side of my body exists, especially the arm and head. When it does, I perceive my facial cheek's existence at an angle to my right side. No feeling exists except numbness, tingling or pain. Those same sensations present themselves all the way down.

Brain sensations of pain, tingling, chills or crawling exist constantly. Any increase in sensations presents a good indicator of upcoming problematic symptoms. Headaches occur regularly. As for attachment concerns, I keep faith for its development as it bears one of my largest emotional pains.

All in all, I manage and feel I have made big strides. I feel rumblings in my brain and body. More intense fallbacks occur monthly and I fail to put more symptoms behind me. I needed time off after Mom's death to recuperate. A full month would have been great. I didn't take a pause, instead placing my loyalty as a teacher to the forefront. The small breakdowns I experience imply more than simple stress and fatigue. I can't put my finger on it, but through all of the progress, the weight of the trifecta begins to wear me down. I should have been more cautious. More wary. I did not take time to pause for me—not mentally, emotionally or spiritually.

Bonnie and I make the rounds at Christmas, once again traveling to visit both families. The holiday tastes more bitter than sweet. Alternating periods of sorrow and numbness set in as I watch Bonnie interact with her mom and family. I sense nothing but emptiness. Subsequently, Christmas with my family in Wisconsin is not the same. How can it be? We make arrangements to stay with siblings as Mom's house sits vacant pending its sale. I find the rapid progression of life after her death hard. I was not ready to clear her house on Labor Day. I was not ready to put her house on the market. I was not ready to begin school so soon after her death. In it all, my recovery sits off in the distance.

As the first semester of teaching comes to a close, I begin to recognize I no longer sense a purpose. I feel lost and my tank nears empty. *Is this grief, recovery or changing priorities?* The murmurs are deafening.

By mid-January 2012, I feel melancholy as the second semester sets in. I perform my affirmations daily: I am far from 100 percent. The method of stating "I AM" with clear intention is ambiguous. I still suffer. How can I continually say "I AM whole" and "I AM healed" when after over two and a half years I certainly am not? I look for a means to propel me forward, but have yet to find a boost.

Life events continue to unfold. February catches Bonnie and me off-guard. We wake one early morning to hear Buster gasping for breath. Both distressed, we try to comfort him as we make calls to emergency veterinarians. Upon later examination, the vet informs us of his congestive heart failure. *How ironic?*

We both noticed walks had become problematic over these past few years, especially months. Bonnie and I cut the length of the walks since then, but had not noticed any other signs.

The veterinarian affords him a few months, possibly into the summer. Bonnie and I bank on it; grace is short-lived as he radically declines within days. We sleep on the lowest level of the house on a blow-up mattress to be near him. We physically walk him outside so he can rest amongst the landscape. He does nothing but gaze into the distance. When it gets to the point where he can only stand with assistance and shows no indications of an appetite, Bonnie and I reluctantly drive him in to be euthanized.

We attempt to soothe him and affirm our affection. "I love you. You are such a good boy," we whisper as we pet his head and stroke his neck and chest.

The injection follows and within seconds his eyes glaze over. Our "big white" crosses Rainbow Bridge. My heart gets stuck in my throat. Neither of us wants to leave; we can't stay with him forever. Speechless, we return home, throw on some comfy grub clothes and close the blinds to darken the house. We don't want visitors today. Downhearted by the quick turn of events, we reminisce while watching old movies and veg out on the couch all day.

Buster served as a constant companion for me during withdrawal and recovery. He frequented my side on walks and road trips and rendered his presence known whenever I found myself on the couch or in bed from symptoms. He often lay up against the side of me, never moving under the worst of convulsions or dystonia. A loyal friend indeed.

With the ever-increasing stress of teaching, my life falls farther out of balance with too many withdrawals and too few deposits. I arrange a meeting with the school district's human resources director to discuss my health status and petition for a transfer. I believe a change in instruction levels will enhance my passion, energy and, without question, my health.

I also desire growth of new methods and ideas. I have taught physical education at the same grade level in the same building for several years. To add to this, in March, my teaching cohort, who talked frequently of departing, terminates his employment. With health issues himself, he considers the stress of teaching here detrimental. The school replaces him with a substitute teacher for the remainder of the year.

The weight grows beyond unbearable. *Do I dare ask what else can happen? No. Situations can always get worse.* I had returned to this school and teaching itself with blinders on. I wanted so desperately to recapture my old life and regain a sense of my identity. Life's circumstances are going to continue to pile up around me until I leave. I feel it. I sense it stronger than I have anything in a long time. I am not supposed to be here anymore.

48 Authenticity

Being your authentic self is the ultimate secret to happiness in life.
~Sheri Fink

I mull over a number of school-related stressors; one sticks in my craw. I am not my authentic self, nor have I been. Authenticity is being yourself without reservation—not pretending to be someone else or stifling parts of yourself to please others, be it family, friends, strangers, society or your job. Who knows if a transfer to another school will allow my authenticity? I doubt it. Not fully. The school district isn't there yet. Society isn't there yet. Either you are authentic or you are not. The latter entails living a lie. That lie tears me up inside. I have had students curiously ask questions about my life from the day I began instruction in middle school.

One of the first questions is always, "Are you married?" soon followed by, "Do you have a boyfriend?"

With a "no" to each, I feel like a piece of raw meat on a hot grill. The students are very perceptive, especially when they intend to be. I cannot display pictures of my significant other—only those of family or friends. Beyond school staff, I am unable to make mention of my partner and, combined with the rest, it draws attention by the students year after year.

Administrators have told me varying things over the past few years, from "Don't tell anyone you are gay" to "I know it must be hard not being able to put pictures up or share parts of your life like we can. Just tell the kids the questions are inappropriate." *Like that makes everything okay. Just another version of "Don't Ask, Don't Tell." Besides, I want to be authentic personally and professionally.*

Time after time, year after year, I tell my administrator I try to skirt the questions. "But it doesn't stop there," I say. "Not answering is an answer."

Worst of all, I observe numerous LGBT students struggle with their own identity. I frequently see them bullied and in need of counseling and support. Thousands of LGBT teens commit suicide each year. What better role model than me? I inform the administration of my torment time and time again. *I can help these kids.*

Students have witnessed me curb questions related to my sexuality year after year. What message does that send to LGBT students? It suggests covering who you are for the sake of your job, of cutting yourself short, and that, even in adulthood, the freedom to live as yourself does not exist. What message does that send to other students, especially the bullies? That being gay is shameful? That it is okay to pick on someone because of their sexuality? I don't want anyone to think I am ashamed—not the bullies, not the LGBT students, not anyone.

I am proud of who I am; however, discussion of the subject falls on deaf ears incapable of understanding. Nobody wants to deal with it. In the scheme of things aren't love and acceptance what all of us want? Yet we don't teach or enforce it.

By the end of April, on my three-year anniversary from the hospital withdrawal, symptoms begin to run back through one by one without explanation. The benzowithdrawal.com site no longer operates and I have lost connection with a handful of friends from the site. *How will I ever get in touch with them again?* Bothered by the turn of events in my recovery, I contact Lisa. She informs me the three-year mark symbolizes "the point at which a recovering person sees daylight." In general, a baseline is attained. Symptoms and fallbacks may continue, but never to the degree prior. Recovery should convert from a roller coaster to a more linear fashion.

"What? It's still here," I tell her. Not only are they here, the symptoms are coming through again with higher intensely. Far from full recovery, I feel burdened by the emotional pain as it kicks my butt. I don't understand what is happening to me. My only deduction rests in the sacrifice of my health for time with Mom. My healing is delayed.

At the school year's end, all attempts to transfer out expire. My head spins initially, then a strong calm takes hold. I accept the outcome and clean out my office. *I can't remain here. It's just not healthy.* Bonnie and some friends talk me into waiting a month to think over my decision for the next school year. In reality, I decisively know the conclusion.

Driving home on one of the last days of school, I ponder a stop at the Columbia Humane Society. I find myself in need of a rescue. I want a dog. I yearn to attach myself to a living part of this real world—something breathing. Something I can cuddle with and love freely as best as I can without expectations of feelings and attachment. Several times over the past month, I have thought of visiting the local Humane Society to view the animals. Since Buster died prematurely, it seems fitting to adopt a rescue animal.

Bonnie and I make a few trips to view the dogs, but we knew after the first visit. Six-month-old Hudson, a beautiful black-with-white-markings mix of Great Dane and Labrador, bonds immediately and captures our hearts. We will save each other.

Bonnie and I decide to take a long overdue, ten-day vacation in June, which is a few months shy of our twenty-year anniversary. The trip will serve as a celebration but, more important, we intend to take time to rediscover each other. I worked on small house projects to re-establish a connection to our home. I hope the trip triggers a better association with Bonnie.

First stop—Yosemite National Park. Waterfalls, rock formations, cliffs and sequoias all summed up in one word: majestic. We spend each morning on the deck with a cup of coffee, observing the coyotes that peruse the area. Thereafter, we make our way to several hiking destinations and explore the grand terrain. Nature and hiking serve as our primary undertakings. Staying on schedule, we road trip to San Francisco. I am pleasantly surprised by the geography and ease of travel. I geared myself up for fast-paced, big-city driving, except for Yosemite. I pictured much of California like Los Angeles. *Too much television.*

I know I will enjoy San Francisco the moment we arrive. Bonnie and I immediately unpack our bags and head out to sightsee. We try to get in as much as possible, rising early and staying up late. Playing tourists, we visit Fisherman's Wharf, the Golden Gate Bridge, Chinatown, Nob Hill and the Castro. We also try out a cable car, although we trek primarily by foot up and down hill after hill. We joke how we have spent more money in one day compared to three in Yosemite.

I could imagine myself living here. A problem lies behind that thought. I do not have a connection to Columbia over San Francisco, or anywhere else for that matter. Correlations are still lost. I make no mention of it to Bonnie. The void of lacking attachment makes me throb with pain.

On intake overload, we drive up the coast along beautiful Highway 1 to Point Arena. Highway 1, not for the faint of heart, runs the winding Pacific coastline, at times within feet of the cliff. The views are like no other. After a short stay, we make our way to Sonoma and Napa wine country and our first ever bed and breakfast. The landscape consists of vineyard after vineyard, row after row of grapes. A quick note about wineries: always sip; don't gulp.

After our mixed adventure of nature and city, we cap our trip with a visit to see longtime friends. While signs of disconnect present themselves off and on, I focus on the celebration itself and on the obvious close friendship we once shared with these people. In addition, I experience shimmers of recollection regarding my relationship with Bonnie. For the first time, I grasp that our connection extends beyond friendship, though I haven't recovered my feelings. At least I have that to go on for now. Attempts to pressure myself to think and feel more toward Bonnie only negate what presently exists.

July features a family trip with Bonnie's side to Estes Park, Colorado. I am always eager to take a trip and see how well my body can tackle the fatigue and activity. I take it as a gauge to my healing. The fewer symptoms that crop up, the more healed I know I am. I set a goal to conquer whitewater rafting. Bonnie's niece tells our group she will sign us up as beginners. The course, however, looked too easy for a few family members and, before I knew it, our trip was upgraded to "intermediate," meaning we would face more moderate rapids and waves large enough to overturn the raft.

My biggest concern comes when one of the instructors explains the method for retrieving someone who has flown overboard. A person in the raft is supposed to grab them on each shoulder, swiftly dunk them completely under, then pull them up forcefully and into the raft. Right away I look at everyone in our group. They know what I am thinking and start snickering. *Don't even think about it!* Without me saying a word, they joke I will come up swinging. *Probably.*

I am happy to announce there are no hiccups and I enjoy every bit of it. Much of the Estes trip involves hikes, sightseeing, shopping and a favorite—horseback riding. For this family, though, games and planning the next meal always take priority. Unlike our previous trip to Estes, exhausting hikes and fatigue do not cause a flare-up with my symptoms.

As we arrive home to Columbia, I discuss with Bonnie my decision on the school year. I have no intentions of going back. It is amazing how long you will stay in an uncomfortable situation just because of the familiarity and for fear of stepping outside the box. Doesn't matter how unhappy you are. I want to resign from the school district. Bonnie talks me into taking a year's leave of absence to check out various options. Wilson's Fitness Center, a local gym, hires me for the opening shift. Scared, I feel as if I am being internally directed. *If I am not a teacher anymore, who am I?*

Just as the dust begins to settle, I get another emergency phone call from my family. My oldest brother has been hospitalized in Indiana with initial reports of seizures or a stroke. Luckily, he pulled his semi-truck off the road, but fell out onto the pavement as he tried to climb out of the vehicle. Once stabilized, he was transported by ambulance from a smaller hospital to Fort Wayne. I sit by the phone waiting for word to travel either to Indiana to meet family members or to Wisconsin. After dilly-dallying all day, I get the word and plan an early-morning departure for Indiana.

Upon waking, I hurriedly map my route and take off. Don't you know it? Once I arrive in Indianapolis I miss marking an exit and continue on to Ohio. My eight-hour trip spins into ten. I think of Mom often and worry my brother's situation will result in the same. Changes occur hours into the drive; whispers return as exclamations. Stressed out, my symptoms erupt. My brain flips radio stations—to ones I have not heard in a while. Irrational thoughts, the "crazies," return to torture my already tormented soul. I focus on the trip and my brother. Control vanishes.

By the time I arrive at the hospital, my nerves are shot. My brother's wife and my older sister and her husband were quick to make the drive to be at his side. I observe his status and compare his symptoms to mine. The doctor performs a three-word memory test. A therapist reads him a story, then asks for a summary. He unknowingly struggles with both. His coordination is off. He suffers irrational rage before an attack. *How surreal!* Memories start to flood my brain, but I resist. Fatigued by the long drive, I head back to my hotel room after visiting hours conclude. As I lie on the bed with intentions of relaxing my body, I fail to detour thoughts of my own health crisis.

49 Last Drug

Reality is a puzzle revealing itself one portion at a time, always where the deepest shroud falls. Waiting to piece the clues together, you are only losing yourself in the maze.
~Mariana Fulger

My brother's predicament triggers memories from four years earlier. September 2008 and I remained on 1.5 milligrams of Lorazepam; the final taper off Zoloft was insane. My body attacked me with hellacious "coherent" seizures for three and a half hours. The vicious mauling eventually caused a blackout. The loss of consciousness lasted over half an hour. I awoke from a deep sleep in wonderment if I was still alive, clueless as to where I was. Motionless, I perused the room. Minutes passed before I realized I was home in my own bed.

For the first month off Zoloft I experienced daily bouts of shaking, lasting one and a half hours in length. Talk about wicked.

Into the new year I continued to decline. I missed two to three school days a month due to body shaking and jerking. I wanted an immediate taper off Lorazepam the moment I was Zoloft-free. The request was refused by Dr. Clifford without explanation. I resided four months past my last taper of Zoloft and he still refused to taper me. None of this made sense. I presumed he wanted to give my body a chance to adjust from the Zoloft taper. During my second appointment after our introduction, Dr. Clifford had implied we would remove Lorazepam from my system as well. Every appointment since then, I explained to him the ongoing body jerks and shaking—even the "coherent" seizures.

I was going downhill fast. I felt I had been riding a roller coaster filled with assorted loops and corkscrew turns. I deteriorated on some level each and every day. I set my alarm two hours earlier than needed each day to allow my body time to shake, rattle and roll. If the electricity subsided in time, I elected to go to school.

When the morning attacks failed to cease, Bonnie called for a substitute teacher and/or notified the school. The school district's substitute hotline became a permanent fixture on the bedside table. To my amazement, I enjoyed a rebound some days by noon and I could navigate the rest of the day with ease, allowing participation in staff and student sporting events. As time passed, however, those days became fewer and fewer. I could no longer mask my symptoms.

My memory muddied to the degree that, each time I traveled the 45 minutes to Lisa's counseling appointment, I struggled to make my way as if it was my first visit. The directions were lost in an inaccessible memory file. At school, I wrote down my lessons on index cards more frequently in case I forget pre-planned steps. Students' names came and went. Headaches that felt like an axe in the top of my head plagued me regularly, with aspirin providing no relief. Blurred vision and dizziness made reading increasingly difficult. My eyes were the depiction of pinballs bouncing about in their sockets. My body and world spun without synchronicity. I lay in the nurse's office during lunch and free periods to let my body release its pent-up energy with hopes of regrouping to finish my day.

Changes in my personality occurred, some self-noted, while others remained oblivious to me. I didn't know if anyone else noticed, with the exception of Bonnie and family members. An extroverted disposition replaced my formerly reserved self. I spoke to everyone I met and sought out social opportunities within the school day, as well as outside of it. I became quite the Chatty Cathy. I organized Thursday or Friday Happy Hours as I yearned to socialize. I discussed with closer school staff my life and how my personality was changing, pondering any similar noticing from them. *Is it a transformation as I approach mid-life? Are my priorities changing? Am I happy how my life is?*

Normally a very private and personal person, I informed school staff of my predicament with the drug. Concerned about people's perceptions, my motive lay in helping them understand the drug problem was not self-induced. I would never do such a thing to myself. Generalized paranoia crept into my interactions with people at times, causing an overreaction and conflict generated by my inability to process clearly. I trusted fewer and fewer people.

Possessing a passionate personality, my strong will displayed prominently in areas of robust feeling; however, I seemed to have lost the ability to think before speaking, often moving from indifference to abrasiveness. A filter did not exist. No impulse control whatsoever. With reasoning ability clouded, I suffered a loss of inhibitions and boundaries in many areas of my life. I was numb to many things, my feelings washed away. Not understanding the melancholy feeling, I faced boredom with my life and searched for change. I sensed a lack of association to the people who played major roles in my life, including my family and Bonnie.

As time wore on, there was another shift as my newly social self dissolved away. I began to isolate myself from family and friends outside of school. The sound of the phone ringing enraged me. I was one of Pavlov's dogs. Plain and simple, I wanted to be left alone. The "F" word populated my speech. I could not simultaneously function at both home and school; it wore on me.

I was a blank slate, unconsciously masquerading as a confident person in search of a happy life. Lorazepam had gradually taken every aspect of me, administering a slow death. My Michael Jordan-wagging tongue, although not near as large or protruding in length, never appeared in moments of deep intensity or focus as it had for as long as I could remember. The knee-bouncing that caused my mother to sternly correct me throughout high school disappeared. Exaggerated eye movements I employed to untangle my upper and lower eyelashes were no longer a necessity. Every little characteristic known to me was gone. I concluded all these to be nothing more than a natural occurrence. How could I possibly comprehend it to be anything else?

One constant remained—my thirst for Mountain Dew. Diet, that is. As time passed from the initial drop in Lorazepam, my caffeine consumption increased to nearly 100 fluid ounces of caffeine-fueled drinks daily. My attempt at excusing the amount rested with the knowledge I also consumed 64 fluid ounces of water daily. Nothing fazed me. I was on an unrecognizable autopilot.

By the time April rolled around, I labored to walk. I felt faint and off-balance all the time. Violent tremors, jerks and "coherent" seizures riddled my body around the clock with no relief. Couch-ridden all day with no strength, I was incapable of the slightest of tasks, such as carrying the trash to the curb. I could hardly drag it. Barely able to stand, I resolved to take medical leave.

Back to the doctor I went. Finally, the broken-down car showed its ailment. I struggled to walk on my own. I sensed Dr, Clifford's panic the moment he lay eyes on me. He labeled the body jerking as dystonia and stated I needed to see a neurologist immediately. His concern lay with the length of time I had been dealing with this symptom—and its permanence.

I behove him to switch me over to Diazepam, a longer-lasting benzodiazepine. The crossover is seen by some a typical procedure to allow for a smoother taper. Diazepam stays in the system longer than Lorazepam, which makes for easier tapering, especially with smaller doses.

His demeanor changed the moment I asked for his assistance. The normally warm, friendly doctor converted to conversation that was short, abrupt and cold. He refused a switchover in drugs and re-emphasized the need to see a neurologist.

Though flabbergasted, I was quick to respond. "What? These are the same symptoms I've been dealing with for almost two years... the same symptoms I came to you with... the same symptoms I bring up at every appointment." Since he would not change drugs, I pleaded for him to contact the manufacturers of Lorazepam, as he had done with Zoloft. Complete refusal. Maybe he never contacted the doctors associated with Zoloft.

I asked for a referral to a neurologist for immediate assistance. His forceful words, "No, they don't listen to us!"

"OK," I asked. "How can I get immediate assistance without a referral? Trying to find a neurologist as a new patient could take months. You said I need prompt attention. Wouldn't I be worse by then?"

My mind kept digging. I wanted to find one thing that would persuade him to help me. I was desperate! "You can explain my history to them. You can help them understand what the problem is. If I go to someone new, I'll be starting from scratch. What if they don't know what to do?"

No response. I beseeched Dr. Clifford, "Will you at least recommend a neurologist? I don't know whom I should go to." I would beg if necessary.

"No!" he said sharply and anxiously as he withdrew eye contact. "You need to find one!"

My mind was helter-skelter. Free of Zoloft, I had been under the misconception that, once I was Lorazepam-free, all of these symptoms would automatically disappear. Dr. Clifford's conduct, however, suggested otherwise. Fear engulfed his face. Disturbed by the events, Bonnie and I left his office, unsure of the next step.

50 Desperation Looms

Never allow yourself to be so desperate that you end up settling for far less than what you deserve.
~Unknown

I researched Lorazepam and symptoms, giving the information to Dr. Clifford's secretary. I somehow thought if I verified my symptoms with medical research, he would continue working with me. I was aware the symptoms lined up perfectly with Lorazepam side effects and withdrawal. Even after offering the research information, I got no response.

I returned to his office in an attempt to get another appointment, but got no farther than his secretary. She would not make an appointment, referencing once again that Dr. Clifford wanted me to seek the aid of a neurologist. I was abandoned. My mind ran amok. *How can this be? How can he possibly do this to me without offering some sort of further assistance? Isn't he ethically liable for me?*

Bonnie and I searched the Internet for local physicians. There was no concern about the specialty area: psychiatry or neurology. I no longer cared about the stigma associated with a psychiatrist. I just wanted someone to help me. Someone with a white medical jacket with an ounce of common sense when it came to drug withdrawal would do. I was running low on fuel and pleaded for help. Time was a major factor for my feeble body.

Friends commented to us about my loss of weight and unhealthy appearance. We assured them we were aware and trying our best to take care of me. I contacted my primary, Dr. Baker. Knowing my desperate state, she referred me to a younger neurologist, Dr. Tyson, who was, in her words, "quick to act."

Three weeks after Dr. Clifford's abandonment, I had an appointment with Dr. Tyson. Within five minutes of meeting him, he stated my diagnosis: anxiety caused by internalized childhood issues. *What? What did you say?*

I lost it. His words tasted like sour milk. I intended to spit it back in his face. Given the long, winding road of my suffering, retribution flowed freely. I was sick of all the doctors and their nonsense.

"I don't *have* any internal childhood issues!" I spewed at him. "I don't suffer from anxiety! Who are you to tell me I do?" Unable to contain myself, I continued without pause. "If there is anxiety, it's from the lack of care I've received. You just met me a few minutes ago. You don't know me from Adam. Drugs have caused all my problems. Drugs doctors prescribed." Years of resentment toward the medical community came unleashed. A peacemaker, Bonnie interrupted my tirade. She subtly bore testimony to my emotional stability.

After her eloquent soliloquy on my long-standing mental state, Dr. Tyson smiled and backed off his original diagnosis and instructed me to cold turkey the remaining 1.5 milligrams of Lorazepam. He seemed to enjoy my opposition. Conscious of the fact this doctor knew little of my previous history, I kept the remainder of my thoughts to myself. *OK! I've been down this path before. Four drug withdrawals from too quick a taper and this quack wants me to cold turkey this one. He's no better than the last doctor. No way am I going to cold turkey!*

I shook my head in disbelief. Making direct eye contact, I responded, "You don't have any idea what you're going to do to me, do you?" His cockiness irked me. He sat at the low end of the totem pole with Lorazepam knowledge, yet thought he was brilliant.

Without hesitation, Dr. Tyson changed the directive as if it was no big deal. With a smirk, he said, "OK! Let's have you go off over the weekend and Monday you will check into the hospital for observation."

Over the weekend? "You still don't get it," I muttered, although I succumbed to this overconfident doctor, faithful that, on Monday, he would become conscious of what I had stated all along. *Can I make it through the weekend though? What are my choices considering the state my body is in?* My options seemed limited for the outcome I was pursuing—switching over to Diazepam for a proper taper. This was going to be bad. Upon leaving the office, Bonnie and I glanced at each other and pondered the decision to go along with the plan.

Bonnie smiled. "At least we'll get the drug out of your system and the doctors will be there to observe what happens."

All I could manage was an anemic, "Yah." I had an idea of what was in store. The doctor had no idea what he was going to put me through.

With my withdrawal materializing over the weekend, I persisted at the doctor's mercy. I wanted to enter the hospital early, but feared the medical staff to be ill-prepared for my admittance and observation. Over the years, I had learned to fear their lack of drug education. My only chance of getting switched over to Diazepam or an alternative drug, to properly taper, was to hold out until Monday. I saw no choice. This type of predicament had come up way too often. My body faltered from the drug-ignorant doctors who didn't listen. I was left in a desperate state. There was nothing safe about a doctor's care under these circumstances.

I knew from previous experience that, within hours of cutting back a 0.5 milligram dose, my life would turn upside down. Clonazepam withdrawal was a nightmare after being tapered a pill a day. Now, I was being instructed to quickly taper Lorazepam, another benzodiazepine. I was only on Clonazepam for two months. I had been on this drug a little over three and a half years. It would not be pretty. I was out of options. God help me.

My body wasted no time showing the disturbance. I quickly found myself sidelined to my upstairs bed. I escalated to a higher level of neurological pummeling. For the first time ever, fear settled in. *The tempest has come ashore. Batten down the hatches.* The intensity and duration of the "coherent" seizures skyrocketed. A blackout seemed plausible. I was under constant attack; sleep escaped me. Twenty-four hours makes for a long period of time when no sleep exists and your body disowns you. Forty-eight hours was downright cruel.

The excitement I once felt about getting off the last stupid drug had fully escaped me. All I could think about was holding on. Constant muscle contractions immersed me in pain. I was nauseous and dizzy. Blurred vision hindered my sight. Bonnie helped keep me abreast of the time, though time was my nemesis. She offered small, bite-sized meals to keep my strength up. My stomach lacked interest in food. So did my mind.

One minute my body heated from the constant motion. I threw the sheet off. The next minute, I chilled and pull it back up. I clinched to the thought of Monday. Bonnie kept herself occupied doing busy work. All I cared about was getting into the hospital for help. I continually prayed for strength to survive the onslaught. Questions of a 911 phone call and a ride with flashing lights remained present.

With God's grace, my body calmed for the ride to the hospital on Monday morning. My life from this point on would never be the same.

51 Post-Benzo Chaos

Let go or be dragged.
~Zen Proverb

I begin to weep. The trauma from four years earlier is still deeply etched in my mind. Life kicked me in the face. I struggle to make sense of it all, even years later as now. Up to this point, I have never allowed myself such a level of compassion. To save my strength for my brother, I turn the lights out and hit the hay. Who knows what morning will bring, or how long his hospital stay will last?

After two days, my brother is diagnosed with seizures and medicated with Levetiracetam, an anticonvulsant. This makes me nervous, given my reaction to them. I hesitantly return my brother and his wife to their home in Wisconsin. I want to stay, but feel I must get on my way, fearful other symptoms will overtake me. The following morning, I road trip back to Columbia. The entire trek, I feel like I am floating down the road and across the countryside. My view seems to go on and on like I could travel forever.

I reach home and put my focus on an upcoming medical appointment. I have stayed clear of doctors as much as possible, avoiding a colonoscopy years overdue. I remained at bay, fearful of drugs and the thought of anesthesia. Hints from my internal medicine doctor during an annual exam push me to get it over with. I had polyps in the past and plan to remain healthy once I recover from withdrawal. The simple procedure functions as a milestone for my otherwise sensitive body and marks the first time I allow another drug into my system.

I stumble, informing the nurse of my drug addiction as I had never used those words before. I watch her reaction; she continues with inconsequence. Good. Hard words to say, but I fear any drug going into my body and stand far from shy, continually asking what drug is being administered to me. Coming out with flying colors only boosts my confidence. *My body is on its way!*

Though I suffer emotional unrest, a window opens for me physically. I walk long distances much of the summer. I feel my body can do almost anything, with weightlifting for my legs and cardio workouts on alternating days. Every now and then, I throw in short interval runs. Yes, running! Both arms still lag behind, with my forearms feeling insubstantially brittle, as if every bone is apt to break. They often feel sucked dry. Use of my fingers, wrists or forearms causes the entire arm to stop functioning, almost as if it doesn't exist.

A noticeable improvement comes from my temperature regulator. Not only can I work out, I sweat. I feel an abundance of gratitude for the physical grace, though the emotional symptoms suffocate me. I don't think about what will happen should the grace period come to an abrupt halt. Then it happens.

Trudging through the forest of my journey, I finally make it to the outlet, but get held in check. I yearn to step across the threshold into the voluminous light. A quagmire appears and the step I pine for will wait another day.

When doing well, I find pleasure in my state; however, when withdrawal symptoms strike again, I want past all glitches. While I realize this is all part of the healing process, I want someone to please tell me the purpose of the lesson so the test can be over. I'll take whatever grade is given. Just get it over with. The journey sickens me.

My inner pain devours me. I feel no satisfaction in the fact I have survived or how far I have come. Morbid thoughts overwhelm me; I apathetically find no value in life. I believe bad things are going to continue to happen time and time again. As my brother slowly recovers, I wonder if God will take him, too, and I will lose yet one more person. I believe Bonnie will be tragically taken as well. I feel everything around me will be removed.

My body feels like a 90-year-old arthritic lady. The roller coaster of symptoms takes over once more. An undercurrent persists 24/7 as I come to realize any symptom can still hit at any time. A growing uneasiness relates to numbness in my entire body. I note little improvement in the three-year span. A major disconnect exists physically, as well as emotionally. My body acts dead to the world.

With this physical unresponsiveness, my sexual capacity halts. The fall isn't far, more like off the first step. A seesaw minor resurgence of libido had occurred over the past year, more dormant than operational. Even then, other symptoms nullified the results. When my libido came back, physical body symptoms prevented me from acting. My lack of body strength and inability to control my limbs caused problems, not to mention the fact that the rare orgasm caused convulsions for hours, as well as nausea, bed spins, electrical shocks and general pain throughout my body.

My body parts feel non-existent. My uneasiness causes me to inquire online for a remedy. I know the answer, yet fear causes me to search anyway. I probe side effects of my earlier hysterectomy, my lack of attachment and feelings, menopause, age and anything remotely related.

Maybe I missed something. In distress over the lack of feeling in every single nook and cranny of my entire body, I study it all again to reaffirm the result—the drugs.

What makes sexual dysfunction so difficult besides my own ego and frustration? It directly affects Bonnie, as does this entire trauma. This symptom, in particular, underlies a level of insecurity—a knock to whatever self-esteem I maintain—and shame. Why shame? I kick myself in the butt for allowing this to happen in the first place.

I realize the only way to heal is to write. I have locked away the entire experience, bolt and key, deep within me. Lisa joked to me about writing a book a year into recovery. Bonnie purchased a book about writing to get me started. At that point, I just wanted through and beyond all of it with little to no intent on looking back. I wished it a part of my forgotten history and continued in a full sprint forward. *Well, baby, it's here now!*

I cry every single day from the excruciating pain. Emotionally shackled, the running is over. The weight of the load overtakes me and brings me to my knees once more. I have nowhere to hide—no amount of distraction to take it away. The symptoms, Mom's caretaking and eventual death, Buster's death, teaching, and then my brother's accident stood as distractions from my own emotional healing. My healing has been delayed. The symptoms sit in me like a cannonball ready to be launched.

Once again, Lisa's words resonate. "As you go emotionally, you go physically." I deem myself in a sad state of affairs all the way around.

With so much change and sensing a lack of control, I find myself holding onto the past, even though I hold no attachment there. I embrace people and things in fear of moving forward into the unknown with the notion all will be lost. I feel indescribably alone. Desperate and extremely vulnerable, I tell a small handful of friends about my condition, nutshell version. *Mistake. Mistake. Oh, my God. A mistake.*

I choose erroneous individuals thinking them closer friends. Due to my lack of attachment and feelings, I have an inability to decipher friendship levels. Numbness prevails; desperation looms. I react hastily.

Desperation yields poor choices. Indifference and shunning result as my story turns upside down. I feel betrayed and violated. Rage ensues. I make no attempt to refrain myself. I uncharacteristically unload on those who have forsaken me. I am angry with people, with myself, with my situation, with the world. I move to isolate myself as a means of self-protection. I cannot gauge situations or people and trust no one.

I delete people from contact lists and defriend individuals on Facebook who I perceive have broken my trust. I allow no further friending from anyone. Quite frankly, I tire of people. The fakeness, the callousness. I need a break. After all that has occurred, my full focus decisively turns to healing—both physically and emotionally.

I prioritize my news feed with positive and spiritual sites on Facebook instead of lingering over people's updated statuses. I read articles on the Law of Attraction and information relating to the vibrational energy each person carries. I take in as much as I can from people I consider positive motivational speakers and spiritual leaders and spend an hour or more each morning investigating as soon as I return from work. I resolve to be a daily boost of positive energy for the 150 to 220 people who come through the doors to work out during my early-morning shift. For many members, I represent the first person they see in the morning, at least the first person they talk to. I want to start each of their days off right, lifting their spirits without ever letting someone's negative energy affect mine.

I find it difficult to stay fully present with people and consciously keep tabs on my symptoms whether at work or play. My attention diverts to fighting through symptoms without letting on to my status, then back to the other person.

Either depersonalization persists more intensely, or I am drastically changing. Maybe both. I feel nothing but utter internal chaos. Major confusion sets in. My mind swirls. I let go of all of my conceived attachments and theorize whatever is truly meant to be in my life, God will keep there. I cannot make sense of anything.

I undergo debilitating fatigue, yet insomnia reigns from a body overburdened with stress. With little energy, I push through and function as normally as possible. Viewing nature's importance, I take Hudson for daily outings as I once did with Buster. Of course, his youth and energy level demand it as well. Unlike Buster, Hudson refuses to stay at my side when symptoms hit, fearfully leaving the room at first sign. I joke that, in a fire, he would be the first to leave the home and wish us best in making it out alive.

Symptoms continue to run through me, almost as a continual jog to my memory. I fill days with handwriting page after page, breaking down and uttering prayers. I write by hand first, then type, to pull more emotions from the gut of my stomach.

Simultaneously, I feel a very strong presence within me—one that keeps my bearings set as I work through my drug-withdrawal demons and navigate this new forthcoming being. There is no doubt in my mind I am being led down this path, but where? Something in my depths yearns to be heard. That strong force sits me back at the computer day after day whether I want to or not.

Before accepting the position at Wilson's Fitness, I had checked into other employment options outside of teaching. I knew my direction the entire time. No other alternatives panned out. I didn't want to write about my journey and stalled as long as possible. Something in the pit of my stomach drives me crazy when I try to shy away from it. *What is that?* If you ask me now if I am a teacher, I will say, "No." I can't explain it, but the role no longer matches me. I have walked into several schools since my resignation. I try to take in the surroundings to get a glimmer of reverence. Nothing. I don't know what happened to that familiar role; it disappeared.

I am at a complete loss. *Was all that time wasted? Was I meant to do something else instead?* I raise countless questions, but have zero answers. I move forward on blind faith. I take small steps with hope that, one day, I will walk out of this suffocating fog into a blissful and purposeful life.

I feel as if I am being pulled away kicking and screaming. I had my life's path all planned out. I may have changed schools along the way, but my intent was aimed at retiring from teaching and engaging in service work thereafter. Of course I wanted to travel the world. I still do. The last thing I wanted was to write about drug withdrawal. In that area alone I had become a world-class sprinter—in the opposite direction of dealing with it.

Lisa declares me in post-benzo chaos. Once again, she reiterates, "You have come out a different person and see life differently. How could you be the same?"

I start my life all over again, with fear of the unknown dominating me. I don't know who I am to become, or which people will remain in my life. I do not feel confident about Bonnie either, due to my inability to feel or attach. I do not expect her to wait around forever. My life feels completely out of order. I exist. I know I am to write. That sums up the depth of my knowledge.

52 Lost Time

Your journey has molded you for your greater good, and it was exactly what it needed to be. Don't think you've lost time. There is no short-cutting to life. It took each and every situation you have encountered to bring you to the now. And now is right on time.
~Asha Tyson

I have spent a majority of recovery with the belief I lost time. It's been eight years since my initial back injury. *How can I get my body back? How can I get my brain back? How can I get what I consider a normal life back?* I yearn so badly to retrieve my health, my vitality, before age takes over. On top of everything else, I remain a wounded caterpillar, unaware of my eventual metamorphosis into a butterfly.

My writing gradually changes me—each page, each topic. Day after day, month after month, I pen my symptoms, what life has been like, and my feelings surrounding the ordeal. Each time I read over the written material I edit it into a more profound level.

Working at Wilson's Fitness fits the bill—except for the part where I have to wake up at 3:45 a.m. The part-time position allows plentiful time for writing and rest. Any day I feel overwhelmed with symptoms, I do what I need to for my body without need for second guessing sick leave or personal days.

The multi-tasking job unconsciously brings forth two hesitations from my past. My old self could not fathom my role as a social greeter; I never wanted to work a cash register. The present me stores few inhibitions and initiates conversation with ease, though far removed from an extrovert. I like to joke around with people, always have. Working with the exchange of money is no big deal. I recognize immediately the lesser degree of stress as compared to teaching and greatly appreciate the manager's compliments concerning my work. I receive more comments of appreciation the first couple of months there than I received over the past five or six years as a teacher.

I notice my gratitude for the freshness of the job and the diverse people I cross paths with on a daily basis. I spoke of this prospective position as transitional during my interview with the manager. In reality, the position represents the first step in a brand-new start. Writing does as well, even though I stop short of envisioning myself as a writer. Writing serves as merely a vessel to inform people of my story.

The only downside to working at a health and fitness center, aside from the early rise, lies with the fact that my inability to work out is shoved in front of my face day in, day out. I hear the music, the clanking of the weights and the sounds of various cardio machines. A mass number of people come in for personal training classes or their own planned regimen. The majority leave with a sense of accomplishment and appreciation for the time they have given to their health. I watch. I wait. My time will come, I hope.

I often concern myself with the ability to remember all that has happened, so I can sufficiently compose a book. I know, with each step, I will be given all I need at the proper time to continue. I do not question my path; I fear it. I use daily journals and postings from the benzowithdrawal.com site, which I printed before its demise, as a reference. Will the book be published? Will I find an editor? I don't know. My mission is to write about my journey with the goal of helping others. If, for no other purpose, the feat serves to heal my tortured soul, then so be it. Plus, it will be a book. My story. How many people can say they have written a book? Words I never imagined coming from my mouth.

It is difficult and time consuming. What a lame sentence. The process challenges me far more than I ever imagined. The composition encompasses more than use of language, organization of thoughts into paragraphs, use of creativity to keep the reader engaged and ability to project a movie of the storyline instead of telling it. I had knowledge of my emotional pain; I failed to understand the depth or multitude of it. I buried, carried and moved on.

Many days, I want to scream at the top of my lungs. "Can you hear me? Can anyone hear me? Is anyone even listening?"

Like a Matryoshka doll, I remove a protective layer with each day of writing, growing closer and closer to my guarded inner core. I do not know how many sheaths exist. My brain protectively impedes memory and thoughts. Some days I manage a paragraph; other days I fill pages. I frequently require respites until the insulating shield lowers enough to continue. Baby steps and self-compassion serve as the name of the game. Self-compassion remains hard for me; I am learning. With banishment of each safeguarding veil, I acquire more memories and more healing. A slow process, I often sit in my own agony. Days are long as the remembrances of all I endured flow through me. Bit by bit, I learn to release and let go. I find the practice daunting. Pain and anger are stockpiled.

The passing months have been difficult with little improvement, though writing converts chaos to serenity. I continue forward, unsure of my destiny, longing for the day it reveals itself.

Christmas nears. The date marks the first year I fail to attend my family Christmas in Wisconsin.

Two weeks following the migraines, Christmas gifts me with a personalized present. Memories materialize and stick—this time with an inkling of actual feelings. The sporadic cognitive fog and impairment dissipate and the world appears a step closer. I toss my Wilson's work notes in the trash, confident of my own recall. Like the old me, once I am told something, I remember it. No need for reminders. Endorphins run wild with this enlightenment. I am far from 100 percent, but each step shines like a diamond as it puts me closer in alignment with the real world. I internally explode, instinctually aware my cognitive abilities shall never falter to that degree again.

The world, however, confuses me. The one I once knew no longer exists. Habitual irritability, anger at past hurts and mystification create unrest. While I have been living in a drug fog and recovering from withdrawal, people have changed, I have changed, and circumstances have changed. I must not only remember pertinent information about people from my past, but dial it forward nearly four years, realizing they are not the same people I remember them to be. I sense my only peace by going within myself, embracing faith and concentrating on this very moment in time. What will be, will be. I am a planner by nature and this moment-by-moment trek this far out in recovery throws me for a loop.

In February 2013, my version of a Stephen King mind makes its presence known. I thought myself removed from this. Nope. I got too far ahead of myself. Call it hallucinations or intrusive thoughts—I don't care. Labels mean nothing. I speak of these illusions to Bonnie, but only make mention to friends. They aren't sure whether to fear for my sanity or just feel sorry for me, maybe both. How can they understand unless they have walked in similar footsteps? If not going through it myself, I, too, would probably think it crazy. Thankfully, these blitzes typically last only a few minutes. I know the hallucinations are just a symptom and, usually when one hits hard over a period of time, it will soon excuse itself from my life. My brain has more healing to do.

People would be more sympathetic and empathetic if I had cancer. My godmother developed cancer in the late 1970s. At the time, she was often shunned by others who feared contracting her condition. Nowadays, people are empathetic with the sheer mention of the word cancer. What has changed? Education. No one knows much about prescription drug withdrawal, addiction or recovery other than what they see on the television news or hear from doctors, many uninformed. Dr. Ashton, now retired, was a leading researcher on benzodiazepines. Why didn't other researchers jump on the bandwagon to validate her revelations about the side effects, withdrawal symptoms and possible permanency? Why hasn't anyone now?

Most withdrawal data is only collected a few months out after the last intake of a drug, yielding information on only the acute stages of withdrawal. Why aren't studies conducted on protracted withdrawal and length of recovery? Why aren't studies done researching structural brain damage in relationship to benzodiazepines and other drugs?

One thing I am learning during the course of this journey is to care less about what other people think. To question me only doubts the hell this journey has put me through. Those with the least amount of knowledge are usually the first to utter opinion. I always find that interesting, yet sad, at the same time. I have gone from the defensive "fuck you" response when someone questions me or my mentality to simply thinking "whatever." Other people's opinions no longer influence my life.

I think people judge others to separate them from themselves; truths are denied. Maybe if people call me or someone else crazy that means a similar incident can't happen to them. Try again. Don't find out the hard way. Ignorance will condemn you, not save you.

Recently, I have experienced daily "a-ha" moments, reminding me to resign my worries and struggle to God. Surrender, even now, serves as an afterthought. I find some days easier than others. I get caught up in fighting life and circumstances, questioning the outcome or path to be taken. I think beyond the moment into tomorrow and the future. When thoughts relate to my recovery, nine times out of ten, unconstructive reflection exists. My work resides in grasping constant faith.

With recovery slow, I fail to enjoy peace and happiness. I grow weary from the constant state of alertness. I fight my chaotic mind and feel like I am still in a pickle, wondering if and when the day will come when I will feel normal. I dream of the day I can be 100 percent present with people and the world around me without the nuance of morbid thoughts and other symptoms butting in. I try to return to that one peaceful spot inside me no matter what happens in the world around me. I, alone, am responsible for my individual happiness and attitude concerning people and events in my life. But how to achieve it—internal happiness and the ability to not care about other people's opinions so their opinions cannot affect me. That is the million dollar question.

It is March 2013. Nearly four years have passed since the hospital observation and drug removal. A big moment of surrender summons my attention. Bonnie has repeatedly mentioned the need for me to get a medical bracelet in case of emergency. Members of the benzowithdrawal.com site envisioned a worldwide emblem to signify benzo addiction, much like pink is used to denote breast cancer awareness. I know the necessity of having an emergency symbol on my body in case of an accident. God knows what would happen to me if I were injected with another benzo. I can't think about it. I honestly believe the drug would kill me.

I prohibited any kind of stigmatizing label up to this point. I did not wish to be subject to people's judgment and misunderstanding of how my addiction occurred; however, pride in my achievement finally supersedes anyone's opinion. It has been a long time coming. What a sense of relief.

Enough is enough. I know the work I undertook to get to this place. As a reserved person, I look to purchase a less-noticeable medical tag. I need personal security—not a declaration. A silver bracelet with a golden medical emblem initiates a sense of ownership I had yet to take. The act of putting the bracelet on my wrist announces strength in survival. I have yet to clear the dark forest and secure my path to declare myself victorious.

I also contemplate—in symbolic gesture—a tattoo scribed onto my body. In early withdrawal, I contemplated a tattoo for confirmation of myself. My current thought heralds new meaning. I desire a small, visual representation of all I have withstood, though I fall flat in determining what the tattoo would express or where I would place it. Unsure, I decide not to get one.

53 Fourth Anniversary

And once the storm is over, you won't remember how you made it through, how you managed to survive. You won't even be sure whether the storm is really over. But one thing is certain. When you come out of the storm, you won't be the same person who walked in. That's what this storm's all about.
~Haruki Murakami

April 27, 2013. Wow! I remain in the healing stages after four years of withdrawal and recovery. I noticed vast improvements in a quickened recovery phase over the past year—physically, mentally and emotionally. Constantly in a changing phase, I wonder who I will turn into by the end of this particular journey. I know my name and my family of birth, but otherwise, I tussle with identity and purpose.

A hard reality of change lies in the realization that other people treat me as the same person I was prior to withdrawal. By the same token, some only know my personality as the one on drugs. My true character combines bits and pieces of both with newfound attributes, as well as those I have yet to uncover. All of the changes have been a difficult adjustment on both sides of the table, no matter the relationship.

I unlock the door I closed months earlier on new friendships. With regained strength and optimism, I relinquish countless self-protective measures. My instinctual capabilities offer a sense of genuine confidence not seen since my initial back injury.

New life shows itself within me. I want it all! I desire an abundant, happy life. I yearn for a career of passionate service. I crave unconditional love in my relationship, both shown and received. I want to travel and to experience other cultures.

In the heat of the moment, I get carried away with my exuberance and develop poor judgment. I ignore frailties and proceed without caution. Another large window appears and I take full advantage. I lift light weights with both legs and arms even though numbness prevails. I try to force oxygen and vitality into my limbs. I do whatever my body allows without forethought of the aftereffects.

I leap full steam ahead into a spinning class. RPM spinning continually challenges a rider in speed, duration and hill work for a full hour. Normally, this would wash me under the bridge, which it does the first few times. In fact, it sends my brain into a continual auto-scan for a couple of days after, with bouts of irritability and confusion. I focus on staying in the present. Unbelievably, a breakthrough arrives and I get to the point where I can spin two to three times a week. I use up every ounce of energy in my body and it recuperates naturally, nearly symptom free. I feel home free.

A little voice reminds me to take it easy—that I should not undertake any other workouts during the week in combination with the spin class. My body limits me, yet I robotically continue. My goal consists of cross-training on alternate days, so I can return to working out like the fitness nut I remain—at a minimum of five days a week. Whenever a window this size opens, increased abilities and euphoria enhance my belief I have moved beyond the nightmare and into the sunlight, never to return to any form of this darkness.

When will I learn? Sometimes, I think never. I usually like a surprise visitor, but not this time. Who would have thought it? Six months marks the longest I have made it between major fallbacks. Coming into June, I feel I am inching closer to one, but figure it will be the typical two- to three-day affair. After all my body has allowed with the workouts, I feel confident of a quick turnaround whenever it does hit.

A major fallback hits that I optimistically believe signals the final onslaught due to the similarities of my first in 2009. I can stay emotionally centered up to seven days but, by day eight, I adopt a fuck-it-all attitude. My hard-headed attempt to retrieve my fitness level has backfired. My eagerness shows the fight in me to recover—not to surrender. The event causes me to miss two weeks of work. Beyond medical leave, I have never missed that much employment due to a fallback.

Advances arrive rapidly, which amazes me considering the degree and longevity of my recent attack. The light always returns after the darkness. The prevalent physical pain moves from my inner core outward and closer to the shell of my being. *All of this is big! Oh, my God, this is big!* Worth the beating? Ask me in a few more months.

Derealization slowly softens. I not only hold interest in going to watch a friend's softball game, I sense what it was like when I played years earlier. I appreciate the smell of the freshly mowed grass in the outfield, the sound of the ball pinging off the metal bats on contact, along with the force absorbed by a leather glove on the other end. I envision myself as a left centerfielder, moving after each ball and preplanning where each ball will be thrown to cut off base runners. I follow the runners on base, imagining myself hustling from one base to the next. These types of visions disappeared for several years. My elated eyes widen with a sense of moving a layer closer to myself—my athletic self.

With the glimpse of softball interest I once maintained, I also notice renewed attentiveness to favored pastime activities. Preferences show clearly, though my aversions appear more subtle. I no longer move through my day impassive.

All of the idiosyncrasies uniquely "me" show their faces again. My knee begins to bounce under the table. My tongue protrudes during thought and my eyes widen to separate the intertwined lashes. The kid at heart peaks through the doorway. For most of this journey, I felt aged way beyond my years in every aspect. The playful side of me has been gratefully rejuvenated. The good-humored, sassy side, too. Nothing wrong with a little sass.

Mentally, my cognitive fog shows up only rarely and I maintain a high functioning level when it does. I still show frustration and shy away from discussions in order to make it less obvious. My poker face dwindles with each fallen protective barrier. I play games daily to stimulate my brain, focusing on continued improvement and maintenance more than anything else. I notice my attention span vastly improve. Instantaneous word recall represents one area where I seek enrichment. Games like Buzzword challenge my word-retrieval skills.

Normally only a card player, I learn to enjoy word games with an occasional board game thrown in. I also play Sudoku, the game I failed miserably with early in recovery. My scores frequent the 75,000 to 80,000 mark on expert level with times averaging around five to six minutes. I note the biggest change as my development of risk-taking. I don't worry about a poor score or losing. I scratch the game, often as soon as I use up turns, and continue on to the next. My best score sits at 86,023 in 3:12 minutes. *Sweet!*

I now have at my disposal most of the crayons in the box of 64. My primary concern involves my emotional blunting of feelings, especially those surrounding deep love. I feel love, though I suffer difficulty with deciphering different kinds of affection. In-depth love itself turns up as a shutter frame. One moment I feel it; the next it is elusive, at times a trigger for confusion by the disconnection. I know healing will return the depths completely again, but when?

I believe unseen layers of bubble wrap protect me from the pain of withdrawal and recovery, my mother's death and family issues, as well as relationships with other people. As I remove layers, I bank on unbridled feelings. To date, my body and mind have been synchronized in healing. Patiently waiting? Nope. Pressure results in nothing but frustration. I have no power over the timeliness of my full healing. *Surrender. Surrender. Surrender.*

54 Single

Single isn't a status. It's a word that describes a person who is strong enough to live and enjoy life without depending upon others.
~Unknown

My body and brain show signs of healing. My symptoms are gradually departing, though one remains strong. Emotional blunting with a lack of attachment angers and perplexes me. I don't understand why varying levels of attachment remain with some people and not others. The frustration and emotional pain from lack of in-depth feelings overwhelm me. I don't want to deal with them anymore and question moving on in life solo. I am unable to decipher if my thought process consists of a flight or fight response.

Most days I want to flee to some other city and start over. I don't know where, although San Diego comes to mind, frequently. Who knows why. I don't feel attachment to our house or to Columbia. Don't get me wrong. We have a beautiful home and a nice piece of property, not to mention a shared lake. From my recollections, I enjoyed Columbia, but I have no attachment. I can't tell if wanting to move somewhere else is a version of running away, like a wounded dog, or trying to find "home."

Bonnie and I find ourselves at a major crossroads. I cannot look her in the eye and tell her with a sense of confidence if or when my full feelings for her will return. She served as a primary source of support through my recovery, yet I fail to envision a life together. It all sucks. I don't know what to do and the uncertainty causes tension. I debate whether or not splitting up exemplifies a detour in my life's path.

I know I love her, but is that enough? Is it fair to continue in this way? I have held anger and resentment from past trials and tribulations since the return of my memory, especially when feelings returned with them. Maybe this conflict serves as the roadblock. We hold discussions almost every night as we sit on our lower deck swing to communicate our feelings, our angst and our needs. We contact each other throughout the day whenever a question or concern arises. It's not always pretty, but we both make the effort.

The process pains both of us for varying reasons. I see Bonnie's love and sorrow, though I cannot feel it. What I do feel is distant and cold for the deficiency. We decide to hit our issues head on. Our relationship tops the daily priority list and we implement an in-depth level of communication.

Bonnie devises a two category list: ego and spiritual. Spiritually, she understands my anguish and suffering through this journey. She realizes my current incapacities and wants what is best for me whether that includes her or not. Egotistically, she feels anger and betrayal I could think of leaving as we approach 21 years together. There is also the fact she served as a constant support system throughout recovery. Bonnie realizes through our recurrent discussions I am not yet capable of full feeling, and pressure to feel something I cannot only pushes me away. I have mentioned this several times. *Does she understand? Is she in denial? Is my recovery taking too long for her? Will she wait for me? I understand if she doesn't.*

Nonetheless, Bonnie builds a protective wall of her own. She doesn't want to get blindsided, believing all is well, and then have the rug pulled from beneath her. We both realize some overdue changes need to occur. Without hesitancy, once we discuss and agree on alterations, we both take steps toward it. Normally, change is hard, but we are both willing and the shift happens quickly. The inclination to work together for the benefit of our future boosts our confidence. We leave no rock unturned in discussing our past, present and future aspirations.

Out of the blue, a small incident makes me aware of how physically and emotionally clouded I remain. A simple movement to rub my face awakens my cognizance. For the first time in over five years, I feel my left hand wipe my left cheek and vice versa—I feel my cheek being wiped by my hand. Once I feel it, I pause to take in the moment. I announce the revelation to Bonnie, who is sitting with me on the couch. My eyes water. It has been so long since I have been able to feel, especially with my left side. I have been numb. The sensation feels so good I continue several more strokes. *Finally!*

This indicator alone puts everything else in perspective. I decide right here and now that no decisions will be made concerning any avenue of my future. I opt for further healing time to decipher my feelings.

With our relationship a work in progress, I stick around to write my book and my first-round draft nears completion. Now, I must find an editor. Synchronicity takes over as a friend of a friend informs me of a freelance editor, Lisa, from our Unity church. As Lisa the editor comes into my life, Lisa the counselor leaves, at least momentarily.

"I plan to stand on my own two feet now with all that life throws at me," I tell her. "I'm coming out the other side. I have dealt with a number of deaths and withdrawal. I can handle anything. I can't imagine much worse."

We spend time reminiscing about my journey and talk of our appreciation for each other. I inquire about friendship. She tells me that, according to standard practice guidelines, any social context must wait two years from my last appointment. And so it is. Words cannot express the gratitude I hold for all Lisa has done for me. I doubt I would be here without her. She will forever hold a special place in my heart.

Once Lisa the editor reads my first draft, we meet to discuss possibilities and a plan of action. We waste no time. A major learning curve takes place as I begin to grasp the ins and outs of changing my story from the "essay" version to the "book" form. I eat it up.

One of the biggest "a-ha" moments occurs when she suggests a total rewrite. "You have the storyline down. Now you must go deeper. The most difficult piece will be going into more depth."

"More depth? Okay. I can do that."

"It will be the hardest part."

"It will be okay," I say. "I've already dealt with much of my pain." *How much deeper can she ask me to go?*

Lisa tells me not to take anything personally and she will be hard on my writing. I show no concern as I want my book to be the best it can be. All I ask is she use something other than red to mark up the pages. *Yellow is cheery!* Remnants of an old teacher, I guess. I go back through each chapter, paragraph by paragraph, sentence by sentence, word by word. I give the facets and gravity Lisa solicits. The scale she requests sends me through the depths of anger, pain and suffering. *Oh my, she was right.*

I thought the original draft excavated all of the agony. As I rewrite chapters, deep-seated memories arise from the shadows, uncovering more protective layers and suppressed anguish. *How deep did I bury this shit?* I run through the same routine as I did the first time around as frequent breaks are needed when barriers fall away. On occasion, my brain still shuts down into a protective mode.

A large obstacle awaits removal. Writing more in-depth produces a need for my medical records. Sounds so simple. Most people would call it in, or do it online, but I feel the need to pick them up in person. I stall and I stall, but know it will aid healing. I get myself psyched up, grab a Diet Mountain Dew and crank up the music on the drive. With a false sense of confidence, I walk into the facility. Those hallways seem like some of the longest ever. I feel my heart slamming against my chest and my breathing increases. I want to shut myself off.

I continue to take in the surroundings and allow flashbacks to occur. I know it's silly after four years, but I feel like I am going to see Dr. Tyson again. I picture the electrodes placed on my head, which only fuels my pace. Walking past the physicians' lounge compounds it more. I sense relief as I approach the door for the medical records department and talk with a polite lady, who takes my request. As I stand waiting, I rest my folded elbows on the counter and attempt to relax my body and shut off thoughts. *Breathe. Breathe. Breathe.*

In no time at all, I find myself turned back around and heading out the same path I had entered from, paperwork in hand. *Whew! Thank goodness that is done. Easy enough*! I exit with the same quickened pace, eager to get into nature for a lengthy walk with Hudson to release the build-up of tension.

No longer wanting to play a victim, I resolve to make retrieval of the records a different story. I have a chance to rewrite the story. As I make my way out, I drop the anxiousness and replace it with genuine confidence. I walk through the corridors and fully take in my surroundings, including all of the people who pass by. I look each and every person squarely in the eye, even those in scrubs. I keep my pace at an assertive gait, undaunted by past events with no flashbacks apparent.

As the months pass, the profound writing and healing unlock an appreciation for Bonnie's love and support. Daylight begins to shine on our relationship. I do not hold the ability for full love yet, but I sense her love for me and acknowledge her sacrifices. I do not yet feel conscious of the full scope of her care.

Reflective writing turns to her journey as a caretaker as well. I better understand Bonnie's angst in dealing with everyday life, work and me. I also key into her current mentality. My emotional blunting previously stuffed the whole kit and caboodle. Even though physical and emotional feelings are slow to return and I remain a prisoner to the inability for attachment, I inform Bonnie I hold both feet in our relationship and move to fully invest in our future.

"I love you," I tell her, because I know it to be true. Then the gloomy caveat. "I won't tell you I'm in love with you until I can more fully sense it. I want total honesty. I'm not going anywhere, but I don't want to tell you things until I feel them. I think it bodes trust as well."

While a strong bond resonates from our past, we move to start our relationship anew. Bonnie frequently reiterates she believed all along we are meant to be together.

"I believe in me. I believe in you. I believe in us," she says.

Even though we have supported each other in various ways since I left teaching, my degree of restoration allows me to heighten my role as an emotional support for her in her daily life and career.

At this time, we both move to refresh close friendships. Both Bonnie and I have people who have always been at our sides through thick or thin. Better communication on our part would have had them at our sides through this patch. These friendships are the kind where you can go for days, weeks or years without speaking or seeing one another but pick back up like it was yesterday. I recognize and appreciate them.

My symptoms continue to fall by the wayside, but my back has a definite demarcation line. There seems to be a functional divide with my spine. The right side of my body—beyond the sense of touch—seems normal. The entire left half nurses pins and needles, chills and pain, with a sense of distortion in my face. The good news? I say goodbye to hallucinations and the lingering radio stations my brain formerly auto-scanned.

Presently, there are just two channels. My brain flips back and forth between the "normal" station—with emotional numbness and lack of connection—and the one fallback station that remains. The recurrent fallback station renders several emotional footprints combined—unprovoked anger flares without warning and I find myself extremely irritable. At times, I weigh issues with someone or something but, more often than not, no rhyme or reason exists.

I feel flighty and non-trusting, waiting for the other shoe to drop as the attachment I entertain weakens during these episodes. Morbid thoughts haunt me and, even though the hallucinations have halted, an undercurrent prevails, which I keep stuffed below the surface. My brain remains on constant alert, allowing no time for rest. The endless effort wears on me. My own worst enemy lies between my ears. *How much longer will I have to deal with the chaos? The journey seems never-ending. Will I heal completely, or will I be like this the rest of my life? When I am blessed with a window, none of these symptoms are present. Surely I will heal.*

I decide to make a list of what I want for myself and focus on it as often as necessary. A sense of wholeness tops the list along with happiness, harmony, health and a sense of abundance. Bonnie definitely fits into that equation. I want to bask in peace no matter what I currently experience from symptoms. I surrender them and my experiences in life with the belief that all exists for my better good. All lead to strengthen me and aid my individual spiritual growth. I work on faith to stabilize my insecurities with my recovery, my path and my persona. What a mouthful. Yes, it is much easier said than done. I affirm each thought.

My ownership of writing has yet to take place as I continually grow into this pair of shoes that has been delivered to me. I have always had a title: student, production worker, teacher, coach. My teaching days were filled with over 250 people on a regular daily basis. I now spend the majority of the day alone. The silence can be deafening.

With healing, isolation overwhelms me and I need more activities to serve as a reprieve from the house, the quiet, my brain. I enjoy writing, but I tire of the memories and yearn to put them to rest. I am slowly learning to love myself without need for classification. I am fine how I am without the need for being something or someone. I come to realize titles do not make the person, as I was once taught to believe.

Increasingly, as memories with attached feelings return, I take my power back from people I bestowed it to. I not only feel unhappy, but angered by my means of dealing with areas of my past life. As a gay person, I played small because others felt uncomfortable with me and with my relationship. I put others' wants in front of my needs and happiness. A person should never give up their dignity; no one should ask them to. I tolerated ignorance or poor treatment as I waited for someone else to take a stand in support of me and us. It never happened. I presently realize that, if you don't stand up for yourself, no one else will.

I take back my power from people who targeted me on a professional and personal level, knowingly took advantage of my poor health and caused my status to worsen. I take back power from the bystanders. I take back power from people who turned my story around for their own purpose. I take back power from the doctors who drugged, ridiculed and abandoned me.

I move from a casualty to an advocate for education and changes within the ménage a trois of the medical field, drug and insurance companies.

I take back my power from the drugs that reduced me to a wretched existence. The phoenix rises.

On the flip-side, I offer apologies to anyone I hurt and everyone I perceived conflict with during this time period. Responses vary. Some say my apology is unnecessary—that our relationship remained amiable. Others accept it and apologize, too. Some offer no response.

Next, I take a large leap in autonomy by executing a heightened sense of self-love throughout each and every day. I desire to live peacefully without any influence from other people over my actions or mindset. Peace equals happiness. Sure, people with toxic energy exist, but I do not have to take on their energy or let their opinions or actions affect me. The attitude they display reflects their own perceptions and has nothing to do with me.

The second feat consists of forgiveness. I start with myself. I allowed certain levels of treatment and nothing can be done without my permission. I paid for it and learned an invaluable lesson. Forgiveness, conversely, never means the act of forgetting. Otherwise, the lesson serves no purpose. I must find a way to remove the anger and hurt from myself while recognizing I was doing the best I knew how to do at the time.

Forgiveness leads to healing, which leads to peace; however, I find forgiveness on personal levels extremely difficult. Toxic anger harms only me. Bonnie and I frequently discuss the need to let go of all the pain and suffering so the events cease to cause an emotional response. As I search through Facebook updates, I catch a clip of Malala Yousafzai on *The Daily Show* with Jon Stewart. She is a Pakistani schoolgirl shot by the Taliban for defending her right to education. As I watch the video, clarity strikes. If a fourteen-year-old girl can forgive the terrorists who shot her in the face without thought of settling the score, what is my problem as a 53-year-old with the doctors?

55 The Miracle

The soul always knows what to do to heal itself. The challenge is to silence the mind.
~Caroline Myss

Then it happens. January 2014 and the most joyful moment of recovery arrives. All of these years... fighting, holding on, praying and surrendering and then fighting again. Don't ask me how, but I can sense a change—a shift in mind and body. A synchronicity I have yet to feel in recovery. Can it be? It has been nearly ten years since my original back injury, and five years and eight months since the last drug, Lorazepam, was removed from me in the hospital. Finally! I have reached a baseline.

I fought through each day of initial recovery to not only function, but survive from one day into the next. I fought to return to my old career, to remain a caretaker for my mom and be present at her death. I fought to drive to my brother's side after his accident. I fought symptom after symptom every day for improvement, healing and peace. Is this the finale? My brain has healed enough to lock in. No further flipping. I know instantaneously and disclose the transformation to Bonnie. Her eyes exhibit relief. She holds back elation as she awaits further confirmation. Tears of joy run down my face as we share a long embrace.

My perceived facial distortion disappears and my vision vastly improves. The splintered left hemisphere of my brain feels connected to my right. I no longer need to stuff morbid thoughts—they have vanished. I can remain wholly present without the need to put partial attention on symptom management. Insomnia comes and goes. A majority of the pain has departed my body and physical numbness dissipates. The magnitude of my physical sensory healing is exemplified by the fact that, after five minutes by the gas fireplace, I feel the heat on my back and know to move. What a change from the 30-minute back burnings I regularly endured.

My mental and emotional statuses also improve. Chaos leaves the building as my brain takes the floor. The enormousness of the change improves my sense of inner peace. Bonnie and friends notice changes in my demeanor as I appear calmer, more engaging and begin to enjoy life again. The unrest I felt from derealization and emotional blunting eases. I experience moments of true happiness during which my heart radiates sensual warmth.

I take ownership of my life, my experiences, my lessons and this trauma. I also take claim to the title of writer, no matter what happens to the copy once I finish. Then again, I never want to diminish myself to a single title. I am capable of many things. We all are.

I encounter fallbacks—but not the ass-kicking, mental, emotional or physical ones like before. The roller coaster ride converts into what appears more of a normal healing process. *Is this real, or is this wishful thinking?* Guarded, I refrain from celebratory antics.

I appreciate Bonnie's awareness. "You understand better than anyone around me what it's taken to get to this point," I tell her. "No one, except those who have gone through drug withdrawal or similar circumstances, can empathize with living in a body and mind that act other than your own. I don't know how people who take drugs for personal demons ever make it through recovery. I feel for them."

It has been so damned hard. I realize that, after each major fallback, I progressed closer to myself and recovery on each rebound. I understand with all of the adjustments I made how important it is for the body to heal slowly. I never realized how many light years away I was from my true self. The difference is sheer absurdity! Pj has yet to arrive; I sense a version of the old, the new and the ever-growing. A level of numbness still exists and I am not sure what is held underneath it.

The healing progression allows glimpses of in-love feelings. Bonnie and I find ourselves gazing into each other's sparkly eyes in disbelief. Now equipped with wings, I sense how the dark forest epitomized a cocoon. Inside the chaotic metamorphosis, I shed my outer layers for transformation. I do not know if I grew into this person or if this is who I always was underneath it all. It does not matter. I want to fly. I will not travel alone; Bonnie and I choose to soar together.

To satiate our desire for travel, we trek to Boston in February for another work-related convention. Let me just say, "Boston, I love you!" The city brilliantly integrates history and modern living. We find the "T" transportation system easy to use, although much is within walking distance. The people show genuine politeness whether we wait with the masses for the subway at rush hour, walk the streets in the daylight or darkness of night, or pause in line at a restaurant. The people impress us both.

Two big advancements take place this trip. For the first time since I began withdrawal, I do not vibrate or shake on the plane. Second, I realize Boston is not home. I love the city and definitely value a return trip, but I can differentiate cities. Columbia is home. Ahhh, what a statement.

56 Perseverance

Don't stop because you are tired. Keep going because you are almost there.
~Unknown

I relish the new baseline. With each passing month, my body continues to heal. With each step, I feel a natural high as if a rush of endorphins saturates my body. My brain maintains a status quo. I begin to understand the concept of peace.

I take only one prescription—Levothyroxine, used to treat my hypothyroidism. I remain convinced that prescription drugs contributed to my condition. Dr. Baker remains my internal medicine specialist, but our relationship has changed. I believe her to be a good person and a good doctor. We have never once discussed my drug withdrawal and recovery since I took medical leave. At each annual checkup, I wonder about her thoughts concerning prior events. I know she notices my medical alert bracelet, but she never comments. Nor do I.

My checkups are excellent, except for cholesterol. It has always been higher than average, but drugs have definitely caused chaotic numbers the past few years. During my last two annual checkups, Dr. Baker has suggested statins to treat it. She suggests baby aspirin out of safety concerns for my heart. I decide to initiate the aspirin supplement. Within two weeks, I notice blood in my stool and burning sensation in my upper digestive tract. Not a happy camper, I call her office to schedule an appointment. She offers a different prescription for the stomach upset. Instead, I choose to let my body heal itself. I do not want to obtain a prescription to deal with the effects of another drug. Turns out no aspirin equals no bleeding.

Though people often tell me I possess a good memory, optimal recall has yet to return. I no longer maintain the type of recall I once had for the hundreds of students I worked with. Does it matter? Probably not.

A major gap still exists in my memory bank. April 2009 marked the date of my hospital stay for the removal of Lorazepam. The entire first semester of teaching in 2008 sits filed somewhere out of my grasp. I coached basketball but cannot remember practices, games or—more important—players. I taught, but I have no memory of it or any events that may have occurred. My recollection of the spring 2009 semester holds only a few tidbits. I doubt the return of it at all.

I experience fewer and fewer fallbacks, which occur for shorter periods of time, averaging one day to three weeks. My quest for a six-month—or even a year's—healing seems like a joke from a lifetime ago. I stay in the moment as best I can, allowing life and healing to come to me instead of forcing the issue. *Surrender. Surrender. Surrender.* I focus on my abundance and stay centered to maintain peace, though this is not always easy. The hospital anniversary date for the removal of Lorazepam loses its meaning. I chuckle to think I once believed each passing anniversary would serve as a signpost of the past—yet this journey continues into the present.

I respect my body and mind for all I have triumphed over. I instill a plan to elevate my fitness level and begin a 30-day ab challenge and "Couch to 5K" running program. This represents my first initiative with core exercise. I learn to modify activities and build up. With both, however, I must stop within three weeks. My body is not ready. *Shock to my system. Shock to my system. Shock to my system.*

No sooner do I instill a fringe of a fitness program than another major fallback ensues. *Now what? Something isn't right!* I feel anxious like never before—lost and fearful of life for no apparent reason.

I experience oversensitivity and intolerance to all suffering happening around me. It's as if the suffering is happening to me. I agonize in far-reaching depths from the tiniest event. Viewing a picture of a dog left on a chain in undesirable circumstances causes me unbearable pain, as does wondering where a homeless person will receive his next meal. Sensitivity to the needs of other living things is good, but my reaction is over the top.

Adjusting to life, especially this new life and its uncertainty, unravels the threads I worked so hard to sew together in recovery. Mindfulness is non-existent. No matter what work I do with cognitive thinking or mindfulness, I can't calm myself.

Frozen. I feel frozen. I've moved beyond withdrawal and far into recovery, yet lack the ability to step forward into the transitional phase. I suffer internalized pain, often feel like crying and lack enjoyment in my activities. Overrun with anxiety, I face insomnia once more. I run worry loops and fail to find my center. *What's happening to me? This makes no sense. I had been doing so well. I was beyond all of this.* I fear life, every aspect of it. Trust is non-existent. I don't understand. I have lost myself; where did I go?

With the ability to feel again, all painful life events return to haunt me. So many memories, painful incidences and present life circumstances convene and overwhelm me to the point of mental congestion. Life overwhelms me: too much stimuli to take in, too much I am overly sensitive to, too much I am trying to process.

I hunt for answers, for people who may possibly understand what is happening to me. I re-read sections of *Finding Life Beyond Trauma* and an "a-ha" moment slaps me upside the head. Post-traumatic stress. I believed I had life in my grips two years earlier when I left Lisa's counseling. I was still numb. I feel frustrated. *Why can't I do this on my own?*

I join forces with Kaye, a wellness consultant who specializes in trauma and post-traumatic stress. In doing so, I realize my brain—and primarily my body—still both carry the trauma. Kaye reiterates most trauma lodges within the right side of the brain. Our focus through bilateral stimulation emphasizes the transfer of memories and thoughts of the trauma between both sides of the brain to deflate their impact. Opposite sides of the brain are continually activated to release emotional experiences "trapped" in the nervous system.

I bear the insecurity of a toddler in foster care waiting for a lifetime family and home. *Is it because of the severity of the trauma? Is it because I feel the suffering of loss and fear more? Is it from the loss of my identity and uncertainty for the future? Maybe it is all of the above.* Kaye informs me the book-writing process surrounding my trauma has served to heal me on many levels. It has also kept me submerged in my brain and the ordeal for the past two and a half years. *Surrender. Surrender. Surrender. This is what is happening to me. How am I going to take care of myself?*

I relish the handful of months I work with Kaye on settling myself and stepping out of the wreckage into ordinary life. I seek normalcy in life beyond the trauma and the book. It is hard for others to understand, but I enjoy no sense of familiarity in regards to anything until I experience it repeatedly. I continue to work on the maintenance of positive thought patterns and mindfulness of the present moment.

I had not truly grieved the loss of my old life and the old version of me. I continued to grasp for aspects of myself I could remember, but not connect with, often causing pain and confusion. I cannot step forward into new light unless I release and let go of what no longer remains. One thing holds firm—the uncertainty of life and unfamiliarity with the present me. It took 44 years to grow into the old version of myself; eleven years to crawl through the entire drug trauma. Fluency will not come overnight, in a week, or a month.

I pick up methods to soothe myself. I attempt meditation daily and appreciate silence. Some days, I meditate for ten to twenty minutes; other days, I sit quietly or take a walk in nature. I also finally understand the importance of self-compassion. What a difference that makes. I have talked about it, talked about it and talked about it. And surrender. Yep, that too. Thank God, these lessons are coming through. I am my own project.

Six years after the hospitalization for the removal of the last drug, Lorazepam, I celebrate the reality I finally sit on the other side of drug withdrawal and recovery.

57 Meaning of Full Recovery

When you can tell the story and it doesn't bring up any pain, you know it is healed.
~Iyanla Vanzant

Full recovery holds many different definitions. The first to my mind acknowledges moving beyond the storm and finding appreciation for being on the other side. While smaller fallbacks threaten, I no longer fear the rug pulled out from underneath me.

Full recovery means the removal of the insulating buffer that separates me from full emergence into relationships, service and everyday life itself. Life dealt me a huge blow. While I have picked myself up, I gradually move forward with faith and trust I can handle whatever comes my way. Does a harsher hand exist? I don't want to know. Passion. I long to experience passion for life like never before.

Full recovery means the drug stations in my brain are incapacitated. Trust in my reasoning is available again, which leads to increased confidence. Self-trust activates trust in other people and in the world around me. I look to empower my once-enslaved brain.

Full recovery means disposal of my poker face and the elimination of fear in communicating my story to others. I try not to concern myself with other people's opinions or judgments. I surrender the mask, a weight of its own, to the past. I realize numerous people walk around in pain with a poker face of their own and ponder how much healthier everyone would be if they opened up and shared their story. No one is ever alone and everyone has a story we could all learn from. I guarantee there are other people out there with similar stories.

Most of all, full recovery means the removal of all symptoms, so I no longer experience fallbacks or dysfunction. As always, a high fitness level tops the chart. I also want to adjust to the new attributes of me and feel comfortable in my new skin as I move into life on a new path.

Oh, what a handful I have been—the extensiveness still unknown. Emotional blunting, memory impairment and confusion, along with a host of other physical symptoms, make it incomprehensible to appreciate the extent of Bonnie's care and loving willingness to stand at my side through thick and thin. Instead of showering her with reciprocal love and appreciation, I challenge her commitment to me and hold past resentments over her head. Self-absorbed, I fail to realize the toxic nature of such actions.

My memory bank accentuates past events and, having little time to work through them, I hold onto anger tightly. Relationship issues prior to the drug withdrawal led me to believe we possibly reached the end of our road. Withdrawal symptoms from the drugs intensified this thought process into recovery. I hurt the one person stationed at my side throughout who inundated me with unconditional love. My lack of recognition and continual quizzical nature cause agony for Bonnie. How could it not?

We invoke a couple's counselor to help us work through our blocks and to bridge the gap. Step one involves looking at oneself first as part of the equation instead of trying to change the other person, no matter the problem. Change is hard and takes work; it does not come easy. We learn about the stages of relationships and come to understand that, as long as both people keep both feet in the relationship and do not allow a third party to intervene, anything is salvageable as long as both are willing. The primary goal focuses on persistently turning toward each other and never away.

I have worked through the guilt and shame of withdrawal. I must now consider my actions toward Bonnie, which confusingly puts me back into the same guilt-and-shame boat. I never intended to cause such pain. I held tightly to black-and-white constructs of behavior and presently fail to have a consistent grip on my thought processes coming out of recovery. Forgiveness starts with forgiving yourself first. Sometimes that is the hardest, even if acts are unintentional. I ask forgiveness of Bonnie as well.

I contemplate the definition of unconditional love, a term I never celebrated prior. Unconditional love is a complete love—it is free of all expectation. Before, we both shared in-love feelings with each other and thought we experienced unconditional love. This journey opened us to the true meaning.

While the journey was arduous, we discovered more about each other throughout this trial than during all of our previous years together. We learned about our individual strengths and the determination to fight through adversity. We continually learn to celebrate each other's differences, as well as our similarities, and love each other's individuality.

Some days, we need reminders as our egos are not always checked at the door. To love only the similarities is to love only the version of one's self in a partner. We understand we both embody works in progress and cannot expect the other person to be perfect. Though partnered, our experiences and realities will never be identical. We are two separate individuals.

As a couple, we grasp how insecurities within ourselves and each other can cause havoc in the relationship. We now understand the importance of keeping our relationship out of the influence of others. We value each other's willingness under dire circumstances to work through obstacles for the betterment of our relationship. Through persistent communication, we develop into better listeners without intent to reply. We listen to understand. We also learn the importance of pausing to check in with the feelings of the other during discussions instead of carrying on with our own storyline. We've also learned to breathe—always, always, remember to breathe.

While we often read each other, we don't expect the other to know what we are thinking and ask for clarification, which frees us from the confusion of invalid perceptions. Our daily in-house relationship counseling pays major dividends. We consider reaching the point of just "being" with each other again after the trauma—a major stepping stone.

We hold individual authenticity and freedom to be ourselves supreme and learn how mutual self-love and confidence feed into a healthy bond. We focus on finding and celebrating ourselves, which combines for a stronger union. Our prior relationship endorsed individual and combined growth. Now, the emphasis sits on greater support for each other.

We let go of each other only to return. Our bond contains an enriched spiritual element. Bottom line? We choose each other today, tomorrow and for our future until death do us part. I found home. Home rests in each other no matter the ZIP code.

Withdrawal symptoms caused confusion as I searched for my identity and people to connect with. The most important person had been a shining beacon at my side all along.

Drug withdrawal and recovery bring out the worst and best of life. The worst encompasses the hellacious journey from withdrawal to this moment in recovery. It reflects the acquired lifetime benzodiazepine drug addiction and dealing with symptoms as I await full healing and function. It also includes the unbeknownst long-term ill effects the drugs and withdrawal have bestowed on my brain and body.

The worst reflects the often distressing quest of learning myself, of figuring out who I am and my place in the world around me. I hope time transforms awkwardness to joy. The worst also entails a societal taboo surrounding drugs, which involves lack of education and understanding, not just for me, but anyone suffering from drug addiction of any kind, whether medically- or self-induced.

The best? Let me explain. I found God—a loving God. I transitioned from questioning aspects of religion into seeking spiritual growth. The answers I sought do not exist in the outside world, but inside me. I exhibit full belief in someone and something greater than all of us and crave more growth and understanding. I understand the relevance in asking questions and seeking greater truth. I am responsible for my own journey, no one else's, just as no one else is responsible for mine.

Surrender continues to be a work in progress. While I am a step closer, I tend to hold on tightly, depending upon the subject matter. I fully understand the concept and benefit of surrender, but the fighter in me goes down hard. I need to let go of the side of the pool, wade into the middle and surf life's ups and downs. Control is nothing but a fantasy.

I learn to focus on self-love and internal peace with faith that everything happens for me, not against me—even with drug withdrawal. All of the times I felt attacked, I was directed toward growth. Life lessons boomerang until I learn them. Some of life's greatest lessons, unfortunately, are learned through pain. Maybe I will get to the point someday where I can learn more through joy than pain.

I know it is up to me to decide the kind of life I want and live it to the best of my abilities. I developed a higher level of self-respect with the ability to stand up for myself without need for approval or retribution. I believe each experience or obstacle is placed in my path for my own evolution. Self-love and the ability to stand up for myself pre-empt my ability to stand up for other people, animals or causes.

I keep up with current affairs in the community, nation and world but filter the intake. I observe atrocities, unsure of my role. It all seems too big and I am overly sensitive. Overwhelmed, I focus my concern on my zone of influence, concentrating on areas where I can make a difference. I then see the world as a more beautiful place filled with hope and potential. If I believe in a bad world, I will find proof of it. If I believe the world is good, I, too, will find proof. I choose good.

I gradually realize my strength emotionally, mentally and physically as I regain my identity and path. I lost all of me through drug withdrawal and recovery—all but my soul, that is. I lacked confidence and security holding onto faith and perseverance to pull me through. Each fallback withdrew whatever level of self-esteem I had mustered trying to recover and identify myself and my world. My mom and sister showed a pronounced inner strength in their suffering prior to their deaths. While they wished life over death, they boasted no complaint of their demise. I looked upon them in awe and want to hold the same level of vigor inside myself. I do.

Through this journey, I learned not only to dream, but to act on those dreams. I am no longer afraid of risk or failure and believe in the life I desire. I no longer wait for what life has in store for me. I attempt to make life happen. I trust my confidence to grow with each step taken. My parents lived through World War II, the Great Depression and several family health crises. I grew up living inside strict parameters, which negated foolish attempts to step outside the box. The play-it-safe philosophy of my lineage sustained survival of life at the cost of true potential. Life eventually turned mundane without purpose. Life seems wasted, living only for the paycheck, for the weekend, or for vacations. Each day is a blessing; tomorrow never guaranteed.

I learned I do not need tons of people in my life to carry me through in times of trauma. Having one or two as an anchor means the difference between falling through the cracks or standing up to live another day. No matter what, I have me and my faith. I have all I need within me to do whatever I want and make it through any of life's challenges. My soulmate, family and friends at my side are icing on the cake.

I never guessed in a million years my life would unfold in such a manner. This experience happened to me, but is not me. I wear my medical alert bracelet as a badge of honor. Topside, the silver bracelet displays nothing more than a gold medical emblem for simplicity and privacy. Engraved on the back and below my name I list "No benzos," with Bonnie's cell phone number underneath it. The book-writing process has enabled me to recognize my story may help other people going through prescription drug withdrawal and recovery.

I used to believe a medical doctor or celebrity needed to be the face for drug addiction and withdrawal. I used to think, *Who am I to contemplate writing a book that could help someone? Who am I that anyone would actually listen to me?* Let me tell you who I am. I am someone who has gone through the depths of drug withdrawal and come out the other side. I not only survived; I seek to prosper. I am someone who understands the ignorance and abandonment of the medical field. I am someone who understands the symptoms of drug withdrawal, the lack of support, the hellish road to recovery and what it takes to get through it.

My ambition is to help people realize their own individual strength. You are not alone in your suffering. You can make it into the daylight on the other side, and your soul can shine brighter than it ever did before. You will never be the same. Your faith will be stronger, your priorities in better order. Authenticity will highlight your life as you live unconcerned with gaining anyone else's approval. You will cast off the shackles of doubt to find out who you are truly meant to be. You will learn a higher degree of self-love and compassion in order to make it through. As you learn self-compassion, it will be exuded toward other people.

You will consider past mistakes lessons toward growth instead of something to be held over your head. Most important, you will appreciate the hell you have gone through opened the doors to a stronger version of yourself.

With that said, the task to move from one end of the forest to the other appears daunting and requires a great deal of faith, patience and hard work. Only you can answer the question, "How badly do I want to arrive on the other side?" I am here to tell you it can be done.

With all of the revelations comes the quest for understanding why I am here. What is my purpose in life? Everyone has one. As the only surviving child of my parents' last four children, I always believed in my purpose; I just didn't know what it was. I was told to follow my passion and, as for the result, the book is written.

58 Aftermath

An enlightened person doesn't ask anyone to believe anything. They simply point the way, and leave it to the people to realize for themselves.
~Unknown

Having undergone several surgeries in my lifetime, I have the utmost respect and gratitude for the doctors who worked on me. All were professional, knowledgeable and skillful in their areas of expertise. I offer the highest recommendations of them and their skill sets. I believe that, under a more exact science, medical professionals perform brilliantly. However, when it comes to areas in which doctors are ill-informed—such as drugs and the mind itself—too many unknown factors exist that doctors are uneducated in, yet they act. During my ordeal, I ran into a pool of inadequacy in my search for qualified medical professionals, but I know top-grade practitioners are out there.

I do not hate the medical profession because of my trauma and lifelong drug addiction; however, I do not look upon the medical community with full trust. I cannot stress the importance of self-advocacy. Never give your power over to anyone unless you fully understand the ramifications. Your life may very well be in their hands. You have every right to evaluate your medical professional and question any diagnosis given. You also have the right to change doctors—as much of a pain in the ass as that may be.

Don't get me wrong. I believe there is a place for prescription drugs in certain treatment areas. My concern is for proper diagnosis, use of alternative methods prior to the prescription of drugs, and ease of disbursement without adequate knowledge of the drugs themselves. I also find it highly unethical for drug companies to pay doctors to use their drugs in their practice.

I fully understand some people will denounce me, my book and my experience. There will be some who criticize the symptoms and experiences since they have never lived in this arena and cannot possibly comprehend my story. I am willing to make a high-stakes bet, however, that the probability of you having a family member or friend face the adverse effects of benzodiazepines or another addictive prescription drug is fairly high. I know they are out there—the benzodiazepine users not presently experiencing complications but who will one day question their use. I failed to realize the difficulties myself.

With the drug's highly addictive properties, the only way to keep it working is to continually increase the dosage. Some will point to anxiety issues as the root of all my symptoms from their own lack of comprehension. Many medical professionals, drug and insurance companies will proclaim my story as untrue. Their profit and liability lie at risk. BUT, those who have—or are presently walking in similar footsteps—know the truth. This is for you!

May my light shine enough to guide you through your darkness. I am only one voice. I hope as a united outcry for our message to be received, understood and dealt with intelligently. The lives of many depend upon it. Our voices must be heard.

H.O.P.E.

HOLD ON, PAIN ENDS!

Contact the Author

I sincerely thank you for reading this book and hope you enjoyed it. I would be extremely grateful if you could leave a review on Amazon.

I'd also love to hear your comments and am happy to answer any questions you may have, so do please get in touch with me by:

Email: PjLaube@yahoo.com

Facebook: Moment of Surrender by Pj Laube

Website: www.pjlaube.com

Twitter: @Pjlaube

LinkedIn: www.linkedin.com/in/judy-pj-laube-7a850910a

To receive notification of my next book, please join my mailing list now: eepurl.com/bJIiIn

If you enjoy memoirs, I recommend you pop over to Facebook group We Love Memoirs to chat with me and other authors there. www.facebook.com/groups/welovememoirs

I look forward to hearing from you.

Pj Laube

Acknowledgements

I would like to thank each and everyone connected with the book or writing in general. First to mind is former college professor, Dr. Kathryn Vonderau, from the University of Wisconsin-Whitewater who held me and all other physical education students up to the highest standards. She wanted us front and center in any classroom we entered. One typo on a page of work meant redoing the entire page. Keep in mind, we were using typewriters. If we already used a certain word on a page, her suggestion was to use the thesaurus to find another word of similar meaning. My love of words and writing improved greatly.

Sincere thanks to the following people for acting as my beta group in reading my manuscript when it was nothing more than a first draft in essay form and providing feedback: Susan Schaefer, April Farmer, Carolyn Cain, Katie Richardson, Lisa Clervi, Becky Reynolds, Gary Smith, Steven Menard and Bonnie Conley.

I am appreciative of Gary Smith in connecting me with another Unity member, Lisa Frick, who would become not only my editor, but friend, mentor and confidant. Her guidance helped me turn my story into a book. She made me search into the depths of myself to pull out thoughts, feelings and emotions I unconsciously protected.

Thank you to Ant Press for believing in me and my story. I love the personal touch the staff, especially Jacky Donovan, has given me from the beginning. Their guidance and support enable me to continue to blossom as a writer. I am grateful, too, to Amy E. Hess for her work in capturing the essence of my book in the cover design.

I would like to acknowledge benzowithdrawal.com even though it no longer exists. The group provided a wealth of information and sense of sanity when I felt none existed. I thank the handful of friends who were a constant means of support and whose contact I lost with after its demise. I was Phoenix25.

I thank Sue Riley and Leddy Hammock for graciously letting me use their songs. The music touched my soul and was inspirational in my healing.

Last, and definitely not least, I want to thank all my family and friends who have stood by my side in recovery and in the process of writing the book. I thank you for your love, encouragement and support.

No words can illustrate the thoughts and feelings I hold for my lifelines, Bonnie and Lisa, in withdrawal and recovery, who got me through my darkest hours.

Appendix A—Food for Thought

I hope society wakes up to the culture of quick fixes. What a novel idea it would be for practitioners to go back to doctoring instead of matching a prescription drug to a symptom. Pills do not cure; they often cause more serious problems than the medical establishment has yet to confirm. Doctors in various specialties prescribe psychiatric drugs outside of their area of expertise. Physicians within their own area are ignorant about the true nature of the drugs they prescribe, relying vastly on the drug makers themselves for education. What a conflict of interest it is for these companies that seek profit to also serve as educators to the medical field. Where is the FDA in all of this? Why aren't doctors listening to the FDA guidelines?

Insurance companies stipulate the amount of time doctors spend with patients—not the doctors themselves. The doctors are often trained in the questions they ask to code the service for insurance purposes. When the diagnosis isn't known, the top three possibilities are listed. In my case, no answer threw the load back on me, signaling anxiety. How often does that happen? Does it occur more often to women than men? How often does it happen to the elderly? Who is knowledgeable enough to speak up for children? Either way, the doctor's office has grown into a production line of short visits to generate more clients for more revenue. Who watches out for the patient in all of this?

Food for thought. Does your doctor know you? Does your doctor listen to you? Have you come upon doctors who make up their minds about your diagnosis and prognosis without your input? Do you ask for all available options or follow through with their instructions without hesitation? How do you know if your doctor is not only highly educated, but knowledgeable in your treatment area and keeps up to date with current research?

When a doctor prescribes medication, do you ask in-depth questions concerning possible side effects, addiction, the duration of time recommended on the prescription and taper method to get you off safely? What will you do if your doctor seems unable to answer those questions? Will you take the drug anyway? Will you allow your child, parent or grandparent to take the drug?

If you are on an addictive drug, have you noticed slight changes in your demeanor? Has a family member or friend mentioned changes in your personality? Realize that, as an outsider looking in, the person addicted to the medication and showing signs of change will have a limited window to realize it for themselves. Later, they will be clueless and unable to understand what you are telling them. Also understand that, once your loved one quits taking an addictive prescription, the person will not change back into themselves overnight just because the medication has ceased. In fact, your loved one may not change back into the same person at all.

As a parent do you bounce your child on and off their medication due to forgetfulness, running out of the prescription or lack of money? Do you notice changes in your child's behavior? Does the child's teacher notice? Do medical practitioners then prescribe more?

Is your parent in a nursing home? Do you keep track of the medications prescribed and the amount? Does the doctor discuss the possibility of new medications with you or other caregivers before prescribing them to the elder adult? In September 2014, the British Medical Journal reported on a study concerning benzodiazepines and the elderly. Researchers concluded benzodiazepine use was linked to an increased risk of developing dementia. In addition, the article cautioned benzo use for the elderly because of side effects—including confusion—that may contribute to falls and fractures. Benzodiazepines are widely prescribed in nursing homes. Before your parent starts taking one, check into the prescription and do your own research for your loved one's sake. The studies and reports are out there.

Appendix B—Timeline of Events

March 2004: Back injury at school.
June 2004: Neurontin prescription.
July 2, 2004: Neurontin withdrawal began.
August 2004: Xanax prescription.
September 29, 2004: Change of doctors. Referred to Dr. McDonald by Dr. Murry. Prescription switched from Xanax to Clonazepam.
December 8, 2004: Referred to Dr. Tucker. Neurontin reinstated. Clonazepam taper @ 0.5/daily begins. Reinstatement and Clonazepam withdrawal issues.
July 2005: Hysterectomy.
August 2005: Depression.
August 29, 2005: Dr. Reynolds prescribed Lamictal, Zoloft and Lorazepam.
Spring 2006: Lamictal withdrawal—one month. Doctor instructed cold turkey.
Fall 2007: Instructed to take Lorazepam as needed. Zoloft taper began, 200 milligrams down to 150 milligrams in a week. Day eight, down another 50 milligrams taper to 100 milligrams.
May 7, 2008: Medical leave from teaching.
June 2008: Appointment with Dr. Clifford; taper off Zoloft continued.
September 24, 2008: Zoloft-free.
April 8, 2009: Abandoned by Dr. Clifford; he would not remove remaining 1.5 milligrams Lorazepam.
April 24, 2009: Appointment with Dr. Tyson. Taper 0.5 milligrams of Lorazepam beginning that day.
April 27, 2009: Hospital observation after last intake of Lorazepam. 2 ½ day observation. Acute withdrawal lasted six weeks.
July 2009: Major fallback signaling protracted withdrawal.
August 2009: Refusal by Dr. Tyson's office for appointment.
September 10, 2009: Abandoned second time by Dr. Clifford.
August 2009—June 2010: Medical leave.
April 27, 2010: First anniversary of being drug-free.
August 2010: Returned to teaching.
October 2010: Mom taken to emergency room by ambulance and beginning of routine runs to Wisconsin for caretaking.

April 27, 2011: Second anniversary of being drug-free.
July 27, 2011: Mom's death.
August 2011: School began.
April 27, 2012: Third anniversary of being drug-free.
August 2012: Brother's accident. Initial steps for book writing; job at local health club.
August 2012: June 2013: One-year leave of absence from teaching.
January 2013: Resignation from teaching.
April 27, 2013: Fourth anniversary of being drug-free.
April 27, 2014: Fifth anniversary of being drug-free: symptoms diminished at a faster rate.
2015: Sixth anniversary of being drug-free. Reached baseline in recovery. Recovered from PTSD. Book completed. Publishing contract signed with Ant Press.

Ant Press Books

If you enjoyed this book, you may also enjoy these titles:

Chickens, Mules and Two Old Fools by Victoria Twead
(Wall Street Journal Top 10 bestseller)

Two Old Fools ~ Olé! by Victoria Twead

Two Old Fools on a Camel by Victoria Twead
(New York Times bestseller x 3)

Two Old Fools in Spain Again by Victoria Twead

One Young Fool in Dorset by Victoria Twead

Heartprints of Africa: A Family's Story of Faith, Love, Adventure, and Turmoil by Cinda Adams Brooks

Simon Ships Out: How one brave, stray cat became a worldwide war hero by Jacky Donovan

Seacat Simon: The little cat who became a big hero (children's version for age 8 to 11)

Instant Whips and Dream Toppings: A true-life dom rom com by Jacky Donovan

Fat Dogs and French Estates ~ Part I by Beth Haslam

Fat Dogs and French Estates ~ Part II by Beth Haslam

How not to be a Soldier: My Antics in the British Army by Lorna McCann

Into Africa with 3 Kids, 13 Crates and a Husband by Ann Patras

Paw Prints in Oman: Dogs, Mogs and Me by Charlotte Smith
(New York Times bestseller)

Joan's Descent into Alzheimer's by Jill Stoking

The Girl Behind the Painted Smile: My battle with the bottle
by Catherine Lockwood

The Coconut Chronicles: Two Guys, One Caribbean Dream House by Patrick Youngblood

Midwife: A Calling (Memoirs of an Urban Midwife Book 1) by Peggy Vincent

Serving is a Pilgrimage by John S. Basham

Second hand Scotch: How One Family Survived in Spite of Themselves by Cathy Curran